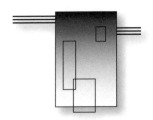

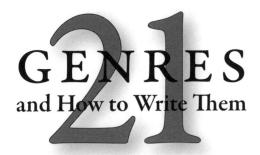

GENRES
and How to Write Them

BROCK DETHIER

UTAH STATE UNIVERSITY PRESS
Logan

The University Press of Colorado is a proud member of
the Association of American University Presses.

The University Press of Colorado is a cooperative publishing enterprise supported, in part,
by Adams State University, Colorado State University, Fort Lewis College, Metropolitan State
University of Denver, Regis University, University of Colorado, University of Northern Colorado,
Utah State University, and Western State Colorado University.

∞ The paper used in this publication meets the minimum requirements of the American National
Standard for Information Sciences—Permanence of Paper for Printed Library Materials. ANSI
Z39.48–1992

ISBN: 978-0-87421-912-8 (e-book)
ISBN: 978-0-87421-911-1 (paper)

Complete cataloging information for this title is available from the Library of Congress.

22   21   20   19   18   17   16   15   14   13   10   9   8   7   6   5   4   3   2   1

To Larkin and Corey
and their future writing

Contents

Part I: Genres

1. ABSTRACT

2. ANNOTATED BIBLIOGRAPHY

3. APPLICATION ESSAY

4. APPLICATION LETTER

5. ARGUMENT

6. BLOG

7. EMAIL

8. GRIPE LETTER

9. LITERARY ANALYSIS

Part II: Moves

29. DRAFT

30. REVISE

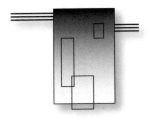

Acknowledgments

The thinking of Donald M. Murray underlies my whole approach. I'd be flattered if people saw this book as an extension of or a distillation of Don's work. Don loved to share, so I know he'd be happy to have me pass on to others ideas he sowed in my mind.

Melody Graulich is always my best critic and strongest support. Denice Turner convinced me to foreground the genres and is thus midwife to the book. Shanan Ballam's close, honest, and insightful readings led to improvements in the text throughout. My writing group—Diane Bush, Christine Cooper-Rompato, Pat Gantt, Keith Grant-Davie, Dave Hailey, Keri Holt, Michael Spooner, and Rebecca Walton—pushed me to rethink drafts of early sections. My son, Corey Dethier, solved my thorny Microsoft puzzles and provided sage advice from a student perspective. Natalie Young's sketches and design ideas helped make the manuscript into a book.

My thanks go to all who have allowed me to use their work as examples in this book, and especially to Greg Brown, for the use of his lyrics. I'm grateful to the following for talking to me about writing in their disciplines: David Dethier, Megan Dethier, Melody Graulich, Chalmers Hardenbergh, Jack Lannamann, Sheila McNamee, Lynne McNeill, Natalie Young.

As anyone in academic publishing knows, Michael Spooner of USU Press is remarkably good at what he does. I consider it a privilege to work with him.

Twenty-One Genres and
How to Write Them

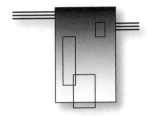

Introduction

Genres, Moves, and Never Getting Stuck Again

What's the hardest part of writing for you? Sitting restlessly in front of your computer, your head full of worry but not words? Trying to come up with a flashy opening? Knowing when it's time to stop? Finding something new to say during the dry endless middle? This book offers you 228 writing *moves*—tools for your writer's toolbox, steps to revive your mind and your momentum, things to DO to solve your writing problems, to get the pages out. Throughout this book, the arrow ➡ indicates "go to this move number." The moves will give you ways to handle everything from coming up with ideas to polishing a final product. Using this book, you will always have options for what to do next, and you should never get stuck for long.

This book is called *21 Genres* rather than *228 Moves* because an easy way to find the best moves for your writing situation is to identify the form, type, or *genre* of writing you need to produce—an essay? a business letter? a blog? I analyze each genre to help you understand it, then suggest a series of moves to take you from start to finish of your writing project in that genre. This book covers more genres and writing moves than you'll ever use. The point is to find the best move for your current writing situation and try to remember successful moves for the future.

If you're not yet sure about your genre or have specific writing problems, ask yourself what you need help with—getting an idea? (chapter 23); focusing? (chapter 27); organizing? (chapter 28). If you're just getting started on a paper, let chapters 23–31 take you through a series of writing steps, from "discovering" to "presenting."

If the prospect of writing anything nauseates you, start with chapter 22, Solve Your Process Problems. You may be surprised at how straightforward, relatively painless, even enjoyable writing can be. And how much you'll learn and discover from it.

Try to adopt an attitude of play when using the moves in this book and when writing in general. It's fun to come up with a dozen openers and discuss with friends which is most effective. It's satisfying to trim five words from a page, making it sparkle. Enjoy it . . . or at least don't fear it. And don't worry. I've got moves for you.

PART I

Genres

The next twenty-one chapters present, in alphabetical order, twenty-one common genres or types of writing. Each chapter starts with an example or two, briefly describes and defines the genre, then suggests a series of moves that might be helpful if you need to write in the particular genre.

A genre is a type, form, or category—for our purposes, a form of writing such as a business letter, a novel, or a resume. We use familiar genres like "lab report" and "personal essay" without thinking about what rules and conventions govern the genre. But analyzing a genre, making sense of such rules can lead to insights. Someone analyzing gripe letters, for instance, will see that most such letters state or at least hint at the kind of response that will satisfy the letter writer. There's little point in writing a complaint if there's no action that can alter the situation. The writer who wants an apology, a policy reconsideration, or a free box of the cookie he found to be moldy has a concrete reason for writing.

The understanding of writing genres has changed substantially in the past two decades. In the old-fashioned view, genres were static and idealized. Writers did their best to follow the form exactly. Recent genre theorists have argued that genres are in fact fluid and evolving. A writer may follow a genre model or prescription, but by creating a new, unique text, the writer also stretches the standard definition a bit, playing a role in the development and evolution of the genre.

Almost all texts mix genres. A simple two-paragraph gripe letter contains description, narration, analysis, persuasion, and summary and may use the memo format and the tone of a business report. The question is not whether you're going to integrate different genres but how you're going to integrate them and which one will be dominant. People pay attention to form, so even if you want to tell a story, if your audience expects a corporate prospectus format, that's what you should give them—saving the narrative form for the "letter to shareholders." Like most good writing moves, the switching and mixing of genres will eventually happen naturally, as long as you can make clear the dominant genre and don't feel constrained to follow it exactly.

One reason to study genres is to learn to distinguish among those elements and processes common to a number of genres and those that are unique to a particular genre. The tools of any particular stage in the process—reading, researching, interviewing, and survey tools that make up most gathering moves, for instance—are similar regardless of what genre the writer intends to create. But what matters to particular audiences and in particular genres DOES change. A moment of personal revelation that might be the core of a personal essay would be irrelevant to a sociological study; the numbers that fill a business report wouldn't matter much to a consultant's assessment of a corporation's culture. So while the moves you've practiced for other purposes will probably serve you well in your next project, the kinds of material you're trying to discover, gather, and organize will change.

Therefore, it's crucial to learn as much as you can about your audience and genre before you get very far into gathering materials. Read as many examples of the genre you're aiming for as possible, with an eye on what matters in that genre. Should you be looking for quotations from famous people, conclusions of the most recent studies, statistics that seem to support your hypothesis, symbolic actions of fictional characters? Does the genre seem to value quantity (lots of references) or quality (just one or two references to important people and publications)? Does personal experience have any place in this genre?

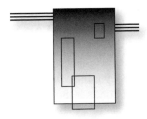

Abstract

EXAMPLE: **Abstract of *Twenty-One Genres*, Brock Dethier**

Twenty-One Genres strives to be the smallest, most inexpensive all-purpose writing text on the college composition market. Author Brock Dethier, director of the composition program at Utah State University, offers descriptions of twenty-one common genres, from abstract to wiki, and suggests for each genre a series of writing "moves." The book presents over two hundred such "moves"—thinking, writing, reading, and researching activities divided into ten chapters, from "Solve Your Process Problems" and "Discover" to "Revise" and "Present." The book is written to be useful to the individual writer, whether or not the writer is currently in a writing class.

Questions about the example:
1. Does it show you anything new about the book or emphasize things that you didn't realize were so important?
2. What details tip you off that the book's author wrote the abstract?
3. Boiling hundreds of pages down into a paragraph as I did here is a specialized writing skill. Can you think of other writing situations where such a skill might be useful?

EXAMPLE: **Using Geophysical Methods to Study the Shallow Subsurface of a Sensitive Alpine Environment, Niwot Ridge, Colorado Front Range, USA, Matthias Leopold,[1] David Dethier,[2] Jörg Völkel,[1] Thomas Raab,[1] Tyler Corsonrickert,[2] and Nel Caine[3]**

This example is the first part of a much longer article. It needs to explain to other experts what's new and interesting in the work discussed, but the authors also hope to give even non-experts a window into the work. Consider the problem these geologists face: how can they learn about the rock beneath the surface of the earth without digging holes or using other such "invasive" techniques?

Abstract

Shallow seismic refraction (SSR) and ground-penetrating radar (GPR) are non-invasive geophysical techniques that enhance studies of the shallow sub-surface deposits which control many geomorphic and biogeochemical processes. These techniques permit measuring the thickness and material properties of these deposits in sensitive alpine area without using extensive pits and trenches that can impact current biogeospheric processes or distort them for future research. Application of GPR and SSR along 1.5 km of geophysical lines shows that layers of fine to coarse, blocky deposits of periglacial origin underlie alpine slopes in the vicinity of Niwot Ridge, Colorado Front Range. Interpretation of geophysical and drilling data shows that depth to bedrock ranges from 4 to >10 m and is not simply related to local slope. Our measurements suggest that ice lenses form seasonally beneath solifluction lobes; ice was not present in adjacent areas. Ice lenses are associated with local ponded water and saturated sediments that result from topographic focusing and low-permeability layers beneath active periglacial features. Geophysical interpretations are consistent with data derived from nearby drill cores and corroborate the utility of GPR in combination with SSR for collecting subsurface data required by different landscape models in sensitive alpine environments.

Questions about the example:

1. This abstract begins the article published in *Arctic, Antarctic, and Alpine Research*. What purposes might it serve for the readers of the journal? For the authors?
2. If you were one of the authors, when else might you use the abstract? Think of situations in which you need to explain quickly what you've been working on.

1.   University of Regensburg, Soil Science and Landscape Ecology, Germany.
2.   Williams College, Department of Geoscience, Williamstown, MA, USA.
3.   University of Colorado at Boulder, Department of Geography, USA.

3. If you're not a geologist, you may find this abstract difficult reading. Yet it's not incomprehensible to a nonspecialist. How did the authors make the technical intelligible?

To see how an abstract fits in the context of a larger work, see the second example in chapter 14: Proposal.

Questions about the Abstract

1. What are its purposes?

An abstract is a miniature version of a much longer document or oral presentation. It presents readers with the highlights of the longer document—its purposes, conclusions, and recommendations. It gives the reader an opportunity to decide, quickly, whether to read the entire text, how to file or catalog it, or who might be interested in it. For the writer, an abstract can be a demanding piece of writing, as it forces the writer to decide what's crucial about the longer text and boil something complex down to just a few words. Writing it can help the writer focus and organize the longer text.

Abstracts are popular on the Internet, since websites like to present readers with a short version of their information to interest the reader in viewing the whole website. The little blurbs that search engines provide along with a title and a web address could be considered abstracts. See how many kinds of abstracts you can find on the Internet and how many different functions they serve.

I wrote the first abstract just for this chapter, but something similar could turn into a book jacket quotation or a blurb that the publisher sends out to distributors. Playing up the book's strengths more would transform this into advertising.

2. Who are its audiences?

The audience for an abstract is generally the same as for the longer piece that is being summarized: readers of genres like business reports, academic journals, and conference programs. While Dissertation Abstracts International and similar publications contain nothing but abstracts, most abstracts are parts of longer pieces and are intended to give readers a good sense of what the longer piece contains. They can be a boon to researchers and casual readers alike.

Given what I said about the purposes of the first abstract, you can imagine that its audience is composition students and their teachers. Who do you think might read the second abstract?

3. What's the typical content?

The content of the abstract mirrors the content of the longer piece, focusing on what's new and/or significant in the piece. The abstract contains nothing that is not in the longer piece and generally reflects the organization of the longer piece. An abstract for a scientific report, for instance, will probably cover, in order, the report's purpose, research questions, methods, findings, conclusions, and recommendations. The abstract should make sense on its own, without reference to the longer piece.

Do you think my abstract fairly represents the book? Can you see report elements in the second abstract?

An **executive summary** is related to an abstract but is generally more complete and longer (roughly 10 percent of the report's length), covering the report's purpose, scope, background, findings, conclusions, and recommendations. Findings and recommendations can be listed first, as a kind of summary within a summary, or they can follow the order of the report.

4. How long is it?

An abstract is usually a paragraph or two, generally not over 350 words.

5. How is it arranged on the page?

Usually the abstract is simply labeled "Abstract," and it often precedes the rest of the paper, sometimes single-spaced or indented to set it off from the body of the paper.

6. What pronouns are used?

The writing in general follows that of the main piece; abstracts in the sciences are likely to use passive voice, avoiding pronouns altogether, while those in the humanities may occasionally use first- and third-person pronouns.

7. What's the tone?

As objective, as neutral, as possible. The writer is not passing judgment or advocating, just clearly stating what's in the document.

8. How does it vary?

Considering purpose is crucial. Is someone making a decision based on your abstract? If so, make sure the recommendation and a key bit of evidence appear in the abstract. Will the abstract be read by researchers trying to decide if they should read the whole article? Then make sure your abstract includes appropriate keywords. If you're trying to catch a reader's eyes, try to work the most startling bit of information into the abstract.

Suggested Moves for Writing an Abstract

I. Discover.

You might think that there's nothing to discover when writing an abstract, but you'd be surprised at what you'll find when you try to boil down an entire report into a single paragraph. You might try **Outline your draft** ➡160 to get a clear sense of what the text says and how different ideas are weighted. Or try **Make ends meet** ➡197 to see what the headings of your paper tell you is important. A different tack would be to **Freewrite** ➡72 without looking at the text—what sticks in your mind as being crucial to the paper? If the different moves lead you to different answers to that question, you may need to revise the text itself.

2. Develop.

There's not much room for development in an abstract, but you do need to make sure that your ideas are developed enough, and specific enough, to be useful. **Answer the journalist's questions** ➡87 to make sure you cover the basics. Try writing a single sentence about the core of the text, then use **Explain your code words** ➡93.

3. Gather.

Consider using a **Double-entry journal** ➡106 with important points on the left side and on the right how they connect to the whole. Try to make sure you're representing the whole text. Go back through the headings or the table of contents to make sure you're not forgetting anything significant. **Skim** ➡103. **Force yourself to read intelligently** ➡154. Look at the beginning and end of each paragraph. Use all the clues the writer gives you about what's important—words like "because" and "therefore" that indicate cause and effect as well as any comparatives ("better"), superlatives ("best"), or keywords ("crucial").

4. Integrate.

Many writers borrow key phrases from throughout the text to use for the abstract. One challenge, therefore, is to integrate borrowed lines with new ones. **Integrate sources** ➡133. And if possible, work with someone: **Check the flow** ➡139.

5. Focus.

Writing an abstract is itself a good focusing activity, since an abstract is all about summary ➡150. **Brainstorming leads** ➡143 can help you with that difficult first sentence and maybe give you some possibilities for sentences two, three, and four. Try brainstorming all the key elements of the text, then group them until you have three to five groupings. **Group, label, and order** ➡162. Then you'll probably have to go through and cut out anything that isn't crucial.

6. Organize.

The abstract can either follow the text from introduction to conclusion or it can highlight three to five main points regardless of where they appear in the text. Put yourself in your reader's shoes and **Answer readers' questions** ➥159, starting with the basic "What's this text about?"

7. Revise.

An error in an abstract might literally drive readers away, so do a lot of rereading and get help from others.

8. Present.

Usually the abstract appears right after the title page and before the table of contents, on a page by itself.

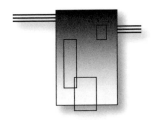

Annotated Bibliography

2

EXAMPLE: **Partial Annotated Bibliography for "The Logan Nunnery: Discovering an Obliterated Site," Allie Anderson**

Bell, Michael Mayerfeld. "The Ghosts of Place." *Theory and Society* 26.6 (1997): 813–36. Print.

> Bell's article argues that ghosts are part of our everyday lives. Their presence exists even if their physical body does not. He goes on to describe how ghosts set boundaries of possession and ownership of place. A ghost will let a human know when his or her presence is not wanted by making them feel frightened, disturbed, or unsafe. Bell also explains his belief that we experience places socially, similarly to how we experience other people. Because ghosts are a part of place they become part of the social experience when discovering that particular locale. Locations that are well known for their supernatural inhabitants are treated differently. They are approached with a measured step and their aura calls out to those with curious minds. This theory very much applies to my topic of the Nunnery. Its landscape is treated differently because people believe it to be haunted.

Bennett, Gillian. *Alas, Poor Ghost: Traditions of Belief in Story and Discourse.*
   Logan: Utah State University Press, 1999. Print.

> In her book, Bennett claims that even though supernatural experiences
> have been demoted to nursery, commercial, or fantasy worlds, people have
> encounters with supernatural forces that cannot be explained or put into
> those categories. She also explores the relationship between narrative and
> belief by interviewing people about their beliefs when it comes to ghosts
> and ghost stories and then analyzing their responses. Bennett believes that
> ghost stories are communal and reflect attitudes and beliefs of the society
> they circulate in. They also help to create and shape a community's folklore.
> I found this last point to be especially useful in my research as the Nunnery
> has greatly impacted Logan's folklore.

Ellis, Bill. *Aliens, Ghosts, and Cults: Legends We Live.* Jackson: University Press of
   Mississippi, 2003. Print.

> In this book Ellis takes a deeper look into legends. He studies how legends
> come to be and what impact they have on society. He describes legends as
> a kind of "living" thing because each version of a legend is somewhat the
> teller's creation. He also says that legends are a process and not just a col-
> lection of texts. Ellis explains that people tell legends in order to define the
> world they inhabit. Legends contribute to the social experience of one's
> surroundings. While conducting interviews on the legends of the Nunnery,
> Ellis's research helped me have a greater understanding of the importance
> of the various legends I was gathering.

Foote, Kenneth E. *Shadowed Ground: America's Landscapes of Violence and Tragedy.*
   Austin: University of Texas Press Austin, 2003. Print.

> This book shows how violence and tragedy have affected landscape in
> America. Foote gives several examples of different landscapes across the
> United States that have been altered because of events that have occurred.
> He discusses what obliteration means and how violence and tragedies can
> cause a landscape to become obliterated. Foote is very clear in the way he
> presents his research and thoughts which was something I really appreciated
> about the book. I drew my main idea from Foote and altered his criteria of
> obliteration to fit that of the Nunnery. I was able to compare and contrast
> the Nunnery with examples he provided to further prove my own theories
> on obliteration of landscape.

Goldstein, Diane E., Sylvia Ann Grider, and Jeannie Banks Thomas. *Haunting
   Experiences: Ghosts in Contemporary Folklore.* Logan: Utah State University
   Press, 2007. Print.

> This book looks at ghost lore from various angles. The authors take a closer
> look at how popular culture affects tradition and belief when it comes to the

supernatural. Ghost stories can reveal different things about personal life, culture, and nature. This book document the authors' field work by giving accounts of ghost stories and pictures of sites that are said to be haunted. I found this book particularly useful because it focuses on how ghost stories affect our culture today, which related to my research of the legends surrounding the Nunnery.

Olwig, Kenneth R. "Recovering the Substantive Nature of Landscape." *Annals of the Association of American Geographers* 86.4 (1996): 630–53. Print.

Olwig's article presents several ideas on the use and meaning of landscape. He discusses how landscapes are not just places but home to nature and customs. He claims that variables such as community, law, and custom shape the human geographical existence. Landscapes are more than just locations they are home to memories, culture, and ways of life. This article was useful for my research because the landscape of the Nunnery has greatly impacted the culture of Cache Valley. It is a place where people go to discover more about their community and their customs.

Tucker, Elizabeth. *Haunted Halls: Ghostlore of American College Campuses.* Jackson: University Press of Mississippi, 2007. Print.

This book is rare in that it focuses specifically on ghostlore in academia. Tucker travels across the United States to discover what ghosts haunt the halls of college campuses. She presents several theories about ghosts and has research to back up those ideas. Tucker's research also includes personal interviews and photographs of haunted sites she visited. It was very interesting to read these students' accounts and see the places that Tucker was talking about. She also discusses the importance of legend tripping and how it adds to the social experience of campus life. Tucker's book was very helpful in my research. Many of the Nunnery's visitors are college students so much of the information in her book related to my topic.

Tucker, Libby. "Legend Quests." *Voices* 32.1 (2006): 1–6. Print.

Tucker gives an in-depth analysis specifically on the importance of legend quests. She states the importance of legend tripping lies not only in the destination but also in the trip. Typically a legend quest involves more than one person, thus making a trip of discovery also a social event. There are emotional components of legend tripping that include feeling afraid, thrilled, and excited. The desire for these emotions also makes legend tripping more enticing. This article was very helpful in my research because it allowed me to gain a greater understanding behind the purpose of legend tripping.

Valk, Ulo. "Ghostly Possession and Real Estate: The Dead in Contemporary Estonian Folklore." *Journal of Folklore Research* 43.1 (2006): 31–51. Print.

> This article focuses on spirits who continue to claim ownership over real estate. Valk discusses the appearance of ghosts when humans stray from their normal, daily routines. He also claims that spirits reinforce social norms, proper behavior, and traditional customs by warning humans when they are participating in dangerous activities. Thus ghosts play an important, stabilizing role in upholding the value system of our culture. Ghosts provide thrilling memories when individuals participate in paranormal investigation. This helped aid my research to give me a better understanding of the cultural importance of ghosts and why they still feel possession over the landscape they inhabit.

Yamagishi, Takeshi. "Landscape and the Human Being." *Human Studies* 15.1 (1992): 95–115. Print.

> Yamagishi's article is about how landscapes affect human beings. He claims that humans aren't just living on landscapes but internalizing them as well. These landscapes affect their personalities and the way in which they live their lives. Place serves as a repository for memory. Events that take place are remembered and stored in the landscape just as they are in a human brain. Landscapes serve as a way for humans to experience life. I liked that this article discussed the importance of landscape when it comes to memories and the human experience and could relate these points to my research.

Questions about the example:
1. Annotated bibliographies are usually double-spaced. Do you see any other deviations from standard form in the example? What stylesheet was the writer using?
2. Annotated bibliography writers are encouraged to include a summary of the work, an assessment of its credibility and value, and an evaluation of its relevance to the project. Do you see these three parts in these annotations? What other kinds of information does the writer provide?
3. How can you improve on the details of this example?
4. How would writing an annotated bibliography be useful to a writer who intended to go on to write a research paper?
5. See an example of an annotated bibliography in context: Alyson Bernhisel and Kendra Homan's proposal in chapter 14.

Questions about the Annotated Bibliography

I. What are its purposes?

A fundamental purpose of all citation information is to help those who may follow your research trail. Researchers build on other research and rely on previous writers' bibliographic information. By creating any kind of bibliography, you guide readers of your paper to your own sources. By annotating your bibliography, you do a service to your readers: you save them from having to find and skim the source to determine its relevance to their own research question. So a main purpose of an annotated bibliography is to provide readers with a short, informative statement that will help them determine the value of the source for their own work.

Annotating the bibliography also serves important purposes for you, the writer—it helps you remember what was in a particular source. If you include some thoughts on the contribution the source makes to your overall project, you'll soon find that your head is full of ideas about what to write.

2. Who are its audiences?

Whoever has asked you to do the annotated bibliography is, of course, your primary audience, so be very sensitive to the nuances of how that audience introduces the assignment. Ask for examples. Another major audience is you in the future, after you've read scores of other sources and need to find key ideas. As you're studying your sources, think about the kinds of things you want to include in your paper—details, facts, connections to your topic.

Outside of the classroom, other researchers read annotated bibliographies, which can appear in books or on the web. You'll never know who might read them and for what reasons. Because you're writing for such a potentially varied audience, you should probably keep the annotated bibliography formal and to-the-point.

Who was the audience for Anderson's bibliography?

3. What's the typical content?

Summary is the most basic annotation. What is it about? *Assessment* might come in a second sentence or paragraph. Is the source authoritative, recent, well-written? A third sentence or paragraph can focus on its *relevance* to the reader or the writer's work. How does it affect your thinking?

Does each entry in our example have these three parts?

4. How long is it?

An annotation can be as short as a few words of summary ("Freud's thinking on dreams") or assessment ("Outdated") and is unlikely to be longer than a page per entry. The length of the whole document depends on the assignment and the length of the bibliography itself.

5. How is it arranged on the page?

Issues like line spacing and indentation depend on the stylesheet you go by (MLA, APA, Chicago, etc.). But you probably want a heading—Annotated Bibliography, if not something more specific—top and center. Then a space and your first entry—alphabetized by author's last name. Can you improve on our example's layout?

6. What pronouns are used?

You won't see much use of "I" or "you" in an annotated bibliography.

7. What's the tone?

Business-like, formal.

8. How does it vary?

The annotated bibliography is largely an academic genre, and like most academic genres, it varies substantially from discipline to discipline, purpose to purpose. Summary, assessment, and relevance are common elements in annotations, but you should analyze the situation and see what's most useful. Perhaps your readers are interested only in whether a particular source is relevant to other research, in which case all of your annotations should focus on relevance. Maybe your professor wants to make sure that you read the source and will be looking for you to mention keywords or concepts from the source.

Suggested Moves for Writing an Annotated Bibliography

1. Discover.

DON'T SKIP THIS STEP. It may be obvious that you're going to create your bibliography about the sources you've gathered for a paper or those that a professor or boss has assigned you to work with. But remember to make the task your own, and keep in mind how much your choice of sources to spend time on will affect your thinking about a project. Do you want to choose the widest variety of sources to work with or the most focused group you can find? **Freewrite** ➡ 72 about why you're doing the annotated bibliography and how your choice of sources could be most useful to you.

2. Develop.

It's tempting to jump on the first good source, use its bibliography as a trailhead, and end up focusing entirely on that line of thinking. But was that the path you wanted to take? **Brainstorm** ➡ 69 on paper the different directions you can imagine your project taking. What would be the most interesting for you? **Answer the journalist's questions** ➡ 87, so you're sure you've covered the basics.

3. Gather.

Obviously you need all your sources and your notes. That's why an annotated bibliography can be a great step toward a research paper—it forces the writer to gather and make sense of a substantial amount of material relevant to the topic. Any source can be included in an annotated bibliography, so unless you're instructed to use a certain kind or variety of sources, you can use your favorite gathering techniques. For starters, **Keep a log** ➡ 105 of all the sources you intend to get. You'll probably need a second list for the things you need, new sources that perhaps you'll find in the bibliographies of the sources you do have. **Reflect** ➡ 102 on the text; what sticks in your mind is probably what should go in the annotation. If you're keeping notes electronically, attach this kind of thinking to the bibliographic entry.

4. Integrate.

A good quotation or example from your source is a fine thing to work into the annotation. **Quote** ➡ 123. If you haven't, skim the source, especially the opening, closing, and cover, looking for passages that would nicely represent large sections of the source. Quotes from the source's authors are good, but sometimes quotes from others—like reviewers or bloggers—may be even more valuable. **Consider your source** ➡ 112.

5. Focus.

As is often the case, focusing can be the most difficult step. It's not easy boiling a source—which can be a thousand-page book—down to a handful of ideas that you're going to assert are typical or representative of the entire work. As soon as possible after you finish reading your source, jot down the three or four most important ideas. **Talk . . . and listen** ➡ 157 about the source. That process will focus your thoughts. Or try reading to discover—use the source's own organizing and highlighting clues to point you to the ideas that the authors and publishers deemed most important. **Skim** ➡ 103.

6. Organize.

If you have an idea of the overall length of your annotation and what kind of information the audience is looking for, how to organize your writing won't be an issue. Unless you've been instructed otherwise, start with the bibliography itself, then a sentence or a paragraph of, first, summary, then assessment, then relevance. Along the way, make sure that you **Answer readers' questions** ➡ 159.

7. Revise.

A picture-perfect annotated bibliography looks deceptively simple. The citation itself can be the source of many tiny errors, and some audiences care very much where you put the dates, the parentheses, and the periods. So it's worth double-checking both the source information and the stylesheet model. Annotations are short, but they cover a lot of ground, so they can be difficult to get just right. Have someone else read yours to see if they make sense.

8. Present.

Your bibliography may come at the end of a paper or may stand on its own, in which case you'd want to follow your normal presentation practice for including your name, the date, and any other necessary information.

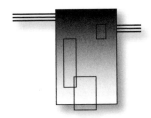

Application Essay 3

The following essay was written as part of a successful application to Harvard University. It was included in the book *50 Successful Harvard Application Essays* 2nd ed. (New York: St. Martin's Griffin, 2005). It is followed by an analysis by one of the staff members of Harvard's student newspaper.

EXAMPLE: **Religion Reconsidered, Alexis Maule**

I had never questioned religion. My father was raised an Episcopalian altar boy and my Colombian mother, a Catholic, only stepped into church for special occasions. In both cases, however, challenging Jesus or "Papa Dios" was as blasphemous as committing murder, even though they couldn't come up for a reason why. The "why" question led me to reconsider my religious beliefs.

After nine years of attending church I had one message drilled into my tiny head: if you were good and prayed to God, He would help you when you needed Him. I remember my first cry for help as if it was yesterday. I made a sanctuary with candles at the foot of my ill father's bed. I got down on one knee and prayed like I had never prayed before. I pleaded with God to save him.

To watch over him. To cure him. The next day I awoke feeling lively because I knew our family would be restored. That same day my father died, and my nine-year-old world came to a stop. I started researching the why of everything, especially religion. My father was one of the most pious men anyone knew. After my father died I hated God. He did not exist to me.

When I was thirteen it came time for Confirmation. I spoke to my deacon about religion before the ceremony because I wasn't sure I wanted to commit myself to the Episcopalian church. Over lunch I asked her tons of questions. How do people talk to God? Why do we worship a work that is sexist and contradicts scientific evidence? The questions that I had when I came into her house remained unanswered when I came out. The only thing she could say was to have faith. As a result, I was never confirmed.

Two years later I took the course European History A.P. and we began to read about the Enlightenment. I felt a great sense of resolution reading everything I had felt about religion scripted eloquently by Nietzsche when I read the works and his claim that religion was for the weak. I picked up Freud on my own and just consumed every word he wrote about religion.

I compare the Bible to the D'Aulieres book of Greek myths—there may be lessons to learn and lively characters to study, but it is more of an imaginative attempt to explain creation. I believe that how I do as a person is not dictated by God. Essentially, people are in charge of their destinies. I have learned the hard way that society is not accepting of these beliefs. Even the closest people in my life reject my lack of religious beliefs. However, I am comfortable with myself and am fortunate to have gone on my very own unique religious journey. The biggest lesson I have learned from my religious journey is to never let anyone mold my beliefs. On any topic I must listen, investigate and form my own beliefs rather than follow the status quo.

Analysis, Zachary M. Seward of *The Harvard Crimson*

At a sparse five hundred words, admissions essays are often sorely lacking the fundamentals of quality writing—narrative detail, character development, even plot. But Alexis manages to include all those elements and then some in an essay which stays within the tight word count yet never feels hurried or deficient.

Clearly, Alexis's essay is focused on her philosophical development with respect to religion. But as she takes us across a span of roughly ten years in just a few minutes of reading, we also learn a surprising amount about her background. Alexis tells us her mother is Colombian, but she tells us even more in two quick words, "Papa Dios," a phrase which brings us right into her home as we imagine a childhood dominated by a cultural, not just religious, deity.

Similarly, when Alexis describes kneeling at her father's bedside, her writing adopts a genuinely prayerful tone. "I pleaded with God to save him," she writes. "To watch over him. To cure him." Those sentence fragments might annoy a middle school English teacher, but they're perfect for this essay. A daughter pleading for her father's life is, of course, permitted to speak in fragments, and Alexis's use of them adds a powerful sense of authenticity.

Professing one's atheism in an essay like this could be considered a risk; after all, who knows what the religious sensibilities of your admissions office might be? But Alexis's strong will is part of her point, and the background she provides suitably justifies whatever conclusions she might draw. And in any event, while the topic here is God, the essay is more fundamentally about Alexis's curiosity and academic spirit. She is demonstrating her ability to question and process her knowledge.

The essay could benefit from some polishing, especially in the third paragraph, where some verb tenses are inconsistent. And proofreading is always important: in the draft she submitted, "Confirmation" was not capitalized, and "Nietzche" was spelled incorrectly.

But Alexis has still constructed a remarkable essay which packs a great deal of information about her into such a maddeningly small space. And her conclusion—"I must listen, investigate and form my own beliefs"—is an unbeatable pitch for admission to any school that values independent thinking.

Questions about the example:

1. If you were a college admissions officer, would you give a thumbs up or a thumbs down to this essay? Why?
2. What do you think of the response to the essay? Did you realize that people care about things like capitalizing "Confirmation"? (I don't see why it should be capitalized.)
3. Do you think it was risky to write about atheism? Are there similar risks that you might take?
4. Do you think Harvard looks for different things in an application essay than does the local community college? What would you look for?

EXAMPLE: **Law School Admissions Essay, Corey Dethier**

I first learned about the concept of the "humblebrag" in one of the three years I spent working at a sandwich shop in Logan, UT. "I got paid so little making what *Salt Lake Magazine* called the Best Sandwiches in Utah" would be a classic humblebrag, in which I snuck a nice piece of bragging into an otherwise humble or self-deprecating statement. Most humblebrags lack in subtlety, but then again, there's basically no tactful way to mention an Oscar nomination or a meeting in the White House, especially in the Twitter form that so many celebrities enjoy these days.

In the same vein, there is no good way to say "I got a perfect score on my LSAT" (a sentence that is, of course, another example of a humblebrag). I do not consider myself to be an overly modest person, nor was I unexcited about the email I received from the LSAC with the nice round 180. But whether influenced by cultural anti-intellectualism, by the twenty-foot-tall eighth-grade math teacher who thought all of his students were too competitive, or by the puritan heritage that has subconsciously drilled the idea of a calling into my bones, I just do not feel right taking praise for how I did on a test.

For me, the reluctance makes sense: accepting praise for good grades or a good test score feels like being praised for hitting well in batting practice. In both cases, the praise is for excelling in activities that might predict or correlate with actual success, but that are not the same as it. That is why, coming out of college, I expect to be most proud of my undergraduate thesis on Hannah Arendt and property law, the poems I have written, and the paper that I am presenting at the New England American Studies Association conference on constitutional myths. These are all things that I have made, contributions—even if they go entirely unseen—to the world.

By the same token, the things that I am most proud of outside of college are the moments when I took a manuscript, whether as an intern at Utah State University Press or as a copy editor for the Wesleyan paper, and made the terrifying claim that there were no more errors in it. Similarly, working for Governor Hickenlooper of Colorado was amazing in itself, but the most exciting part was working on Colorado's application for the third round of Race to the Top grants. If Colorado does win in this round, my contribution to a better education system there, though minimal, will feel like more of an accomplishment than any of the hands I shook or people I took notes for.

The distinction that I am making is between those accomplishments that I think are meaningful and those that are only fodder for humblebrags. It is also why I want to go to law school. I find legal doctrines—especially those of the constitutional variety—fascinating, but I have other interests and options that I could follow or pursue instead. What separates law school from those other options is the way that the former can offer me something other than a career title: when someone asks me what I do, I want to answer not by saying that I am a teacher, or a lawyer, as impressive and worthwhile as those jobs are, but by pointing to something that I have done. I want to point to a case that I won, a client I helped, or a constitutional argument I crafted and say I did that, that is what I do.

This summer, I was told by a Harvard Law alum that I didn't need to worry much about the personal statement, because my LSAT scores were what was really important. I received similar advice, once, while working at the sandwich shop: I was told by another employee that if you got the customers what they were expecting quickly, they would slather it in mayonnaise and the quality would be inconsequential. I could not do that: adding another sandwich to the world was not worth much, it was not something to be proud of. Making a sandwich that would keep people coming back, that they would look forward to and miss on Sundays—that was something worthwhile, something that I'm proud of. I feel the same way about my LSAT: it does not mean a thing unless I do something—something really praiseworthy—with it.

Questions about the example:

1. If you were a law school admissions officer, how would you react to this essay?
2. What word pops into your head to describe the author's tone or attitude? Do you think that's how he would want you to react?
3. What's the organizing principle behind the essay?

Questions about the Application Essay

1. What are its purposes?

If you're in college, you may think you're done with the application essay, but many more may lie ahead of you—applications for graduate or professional schools, for scholarships, for study abroad, for transfers, perhaps even for jobs. Application essays are a study in following directions, in being honest but also appealing to an audience, and in answering a question in depth and with intelligence but in short space.

2. Who are its audiences?

Only one person or a small group will read your essay, but they will almost certainly be strangers to you, so you have to treat them like a big nameless "anyone"—an anyone who may be looking for reasons not to accept your application. Your audience will generally be representing an institution, so the best you can probably do in terms of figuring out your audience is to try to determine what the institution might like to hear.

3. What's the typical content?

Most often, you'll be given a prompt, something like "Write about a decision that changed your life" or "What can you contribute to our company?" Whether or not you're given a prompt, try to choose content that will reveal in you qualities that the university/program/organization will want to see, qualities like taking responsibility, ability to solve problems, reliability, and outside-the-box thinking.

4. How long is it?

The standard college application essay is five hundred words—a little less than two double-spaced pages. That's probably a good length to shoot for if you're not given a length limit.

5. How is it arranged on the page?

Use a standard English essay form, with your name, the date, and the purpose of the essay (for instance, Semester at Sea application essay) at the top left.

6. What pronouns are used?

Like its cousin the personal essay, the application essay is a personal statement that naturally uses "I." References to "you" are less common.

7. What's the tone?

Think of people reading scores or hundreds of these letters. What's going to catch their eye . . . or ear? Humor—but not sarcasm—might do it, though you need to make obvious that you're taking the essay seriously. Put on your most confident, upbeat, can-do hat.

8. How does it vary?

Read the kind of book from which our first example came and you'll see an array of styles, subjects, attitudes. Unless you have inside knowledge of who will be reading your essay, you're at the mercy of the whims of the reader, and those whims may not be predictable even though you know the institution the reader represents. So at a time when you're trying to show yourself off to best effect, you know less about your audience and the audience's desires than you do in almost any other kind of writing. Maybe you can "psych out" the reader and create an insincere but convincing persona. I would rather try to write something that I thought truly represented me.

Suggested Moves for Writing an Application Essay

I. Discover.

Freewrite ➡72 for five minutes a response to the prompt without any consideration of audience or civility. You may need to get some silliness or bitterness out of your system. Reread your freewrite, circling any ideas you want to keep. You might want to repeat the process three or four times, at different hours of the day or when you're in different moods. Just the right memory or just the right perspective on the question can make all the difference in an application essay, so it's worth spending a little time combing your memory and imagination for connections to the question. **Analyze your strengths as a writer** ➡57. Are you good at telling stories? Making arguments? Describing? Tugging on the reader's heartstrings? Organizing and bulleting? How can you use that strength in this essay? Try freewriting again on your strength and this essay: "In this essay, I can use my strength as an arguer to . . ."

2. Develop.

Once you've discovered a scene or moment or change or quality for your essay, you need to write down as much as you can. **Answer the journalist's questions** ➡87, but also do more freewriting and brainstorming. Details that might move a reader? ➡88. A quotation that relates to your story? ➡123

What are the key **Code words** ➡93 in the job description? Does it ask for evidence that you're a "responsible" person? A "self-starter"? What do those words mean? Make a list of evidence you can present in your essay to show you're the right kind of person. You may have hated your summer as a nanny, but think of all the different kinds of *responsibility* it entailed and how much *trust* the parents had in your *maturity* and *good judgment*. Or consider the *organizational skills* and *word-processing expertise* required to head the Current Events club, the *self-motivation* and *people skills* it took to be class treasurer. Anyone can claim to be "disciplined" or a "hard worker." The applicant who presents convincing details to back up such claims will get the job.

Once you have a list of evidence and some convincing details **Brainstorm a list of contexts** ➡89 in which your evidence is relevant. Do you want to emphasize your athletic prowess as captain of the volleyball team, or the people skills required to keep the team from mutiny? Will your conquering of the Spirit Gnome in the Proteus World Tournament impress your audience with your perseverance and skill or depress them about your academic future?

3. Gather.

Most application essays won't require research or outside sources, but no one's going to complain if your essay makes clear that you've done your homework on your subject. If you're going to gather some outside material, don't settle for the celebrity sound bite; try to build on someone's ideas. Get more material than you can fit; it's great to be choosing the best rather than using what you have. **Reflect** ➡102. **Interview** ➡113 family members or friends who might have insights about your life and the ideas you're trying to get across.

4. Integrate.

The most difficult type of integrating you'll probably have to do with an application essay is successfully mixing details about events and actions and explanation of how those details and actions are significant. **Integrate showing with telling** ➡134. Also, consider *Pathos, logos, and ethos* ➡135. Have you made each kind of appeal as strong yet subtle as possible?

5. Focus.

A crucial step. You have two pages to make one single strong positive impression. Try to **Find a focusing detail** ➡146 and **Talk . . . and listen** ➡157. **Brainstorm leads** ➡143 and see how you can **Frame** ➡151 each one to put yourself in the best light.

6. Organize.

The five-paragraph essay may well have been invented for purposes like application essays. Think through what your essay would look like with a five-paragraph structure, then ponder how to expand or twist that structure to make it your own. A catchy lead is crucial, so you might want to come up with the best lead possible and then build the structure on that lead. Make sure you're **Writing reader-based prose** ➡158. Ask "What will grab my reader's attention?" not "What came first?"

Try to briefly **Answer the readers' questions** ➡159, and see if your answers might form the skeleton of the essay. Or **Try standard organizing patterns** ➡166.

7. Revise.

Read aloud ➡189. **Revise for voice** ➡191. **Let it sit** ➡193. **Start as close to the heart as you can** ➡194. Get everybody you can to read this over for you and respond (➡220, 221). You want it as close to perfect as possible.

8. Present.

Don't go overboard, encasing the letter in plastic or printing it on all-rag paper.

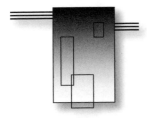

Application Letter

4

EXAMPLE: **Fantasyland Application**

Brock Dethier
Anytown, USA[1]

January 1, 2010
Mr. Cedrick Smee[2]
Fantasyland, USA

Dear Mr. Smee:

I would like to apply for a position as a face character at Fantasyland, USA. I have experience[3] at two other theme parks, where I played first a coachman for Cinderella, then the Headless Horseman. I have also had many speaking and singing parts in plays and musicals at my high school, most notably the announcer in *Wonderful Town*. My resume[4] lists all the roles I have played as well as my references, two employers and two teachers. I believe I can bring to Fantasyland[5] experience, a can-do attitude, and a talent for acting, and I could fill almost any male role.

I am ready to start immediately, and I can be reached anytime via telephone or email.[6] Thank you for your time.

Sincerely,

About this example (numbers below correspond to those in the letter):
1. Yeah, ok, in real life you need to give all the contact information you can.
2. If you can find the name of a specific person to apply to, use it.
3. If you've got it, talk about it.
4. One of the functions of the letter is to draw attention to your resume.
5. What do you have to offer the potential employer? Be as specific as you can.
6. Important information.

EXAMPLE: **Independent Living Coordinator Application**

P.O. Box 1234
Wellsville, UT 80000

December 29, 2009

Options For Independence
1095 North Main
Logan, UT 84341
Subject: Independent Living Coordinator

To Whom It May Concern:[1]

In April 2009 I was fortunate enough to secure an internship with the Logan, Utah BRAG[2] office. During my internship I was able to be introduced to several areas within the Area Agency on Aging. Because I demonstrated excellence in all areas of my work as an intern, I was recently offered a part-time position as a case manager for the BRAAA caregiver program. I accepted this position eagerly because my experience working for BRAG has been extremely rewarding. I deeply admire and support the work that BRAG does for the community. I have also had a wonderful experience working with all of my dedicated managers and colleagues at BRAG. Working with BRAG has given me the opportunity to work with individuals in the community and truly make a difference in their lives. For all of these reasons I am hoping to be hired as a Regional Coordinator/Caseworker for BRAG.

I believe I would make an excellent candidate for this position for many reasons. I have the necessary leadership skills to effectively perform as a Regional Coordinator / Caseworker. Through work at BRAG, volunteer work, and academic work, I have successfully coordinated community outreach programs, organized and led meetings, taught workshops, and made various contacts in the community. I have the energy and dedication necessary to be an excellent Coordinator. Additionally, I am a kind, compassionate, and empathic individual. I have the ability to listen to individuals' needs and connect them to the appropriate resources. I work extremely well with my co-workers, and I have the capacity to encourage a healthy, open, and productive working environment.

Please find attached my résumé and references. Please contact me if you have any questions whatsoever. I look forward to meeting with you to discuss possible employment. Thank you very much for your time and consideration.

Sincerely,

Alyson Frederick
(435) 245-0000
Alyson.c@aggiemail.usu.edu

Questions about the example:

1. I find "to whom it may concern" so impersonal that I try to avoid it when I can, even if it's only to say, "Dear Selection Committee," or in this case, "Dear Options for Independence." And I'd probably change the comma to a colon for formality.
2. Should Frederick spell out whatever BRAG stands for? Normally I would say yes, but in this case, if she's sure that her readers speak of "BRAG" that way, she might seem condescending if she spelled out Bear River Association of Governments.
3. How does Frederick convey her best qualities?
4. Many people find it hard to write about their strengths because they fear they'll be seen as bragging. How does Frederick achieve a tone that is enthusiastic but not arrogant?
5. Can you see examples of the three types of rhetorical appeals?

Questions about the Application Letter

I. What are its purposes?

An application letter may be the most important writing you ever do because it may determine whether you get into the college or graduate school of your choice, or whether you get the job. It needs to hold the reader's interest long enough to persuade the reader to take the next step—read the resume or make the phone call. Writing one can also clarify the writer's hopes and intentions.

2. Who are its audiences?

On campus, you might write an application letter to a scholarship committee, to an office secretary for a work-study job, to get into a fraternity or overseas program or join a club.

3. What's the typical content?

An application letter presents a person in the best possible light. Don't exaggerate or make things up—a reader who catches a minor overstatement may think that the whole letter is bogus. But you don't need to say how nervous you were during the presentation you're highlighting or that it took you seven years to get your associate's degree.

As our sample letters demonstrate, an application letter includes:

a. Standard business letter format: your address, the date, inside address, Dear Somebody: opening. (Get a specific person to send it to!)
b. Specific position you're applying for.
c. Aspects of your education and experience that most suit you for the position.
d. What you can offer the audience.
e. When you're available.
f. How you can be reached.
g. What else you've sent (perhaps a resume or samples of your work).

4. How long is it?

For a high-level job, an application letter might run to two pages or more, but most application letters are a single page long, some only a single paragraph.

5. How is it arranged on the page?

Just like a standard business letter.

6. What pronouns are used?

"I" and "you" are common in application letters. There's no getting around it: one person is asking for something from another.

7. What's the tone?

Humble without being smarmy; confident without arrogance; straightforward.

8. How does it vary?

Application letters vary as much as the jobs they target. If you were applying to work for me, your letter would need to say smart things about teaching writing and be error-free. Most employers would be more interested in your personal characteristics—like responsibility, reliability, and honesty—than in your knowledge of theory or writing skill. Put yourself in the employer's shoes and figure out what the employer wants to hear. And be prepared with some well-written self-promotion that you can paste into the tiny box that an online application may give you.

Suggested Moves for Writing an Application Letter

1. Discover.

Preparing to write an application letter can tell you how much you really want the job or scholarship, so be reflective as you start thinking about the task. If you really want the job, you need to be ready not just to jump through all the hoops, but to do it with enthusiasm. If you have the chance to choose from among several options, **Brainstorm** ➡69 the advantages of each one. You might even **Freewrite** ➡72 about what your life would be like if you got what you're applying for.

2. Develop.

To a large extent, all application letters look the same. So it's crucial to make the unique material as strong and convincing as possible. What are the most important attributes that you can offer? What details from your past can demonstrate such attributes ➡88? **Show**—"My election as Grand Wazoo at our camp demonstrates"—and **tell** ➡134—"that I'm popular with my peers." **Take the other side** ➡82—spend a few minutes brainstorming about the situation from the employer's point of view.

3. Gather.

If you've written a resume, you probably just need to gather the names of the people and places you're applying to. It's worth a phone call to find out to whom you should address your letter. Make VERY sure that you copy down the names perfectly. Try **Memory joggers** ➡100 to make sure you don't forget anything important. **Read from the Internet** ➡108 everything you can about the people or institutions you're applying to. If you discover that the head of human resources is from San Antonio, you might find a way to mention in your letter the Habitat for Humanity work you did there.

4. Integrate.

A **Quote** ➡123 about you from a former employer, teacher, or student might be a very appropriate part of the body of the letter.

5. Focus.

An application letter is a focusing document, intended to draw the audience's attention to some aspect of your life and qualifications. Try some

Fill-in-the-blanks ➡141 like "My strongest feature in this competition is _____" or "I want this particular job because _____" or "What I can offer to the company is _____." Coming up with the first sentence of the letter can be difficult; **Brainstorm leads** ➡143. Get your strongest asset into the first sentence or two.

6. Organize.

The organization of the letter is simple and traditional: you start by saying what you're applying for, give some reasons that you're an excellent candidate and will offer much to the program, and close by giving contact and availability information. The only real organizing issue is in what order to put your accomplishments and qualifications. Make sure you're **Writing reader-based prose** ➡158, thinking from your audience's point of view.

7. Revise.

This one is worth a lot of proofreading. Some readers will reject any application that makes a grammar mistake. It's especially important to have a reader for an application letter. Tone is crucial; ask your reader if your letter seems too casual, too desperate, not focused enough on the specific job. In terms of its long-term effects on your life, an application letter can be the most important writing you ever do, so it's worth taking plenty of time on it, even though it may be very short.

8. Present.

Spring for a full-sized envelope, use company letterhead if you have it, fold neatly, sign neatly.

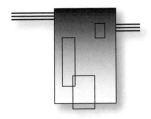

5 Argument

EXAMPLE: **What Price Clean Air?, George Will**

The federal government is a bull that has found yet another china shop, this time in Arizona. It seems determined to inflict, for angelic motives and progressive goals, economic damage on this state. And economic and social damage on Native Americans, who over the years have experienced quite enough of that at Washington's hands.

The gain from this pain? The most frequently cited study says "research to date ... is inconclusive as to whether" there would be "any perceptible improvement in visibility at the Grand Canyon and other areas of concern." The Environmental Protection Agency says that the Navajo Generating Station (NGS) is "near" 11 national parks, several of which are 175 miles distant.

The NGS on Navajo land in northern Arizona burns coal from the Kayenta Mine, which is co-owned by the Navajo and Hopi nations. The EPA is pondering whether all three units of the NGS should be required to install the "best available" emission-control technologies, perhaps costing more than $1.1

billion. More than 80 percent of the power plant's employees are Navajo, many of whom speak Navajo to help preserve the nation's culture. In 2007, the percentage of the Navajo Nation's population living in poverty was 36.8.

But the Navajos, the plant and the mine that powers it may be sacrificed to this dubious environmental crusade. The new technology would reduce nitrate aerosols. They, however, are responsible for just 4 percent of what is called "light extinction" over the Grand Canyon.

Water falls unbidden from the sky but must be pumped to Arizonans—Tucson is 2,500 feet above sea level. The NGS provides 95 percent of the power for the pumps of the Central Arizona Project (CAP), which made Phoenix and most of modern Arizona possible. A study sponsored by the Interior Department estimates that the EPA's mandate might increase the cost of water by as much as 32 percent, hitting agriculture users especially hard. They might be driven back to using scarce groundwater—which was supposed to be protected by the CAP. That is why many environmentalists supported the CAP, one of the largest reclamation projects in US history.

An Arizona State University study estimates that between now and 2044, the NGS and the mine will contribute $20 billion to the state's economy and provide 3,000 jobs each year. If there is an NGS. Its site lease expires in 2019. If the EPA mandates the most expensive technologies, each of the NGS owners would have to weigh whether it is sensible to make large capital investments in a plant that might not operate after that. Furthermore, one of the six owners of the NGS is the Los Angeles Department of Water and Power, which may be prohibited by California law—the state may be destitute, but it is determined to fix the climate—from making investments that will extend the life of coal-fired plants.

Testifying to Congress last February, an EPA official uttered the six-word incantation that summarizes Obama administration policies and progressivism generally: "We do not have to choose." It is, the official said, quoting President Obama, a "false debate" that we have to choose between the "public health benefits from reducing air pollution from power plants" and "growing this economy in a robust way."

But benefits usually have costs. And in reality—which is the region contiguous to Washington—two pertinent questions usually are: How much government do you want, and how much are you willing to pay for it in diminished economic growth? The Obama administration consistently favors more government and, believing that "we do not have to choose," is mystified by stubbornly sluggish growth.

In 1990, Congress passed the Clean Air Act amendments, which high-mindedly mandated restoration of visibility in parks and wilderness areas *to natural conditions.* "Natural" meaning what? Before humanity? Anyway, the EPA is empowered to make this happen, so it empowers its professional writers of regulations—sometimes 26-year-olds fresh from law school—to *maximize regulations* to that end. These are regulations that others must live with while minimizing the damage the regulations cause.

The Navajo have been here before. EPA regulations caused the closure of the Mohave Generating Station near Laughlin, Nev., which was the sole buyer of coal from the Black Mesa Mine, leading it to cease operations. The mine's land is co-owned by the Navajo and Hopi nations.

This story has become as American as *The Great Gatsby*, wherein Tom and Daisy Buchanan "smashed up things and creatures and then retreated back into their money or their vast carelessness . . . and let other people clean up the mess they had made."

EXAMPLE: **What's the Matter with Creationism?, Katha Pollitt**

Do you know what the worst thing about the recent Gallup poll on evolution is? It isn't that 46 percent of respondents are creationists ("God created human beings pretty much in their present form at one time within the last ten thousand years or so"). Or that 32 percent believe in "theistic evolution" ("Human beings have developed over millions of years from less advanced forms of life, but God guided this process"). Or that only 15 percent said humans evolved and "God had no part in this process." It isn't even that the percentage of Americans with creationist views has barely budged since 1982, when it was 44 percent, with a small rise in the no-God vote (up from 9 percent) coming at the expense of the divine-help position (down from 38 percent). Or that 58 percent of Republicans are creationists, although that does explain a lot.

It's that the proportion of college graduates who are creationists is exactly the same as for the general public. That's right: 46 percent of Americans with sixteen long years of education under their belt believe the story of Adam and Eve is literally true. Even 25 percent of Americans with graduate degrees believe dinosaurs and humans romped together before Noah's flood. Needless to say, this remarkable demonstration of educational failure attracts little attention from those who call for improving our schools.

My brilliant husband, a sociologist and political theorist, refuses to get upset about the poll. It's quite annoying, actually. He thinks questions like these primarily elicit affirmations of identity, not literal convictions; declaring your belief in creationism is another way of saying you're a good Christian. That does rather beg the question of what a good Christian is, and why so many think it means refusing to use the brains God gave you. And yes, as you may have suspected, according to the Pew Research Center, evangelicals are far more likely than those of other faiths to hold creationist views; just 24 percent of them believe in evolution. Mormons come in even lower, at 22 percent, although official church doctrine has no problem with evolution.

Why does it matter that almost half the country rejects the overwhelming evidence of evolution, with or without the hand of God? After all, Americans are famously ignorant of many things—like where Iran is or when World War II took place—and we are still here. One reason is that rejecting evolution expresses more than an inability to think critically; it relies on a fundamentally paranoid worldview. Think what the world would have to be like for evolution to be false. Almost every scientist on earth would have to be engaged in a fraud so complex and extensive it involved every field from archaeology, paleontology, geology and genetics to biology, chemistry and physics. And yet this massive concatenation of lies and delusion is so full of obvious holes that a pastor with a Bible-college degree or a homeschooling parent with no degree at all can see right through it. A flute discovered in southern Germany is 43,000 years old? Not bloody likely. It's probably some old bone left over from an ancient barbecue. To celebrate its fifth anniversary, the Creation Museum in Petersburg, Kentucky, has installed a holographic exhibit of Lucy, the famous proto-human fossil, showing how she was really just a few-thousand-year-old ape after all.

Patricia Princehouse, director of the evolutionary biology program at Case Western Reserve University, laughed when I suggested to her that the Gallup survey shows that education doesn't work. "There isn't much evolution education in the schools," she told me. "Most have no more than a lesson or two, and it isn't presented as connected with the rest of biology." In fact, students may not even get that much exposure. Nationally, Princehouse said, at least 13 percent of biology teachers teach "young earth" creationism (not just humans but the earth itself is only 10,000 years old or thereabouts), despite laws forbidding it, and some 60 percent teach a watered-down version of evolution. They have to get along with their neighbors, after all. In Tennessee, home of the Scopes trial, a new law actually makes teaching creationism legal. "No one takes them to court," Princehouse told me, "because creationism is so popular. Those who object are isolated and afraid of reprisals." People tend to forget that Clarence Darrow lost the Scopes trial; until the Supreme Court ruled otherwise in 1968, it was illegal to teach evolution in public schools in about half a dozen states.

Kenneth Miller, a biology professor at Brown University and practicing Catholic who is a leading voice against creationism, agrees with Princehouse. "Science education has been remarkably ineffective," he told me. "Those of us in the scientific community who are religious have a tremendous amount of work to do in the faith community." Why bother? "There's a potential for great harm when nearly half the population rejects the central organizing principle of the biological sciences. It's useful for us as a species to understand that we are a recent appearance on this planet and that 99.9 percent of all species that have ever existed have gone extinct." Evangelical parents may care less that their children learn science than that they avoid going to hell, but Miller points out that many of the major challenges facing the nation— and the world—are scientific in nature: climate change and energy policy, for instance. "To have a near majority essentially rejecting the scientific method is very troubling," he says. And to have solidly grounded science waved away as political and theological propaganda could not come at a worse time. "Sea-level rise" is a "left-wing term," said Virginia state legislator Chris Stolle, a Republican, successfully urging its replacement in a state-commissioned study by the expression "recurrent flooding."

The group Answers in Genesis, which runs the Creation Museum, has plans to build a full-size replica of Noah's Ark as part of its Ark Encounter theme park. If that "recurrent flooding" really gets going, you may wish you'd booked a cabin.

EXAMPLE: *Dulce et Decorum est,* **Wilfred Owen**

> Bent double, like old beggars under sacks,
> Knock-kneed, coughing like hags, we cursed through sludge,
> Till on the haunting flares we turned our backs
> And towards our distant rest began to trudge.
> Men marched asleep. Many had lost their boots
> But limped on, blood-shod. All went lame; all blind;
> Drunk with fatigue; deaf even to the hoots
> Of disappointed shells that dropped behind.
>
> GAS! Gas! Quick, boys!—An ecstasy of fumbling,
> Fitting the clumsy helmets just in time;
> But someone still was yelling out and stumbling
> And floundering like a man in fire or lime.—
> Dim, through the misty panes and thick green light
> As under a green sea, I saw him drowning.
>
> In all my dreams, before my helpless sight,
> He plunges at me, guttering, choking, drowning.
>
> If in some smothering dreams you too could pace
> Behind the wagon that we flung him in,
> And watch the white eyes writhing in his face,
> His hanging face, like a devil's sick of sin;
> If you could hear, at every jolt, the blood
> Come gargling from the froth-corrupted lungs,

Obscene as cancer, bitter as the cud
Of vile, incurable sores on innocent tongues,—
My friend, you would not tell with such high zest
To children ardent for some desperate glory,
The old Lie: *Dulce et decorum est*
Pro patria mori.

EXAMPLE: **Problems for Atheistic Evolutionists,
www.creationtips.com**

Good Arguments against Evolution

Evolutionists who reject God and miracles have some huge problems to explain.

Problem No. 1
How did the universe come about?

There is, of course, no scientific law or demonstrable process that would let something evolve from nothing. If there was nothing in the universe to begin with, obviously nothing could happen to cause anything to appear.

Atheistic evolutionists often try to duck this problem—which is impossible for them to answer satisfactorily—by saying that evolution is not concerned with the origin of life, only how life progressed after it appeared. But assuming the existence of an intricately working universe with some sort of life-forms already in it is not a minor assumption, and puts more faith in an unknown, counter-intuitive process than Christians put in God.

The problem is that if you can't get something from nothing, it's pointless thinking you can accurately explain the next step. Juggle the figures any way you like, but without a Creator you are not going to get anything, let alone *everything.*

For more information on the origin of the universe, see *Models of the Origin of the Universe,* by Dr. John Rankin.

Problem No. 2
How could living creatures come from non-life?

Again, there is no scientific law or demonstrable process that can account for non-living objects coming to life. The non-living soil in your garden didn't turn into living trees and flowers. They came from seeds, cuttings, or grafts from other living trees and flowers. Life invariably comes from something that is already alive.

Atheistic evolutionists have long believed that at some time in the distant past, life arose from non-living substances. British biologist T. H. Huxley in 1869 and physicist John Tyndall in 1874 were early promoters of the idea that life could be generated from inorganic chemicals.

But biology has found no support for this, and much against it. The invariable observation is that only living things give rise to other living things. Life could not begin if God and miracles took no part! Dr. Kenneth Poppe says in his book *Exposing Evolution's Weakest Link*, "There are no provable mechanisms for how molecules could increase in complexity without cells to produce and utilize them. For example, you cannot assume proteins before you have the DNA that codes for them."

Imagine all life on earth disappeared. There are no trees, plants or animals. All we have is rocks, dust, and lifeless matter. So how does the earth get populated with living things? That's the atheist evolutionist's unanswerable dilemma, and shows the massive faith they have to hold in preposterous answers.

For more information on abiogenesis (the theory that contends organisms originated from non-living material), see the CreationWiki article, *Abiogenesis*.

See also *Origin of Life Questions and Answers*, by Answers in Genesis.

Problem No. 3
How could new genetic information arise?

There is no known scientific law that would allow one kind of creature to turn naturally into a completely different kind. Insects don't evolve into more *complex non-insects* for instance, because they don't have the genes to do it.

To show that all life evolved from a single cell, which itself came from some type of chemical soup, there would have had to be massive genetic information gains.

But evolutionists have failed to show how this gain of new information occurred. Where did the information come from for the first bristles, stomachs, spines, intestines, complex blood circulation systems, intricate mouthpieces to strain special foods out of the water, and so on, when these were supposedly not present in the ancestral species?

The theory of evolution teaches that *complex life-forms evolved from simple life-forms*. There is no natural law known that could allow this to happen. The best that evolutionists can come up with to try to explain how this might have happened is to propose that it happened by mutations and natural selection.

But mutations and natural selection do not show *gain* in information, just rearrangement or loss of what is already there—therefore there may be beneficial mutations without an increase in genetic information.

Mutations overwhelmingly destroy genetic information and produce creatures more handicapped than the parents. (See our article on *TNR, the Totally Naked Rooster*.) And natural selection simply weeds out unfit creatures. Natural selection may explain why light-colored moths decrease and dark moths proliferate, but it cannot show that moths could ever turn into effective, totally different, non-moth creatures. Moths do not have the genetic information to turn into something that is not a moth, no matter how much time you give them. Nor could they evolve from something that was totally different from a moth.

For more information on macroevolution, see the CreationWiki articles *Macroevolution* and *Macroevolution has never been observed*.

See also *Speciation Questions and Answers* by Answers in Genesis.

Problem No. 4

Where is the proof that apes turned into humans?

Despite the evidence being pathetic, even if you claim the title of World's Biggest Optimist, evolutionists still tell the story that once upon a time humans evolved from ape-like creatures.

Many years ago this argument seemed credible to a lot of people because there was so little hominid fossil evidence that it was easy to imagine evolutionary links everywhere.

But things have changed. Thousands of fossils and fossil fragments of apes and humans have now been found—and they don't show a steady progression from apes to humans at all. Fossils have been found in the wrong time-frames, put into the wrong categories before all the evidence was in, and what was once thought to be the ape-human family tree now actually has no trunk—just unconnected branches.

Because evolutionists can't change their theory, they are stuck with the evidence looking more confusing for them with each new hominid/homin/hominine fossil discovery. Instead of *clarifying* the alleged link between apes and humans, new fossil discoveries are making it *harder* to show which type of ape or ape-like creature evolved into a human.

For more information on ape fossils making monkeys out of humans, see the article *Humans are not descended from apes*.

Alternative view

We believe that the evidence is stronger for those who believe the Bible's account of creation—that in the beginning God created the world and all the major types of creatures to reproduce "after their kind."

Related topics:

- Ape-human evolution never happened.
- Lucy is not the missing link.
- Ida, the "missing link" dud.
- Human babies born with tails are not evidence for evolution.
- Evolution trees: The problem with those dotted lines.
- Pests and germs do not evolve resistance to poisons and antibiotics.
- Neanderthals were humans—not ape-men or missing links!
- Human embryos do not retrace the stages of evolution.
- Why dogs and finch beaks don't prove evolution.

- Could God have created using evolution?
- Is evolution a fact, like gravity?
- Why does evolution breed tyrants?

EXAMPLE: **Cigarette Warning, FDA**

Google something like "images cigarettes addictive" to find images that the FDA has considered putting on cigarette packs. Analyze some of the images. What argumentative strategies are at work in the choice of these images to persuade people not to smoke?

Questions about the examples:

1. Is the FDA warning an argument?
2. Who are the audiences for the examples?
3. Blogger Mark Edson (chapter 6) took a stance on global warming that could be seen as politically opposite George Will's stance in his essay. Can you imagine common ground between the two? Which type of persuasion do you find more effective?
4. In terms of changing people's behavior, do you think a picture is worth 1,000 words? How about a poem?
5. Which examples use *ethos*, *logos*, and *pathos* most effectively?
6. Which argument do you disagree with most strongly? Which of its points came closest to changing your mind?
7. Almost every writing sample in this book could be considered an argument. Look at some of the samples outside this chapter. What are they arguing, and how?

Questions about Argument

I. What are its purposes?

We argue to persuade, to demonstrate our skill and knowledge, to right wrongs, and to give credit where credit is due. A popular writing text is called *Everything's an Argument*, and certainly every piece of writing has a persuasive component, from the college application essay with its implied message "Please take me" to the grocery list, which is a series of commands: "Don't forget the eggs!" You can make an argument for your interpretation of a story, for your choice of candidates, for a change in registration procedures.

The purpose of an argument isn't necessarily to win a debate or persuade someone to a particular way of thinking. In the world outside school, most arguments end in compromise, with participants forced to find common ground.

Many writers follow the principles of Rogerian argument to see the issue from multiple perspectives, acknowledge the reasoning of their opponents, find the overlap in the different positions, and work toward a win-win solution.

Your integrity is on the line when you argue. It may seem convenient to exaggerate or make up facts, but doing so can destroy your credibility. Your reputation as a writer and thinker—your *ethos*—is more important than scoring a few points in a debate.

What purposes do you see behind our example arguments?

2. Who are its audiences?

In a classroom setting, the argument is likely to have at least two primary audiences: the teacher and the (usually imagined) people whose opinion you're trying to change with your paper, people on the other side of some debate. You probably won't persuade your teacher to change views of gun control or the university parking problem, but you might well impress your teacher by how well you research your facts and marshal your evidence.

"What Price Clean Air" first appeared in a newspaper, *The Washington Post*. Who is the author trying to reach? Who is the FDA trying to reach with its cigarette pack ads?

3. What's the typical content?

An argument makes a claim based on certain assumptions and backed by facts and details presented in a way to make them seem logical. It may help the writer's motivation if the writer really cares about the topic, but your teacher may assign you to write on the side opposite the one you really believe in. The subject of the argument is limited only by imagination. If you dislike the word "argument," think "thesis": a paper with a clear thesis and support is an argument.

4. How long is it?

As long as it needs to be, from a sentence to a book.

5. How is it arranged on the page?

You might use bullets for a series of facts, and in general you want readers who skim to be able to grasp your point.

6. What pronouns are used?

"I" is common, though some writers feel that "we" is stronger, and some like to pawn off their opinions as those of "the American people" or "most reasonable people."

7. What's the tone?

Some people conceive of arguments as what happens before a brawl, but in fact written arguments are often understated and try to convince an audience through an accumulation of evidence and logic, not with a threatening or nasty tone. Assume your readers are reasonable people, and you want to invite them to your side, not make them defensive.

Describe the tone of each of our arguments. Which is most effective?

8. How does it vary?

Think of the range of arguments you see in a day, from billboards to emails trying to convince you to go to an event. Few of them would announce themselves as "argument," yet they're trying to convince you of something, and they use many of the techniques of argument. If you want to study the range of kinds of argument, look at every reading in this book and identify the claims and the evidence and the techniques used to present them. What works for you as a reader?

Suggested Moves for Writing an Argument

I. Discover.

If you're trying to find a subject, **Inventory** ➡61–68, making each list at least twenty items long. If you have a subject, **Analyze your purposes** ➡55. Is impressing your friend a more important purpose than getting a good grade or persuading some imaginary opponent to agree with you? Get as clear as you can about what you're actually trying to accomplish. **Brainstorm** ➡69 all of your arguments and evidence and all you can think of for the other side as well. Then talk to people about it: **Tell me what I'm saying** ➡79 or **Pass the ideas, please** ➡80.

2. Develop.

Anyone making a serious argument needs to be aware of what the opposition is thinking and saying. **Take the other side** ➡82. And you need to have your facts straight: **Answer the journalist's questions** ➡87. **Adjust distance** ➡85 for maximum persuasiveness. **Explain your code words** ➡93. **A tree diagram** ➡99 might help you ask all the right questions.

3. Gather.

Along with gathering all the material upon which you'll base your argument, find the latest on the Internet. **Read from the Internet** ➡108–112.

4. Integrate.

Be sure to **Integrate your own ideas** ➡131 into your argument but keep in mind that others' ideas probably carry more weight, so **Quote** ➡123 and **Integrate sources** ➡133. Work to establish a positive *ethos*, argue logically for a position, and appeal to the audience's humanity: *Pathos, logos, and ethos* ➡135.

5. Focus.

Brainstorm titles, leads, and ends ➡ 142–144. **Find the problem/tension/ conflict** ➡ 145. **Find a focusing detail** ➡ 146.

6. Organize.

You want your argument to be clear and easily understood, so you might **Try standard organizing patterns** ➡ 166, because readers are used to patterns like "compare and contrast" or "chronological order" and will follow them easily. If the audience is likely to agree with your argument, spell it out early and then provide backing. If the audience is skeptical, pile on the details and arguments before you take your stand. Work with a partner to **Analyze your thesis** ➡ 169 and make sure it's coming across.

7. Revise.

Revision at all levels is crucial for an argument; the smallest mistake can give your opponent a chance to undermine you. **Learn the red flags of your prose** ➡ 196. Check your structure and focus with **Make ends meet** ➡ 197 and **Examine the links** ➡ 198. Be sure to **Revise your verbs** ➡ 208–216, since they're so important for making a forceful argument.

8. Present.

Maybe you'll be lucky enough to present your argument to people who have power to make changes.

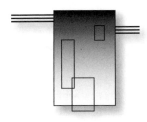

Blogs

EXAMPLE: **Weather or Not We're Ready, It's Here, Mark Edson**

Sunday, June 10, 2012

I've been thinking, again, about the weather. This time, though, I mean the external meteorology, climate change, not the solipsistic this-is-how-it-looks-inside-so-that's-how-I-see-the-outside stuff. I know I've written about things climatic before, at least tangentially, but it's getting harder to deny that we're entering a strange new world unless you're a multi-billionaire already, someone who's made your fortune on environmentally-degrading endeavors and wants still way more money and so you spend barrels of cash on having "experts" plant the seeds in the minds of average people that this whole climate-change thing is a hoax and no, this isn't a run-on sentence, just a lengthy and barely-controlled one.

But really, is there any plausible deniability left? David Letterman started his TV career as a weatherman in Indianapolis and once said that there were hailstones the size of canned hams falling in his broadcast area. I don't guess that's accurate even now, but as Jackson Browne said, "Don't think it won't happen just because it hasn't happened yet." We've had at least 3 hailstorms in the last couple weeks in this area, some quite damaging; I certainly can't remember belonging to the hailstorm-of-the-week-club ever in the past. And in case you're wondering, I got a great deal on hyphens on E-bay recently, so I've got plenty to use willy-nilly (see?).

I know, too, that I mentioned Kurt Vonnegut's *Cat's Cradle* a while ago, so I'm sure I've given you all a chance to reread it. As you'll recall, then, the book's basic premise is that, the US military, grown tired of being mired in swamp after swamp in their various wars, have (that may be a more British verb form there, the "have" rather than "has," "military" for them being a collective noun rather than a single entity, thus "they have" rather than "it has," leading to the awkward-sounding, to our ears, use of the singular v--oh, never mind) commissioned their scientists to come up with something that dries up any mud they might encounter. The result is something called "Ice Nine" (Jerry Garcia named his music publishing company "Ice Nine," for what it's worth). It works great, essentially freeze-drying the water in the mud and allowing their vehicles to ride atop the suddenly hard ground.

The problem, of course, one which no one considered, is that Earth is a closed system and all water on the planet is ultimately connected to all other water. Hence, the entire planet becomes a rime-covered waterless uninhabitable desert. Oops! As Vonnegut describes it: There was the sound like that of the gentle closing of a portal as big as the sky, the great door of heaven being closed softly. It was a grand AH-WHOOM.

I opened my eyes--and all the sea was ice-nine.

The moist green earth was a blue-white pearl.

The sky darkened...the sun...became a sickly yellow ball, tiny and cruel.

The sky was filled with worms. The worms were tornadoes.

When my kids were babies and I'd stop in their rooms to kiss them one more time on my way to bed, I often took the opportunity to apologize to them (they were asleep--I wasn't trying to give them nightmares. What kind of person do you think I am, for chrissakes?) for having brought them into this world. The only reasons, it seems to me, to have kids intentionally are the biologically-encoded drive all organisms have, to propagate to ensure the continuation of the species (hardly necessary in our case, what with seven billion others around to handle that) and ego: the need to ensure a specific genetic line's continuation, or to attempt to ensure one's own immortality, or whatever other socio-psychological theory is currently in vogue about that issue. But I don't think it's 'cause we think we're giving these new beings a slice o' paradise.

Maybe the sky's not falling, maybe it won't soon be filled with worms of tornadoes, though I bet there are people in this country who'd say it already has been. But it sure seems to me that we're at least dipping our toes into waters we know nothing about. We're changing the sky above us with greenhouse gases and the very ground beneath us with our hydrofracking experiments to feed our fossil fuel dependency which will then put more gases into the atmosphere which will then, you get where I'm going. I guess what baffles me most is this: where do the Koch Bros. and all of the other billionaire anti-climate-change propagandists and fanatical, dissembling environmental deregulators think they're gonna go if cataclysmic events caused by our behaviors do happen? Are they so insulated by money and privilege that they think they're somehow immune? Must be, but wow. And what of their children and children's children?

All of this sparked by a few hailstones--what a whackjob I must be. But the music'll be good: lots of weather-related stuff--"Stormy Weather," "Bless the Weather," "Earthquake Weather," "Hail, Hail, Rock 'n' Roll," and many "nowhere" songs, 'cause we don't really know where we are anymore and there's nowhere else to go, and Bruce Cockburn's "The Trouble With Normal." Join me Tuesday, noon-till-two, won'tcha? And "Hi," Rybie!

"Pay attention to the open sky/You never know what will be comin' down...."

Questions about the example:

1. Unlike the author of a printed book, whose work has been approved by editors and reviewers, a blogger has not been reviewed by anyone, and a blog can be as fanciful and false as the writer wants to make it. How does Edson establish his authority on the subjects he's discussing?

2. How did you feel when you got to the end and realized that Edson also has a radio show?

3. Do you like reading someone's strong personal feelings, or would you appreciate a more "objective" or balanced presentation?

4. Do you imagine that writing a post like this makes the writer feel better? Here's how blogger/contractor/ex-writing teacher Edson answered that question: *Weirdly, yes, I do feel better, though I'm not sure I can really say why. There's all of this anger and outrage and bafflement and bemusement and sadness spinning around inside of me and being able to put it down and out seems to assuage it if only briefly. I've always just wanted people to get me and know what a wonderful and valuable and amazing person I am and carry on accordingly, which is to my mind simply the flip side of screaming, gnawing, nearly-debilitating-at-times insecurity. I also like to think that, while I'm not ever gonna change anything significantly, maybe someone will think differently about something I write about, or just think about it, or maybe realize there are others who think similarly. And some of it's just a chance to show off stuff I've got that others maybe don't. It ain't pretty between these ears on the inside, either.*

Questions about Blogs

1. What are its purposes?

The purposes for which someone starts or contributes to a blog are as diverse as the subjects of blogs themselves. Some blog, certainly, in the hopes of making money. But most bloggers also spend the time and energy to express themselves, to make the point THEY want to make about basketball statistics or race relations. Some bloggers want readers; others don't seem to care about an audience. But they DO care about making their point. Mark Edson clearly wants to make himself heard about climate change. What other purposes does his blog serve?

2. Who are its audiences?

The answer to that question seems to change by the day, as more and more people find blogs useful sources of ideas, useful outlets for expression, or both. Bloggers seldom know who might read what they write, though most have a core readership. Beginning bloggers imagine a readership and write for it . . . and sometimes it materializes.

3. What's the typical content?

Most blogs contain a large measure of opinion. Many also contain information, though that information usually hasn't been checked by anyone and should therefore be considered less reliable than information from most printed sources and even wikis.

4. How long is it?

As long as the blogger wants to make it.

5. How is it arranged on the page?

Most blogs scroll straight down but they may highlight or downplay the text and the surrounding material. People writing for someone else's blog don't usually have much control over how their words appear.

6. What pronouns are used?

Most bloggers use "I."

7. What's the tone?

It depends on how the blogger wants to be perceived and can range from purposefully obscure or offensive to business-like and formal.

8. How does it vary?

Literary journal editors always say "read an issue before submitting a piece to us," and that advice is probably even more true for bloggers. You don't want to blog in a tuxedo about gardens if others are blogging in cutoffs about Dr. Seuss.

Suggested Moves for Writing a Blog

Creating your own blog is just about as easy as opening a new document in a word-processing program. Use something like Google's Blogger, tailored for newcomers. It will take you step by step through the process that results in your blog becoming available on the Internet. For free. A slightly more complex process involves downloading software like WordPress and then finding a web host for your blog. (One of WordPress's favorite hosts is Laughing Squid.) Or you may be able to use social media as a blogging tool.

I. Discover.

First, **Shut up the critic** ➡47. Your first attempt at a blog will likely feel awkward, as does any new genre. **Freewrite** ➡72 about what motivated you to blog in the first place or about what you know about the subject of the blog. If you're supposed to blog as an assignment, **Inventory** ➡61–68. There's bound to be something in those lists that you want to tell the world about. Consider **Creating a persona** ➡75. Is there a particular aspect of your character or your opinions that you'd like to give voice to? It can be fun and liberating to write as someone else. Early in the process, **Share your story** ➡78 or 79.

2. Develop.

The next generation of bloggers may blog in textspeak, but many writers today approach writing a blog as they would approach an essay. Follow the **Accordion Principle** ➡152. Write your ideas out in full the first time, not worrying about word count. Then go back and save the good parts. You need to consider your multiple potential audiences and how they might read your blog. **Brainstorm a list of contexts** ➡89. Your audience may see your ideas in a context you never imagined. People may not be able to hear the virtues of the golf course you're proposing if all they're thinking about are potential wild parties at the clubhouse. As soon as you've got a draft to work with, **Explain your code words** ➡93.

3. Gather.

Try **Memory joggers** ➡100 and **Brainstorm songs and song lines** ➡101. Finding a song that connects to your post can both help your thinking about it and give you a way to hook your readers.

Even if you've chosen a subject you know a lot about, you may need to do traditional research. You don't want to spread inaccuracies to a potentially huge audience.

4. Integrate.

Your ability to **Summarize** ➡125 may be important at this stage. Can you quickly and fairly boil down a book or an interview into a couple of sentences? Can you take a paragraph of your own and turn it into a single sentence? **Integrate your own ideas** ➡131.

5. Focus.

It's up to you—and perhaps the blog's traditions—whether your blog has the same kind of focus and point you'd want in a personal essay. Try **Filling in the blanks** ➡141 to come up with potential focal points. If that doesn't work, **Find the problem/tension/conflict** ➡145. And once you've got some kind of direction, **Brainstorm leads** ➡143. You only have seconds to catch the eye of hyperactive Internet readers. If you haven't yet systematically considered all your possible audiences, **Focus for different audiences** ➡148.

6. Organize.

A blog post may not need as tight a structure as a formal essay, but you should still **Answer readers' questions** ➡159. If you're interested in communicating with readers, not just in expressing yourself, make sure you're **Writing reader-based prose** ➡158. Is your post long and complex? **Use headings and subheadings** ➡165.

7. Revise.

Imagine that your post is to be read by thousands. Make it as good as possible. **Revise your process** ➡189–194. To make sure that the whole thing holds together, **Make ends meet** ➡197. Be sure to **Share** ➡219.

8. Present.

You may not have much control over how your post looks, but you can look at other posts on the blog and try to imagine how you can use its color scheme and highlighting techniques.

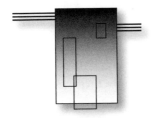

Email

EXAMPLE: **To Professor from Student**

HEY HOW R U THIS IS XXXXXX AND MY PT TOLD ME THAT I WS DOIN BAD IN CLASS AND I DIDNT REALIZE IT UNTIL TODAY LIKE 4REAL AND SHE SAID U SAID U WAS WILLING TO HELP ME DO MY HOMEWORKS ASSIGNMENTS. OR WHAT EVER I GOT TO DO IN THIS CLASS TO GET A (C) OR BETTER IN THIS CLASS. IF I COULD DO EXTRA WORK WHICH I PROBLEY CNT BUT I HAVE TO PASS THIS CLASS SOWE NEED TO MEET ASAP IM FREE 2MORROW AFTER 330. AND IF I DO GOOD ON THE NEXT TWO TEST I SHOULD BE GOOD AND GET 20/20 ON MY ASSIGMENTS JUST PLZ LET ME KNW CAUSE WE ONLY HAVE 4 WEKS AND I REFUSS TO FAIL THIS CLASS SO GOT TO GET TO WRK AND I REFUSS TO GET A C- OR C+ I NEED A C OR BETTER SO IM ABOUT TO MAKE THIS THIS BEST 4WEEKS OF MY LIFE TO PASS THIS CLASS WITH A C OR BETTER THANKS JUST LET ME KNW WHAT I CAN DO IM FREE 2MORROWAFTER 330 SO WHENEVER WE CAN MEET THANKS

Questions about the example:

1. What do you think the professor who received this email concluded about the student who wrote it?
2. Nobody has told you, "These are the rules of email." Yet what implicit rules does this email violate?
3. If you were a writing teacher working with this student, would you despair? (Hint: there's VOICE in this email, and that's the single most important ingredient in great writing.)

Questions about Email

Email is a medium through which almost anything can be transmitted, but it also shares many properties with genres: it has its own conventions that writers must be aware of and generally adhere to. Our sample email is an actual message sent to a professor by a student. You may have thought that anything goes in email, but how many writing conventions did our sample ignore? Did it communicate successfully? If you had been the recipient of the email, what would you have thought of the sender?

1. What are its purposes?

Email is used for communicating any message that doesn't require the formality of a hard-copy letter or the instantaneousness of a phone call. Because email is fast, permanent, and easy to file and to search, many people use it almost exclusively for their business correspondence. But you should never email something you're not willing to let the world see. Once released on the Internet, your words take on a life of their own. Writing an email to a friend may feel as casual as a dorm-room conversation, yet the email may be permanent and find its way to the wrong people. So don't say things in an email that you can't stand behind.

As compared to other forms of writing, email is particularly susceptible to being sent in haste, before the writer has fully thought through all the implications and eliminated as much potential misreading and confusion as possible. Many people create an email rule for themselves: Don't SEND until morning.

2. Who are its audiences?

Anyone who can read. Because email can be so easily forwarded and copied, you always need to be thinking, "Whose hands might this get into?"

3. What's the typical content?

Email is more formal, personal, and individual than social media. Some use it to keep in touch, others just for business or to do research. There's no "typical" content.

4. How long is it?

There are no limits, though someone preparing a multi-page document would be smart to write it with a word processor and send it as an attachment rather than as an email.

5. How is it arranged on the page?

Email text goes through several conversions before it appears on the receiver's monitor, and all formatting, including paragraph breaks, can be lost without the sender's knowledge. So there's not much point in trying to make email text look good, though I double-return between email paragraphs in hopes that a paragraph break will be retained.

6. What pronouns are used?

"I," usually, though some dispense even with that.

7. What's the tone?

Anything's possible. Hostile emailing has helped create a new term—"flaming." No matter how angry you are, you don't want to get a reputation as a "flamer."

8. How does it vary?

Every element of an email can vary as tremendously as the audience varies. The weightier the email, or the higher-up the recipient, the more the email should resemble a formal business letter: "Dear Professor" or at least "Hello." No "LOL" or "IMHO." Use appropriate punctuation and capital letters.

Some people seem to feel that email puts everyone on the same plane. But don't assume with your words or tone that you and the receiver are buddies. Be respectful and put on your snappiest outfit. It will seem odd, even stuffy, if you usually email only friends, but that little jolt of discomfort is a useful wakeup: Are you approaching this recipient in the most appropriate way? Have you made all the points you want to make?

Suggested Moves for Writing an Email

Because of the huge variety of ways that people use email, and our general impatience to "send it off," I'm not going to pretend that most people will conscientiously follow a ten-step process every time they write an email. Instead, I will suggest a few moves crucial to creating any email that matters to you.

Analyze the writing situation ➥ 1. Yes, we do this unconsciously, more or less automatically, but I get enough totally inappropriate emails to know that we all need to take the extra seconds that this move requires. If this is a casual email to a friend you trust, you might be able to skip all the suggested steps and just "talk." But if the friend you trust, A, is friends with B, someone you don't trust, you'd better be careful what you say to A about mutual friend C, or within seconds B might be reading your email and plotting to blackmail you.

Ask the assigner for ideas ➥2. With emails, the "assigner" is often a previous email; that email will determine exactly what you need to say in yours. Most writers make a point of rereading and replying to the most recent message about the subject rather than starting a new thread. Similarly, it makes sense to gather all relevant emails and printed documents before you begin composing the email.

If you've got more than a couple of things to say in your email, **Inventory** ➥61 on a piece of scratch paper your reasons for writing. Save yourself from having to write a "PS" email. If your list is long, consider writing on a word processor first, using a series of your favorite moves with the document, and then attaching your revised and polished document.

Most people write emails in one short sitting, but that doesn't mean that important emails should be written stream-of-consciousness and sent off without a second thought. You've got to reread any piece of writing that you care about. If you have a tendency to send before you think, **Draft recursively** ➥176.

If it's an important subject or an important audience, quickly **Freewrite** ➥72 about what you want to accomplish with the email. What kind of response will be useful to you? You may find that you're writing not to accomplish something but just to vent, in which case you need to obey one simple rule: don't click *Send*.

Learn the red flags of your email writing ➥196.

Have a friend read a few of your emails looking for issues of tone and clarity. Do you sound like you're yelling or irritated? Do you have habits of typing or abbreviation that make your readers' jobs difficult? Should you make a resolution to wait at least an hour before replying to any irritating email?

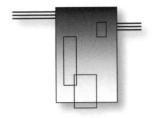

8

Gripe Letter

EXAMPLE: **Refund Request**

Brock Dethier
Anytown, USA

January 1, 2010

Mr. Cedrick Smee
Fantasyland, USA

Dear Mr. Smee:

I am enclosing two tickets[1] to Fantasyland, USA, for which I paid a total of $135.63 on December 9, 2009.[2] I deserve a refund for the full amount paid[3] because of my bad experiences at your park on that day.

Two of your employees dressed as clowns went out of their way to give my son frightful experiences from which he may never recover. Both times, I saw the clown coming and steered away from him as much as I could. But they were relentless in their drive to cause terror. During the second attack, my son soiled himself, something he hasn't done for over two years. Of course we weren't going to stay after that, so we retreated to our car, my son with his hoodie pulled tight over his face.

Sincerely,

About this example (numbers below correspond to those in the letter):
1. Use your evidence . . . but keep copies of everything.
2. If you don't provide specifics, they'll stall by asking for them.
3. Be specific about what you're asking for.
4. Can you locate uses of *ethos*, *pathos*, and *logos* in this letter?

EXAMPLE: **Complaint**

1377 South 1200 East
Batham ID 83241

December 4, 2004

Claudia Sorensen
Montrose-Pierce Library
109 North 5th East
Batham ID 83241

Dear Ms. Sorensen:

This past Wednesday I attended the pre-school story hour for the first time at the Montrose-Pierce Public Library with my infant son. Three books were read. The third book, a book on the history of candy canes, was ultimately a book about Jesus. It suggested that the red in the candy cane represented the blood of Christ's sacrifice. I left before finding out what the white symbolized. I am not a member of the Church of Jesus Christ of Latter-day Saints. I am not Christian. And it is against state and federal laws to use a public service like the library to promote or endorse any particular religion. I am angry that such a book was selected. It is both inappropriate and illegal.

Choosing a Christian book for story hour is symptomatic of a much larger and systemic problem plaguing the Jefferson County Library. While the library's collection is fairly small, it is dominated by LDS books and books published by LDS authors and presses. To the point, in the online catalog I can find only five books by Nobel prize-winning author Toni Morrison, one book by Alice Walker, and zero books by Sandra Cisneros, Gabriel Garcia Marquez, or Louise Erdrich. These are important contemporary writers whose work is changing how we think about the world and the way we want to live our lives. At the same time, there are forty-two books available by LDS author Jack Weyland. How is that possibly justifiable? The library is a public service, meant to serve the needs of a diversity of people and interests.

At a time when newspapers and media outlets are all owned by a few giant conglomerates and the independent bookstore has fallen to mega bookstores who control what gets bought and sold, libraries are the last spaces supporting a broad range of ideas and thoughts. They must remain committed to free speech and democracy. Censorship does not just mean banning a book. Censorship occurs through omission and absence. Children, adolescents, and adults depend on the public library to offer books and services that explore the world of ideas. The Montrose-Pierce library is failing the public it serves. It is engaging in censorship and blurring the lines between church and state.

I see two problems. The first is relatively easy to address. In the future, unless you are going to read stories that represent all religions and points of view, you should not allow any stories that promote one religious viewpoint. The second is much harder but, in the end, more important. You need to rethink the books that you purchase for the library. You are a state institution and your collection should represent the diversity of the country.

I ask that you respond to my concerns. If I do not hear from you, I will write the county, the state, and the local chapter of the ACLU. As an English teacher, I take access to books and the potential for empowerment found in literature very seriously.

Sincerely,

Jennifer Sinor

Questions about the example:

1. Do you think Sinor's complaint is justified?
2. What do you think she hopes to accomplish by writing the letter?
3. What elements make her letter effective? Does anything undercut her point?

Questions about the Gripe Letter

1. What are its purposes?

To set things right, to feel as though you CAN be heard, to blow off steam in a productive way, to get free products or services, to improve the product or service for future customers.

2. Who are its audiences?

The customer service people at a big company or whoever opens the envelope at smaller organizations.

3. What's the typical content?

As our sample letters demonstrate, a gripe letter needs the following:

a. Standard business letter format: your address, the date, inside address, Dear Somebody: opening
b. All available details about your gripe
c. Specific action you would like taken (for instance, refund or apology)
d. How you can be reached

4. How long is it?

No longer than it has to be. There's little point in carrying on about how outraged you are. A succinct, biting sentence probably has more kick than pages of rambling anger.

5. How is it arranged on the page?

Just like a standard business letter.

6. What pronouns are used?

"I" and "you" are common, though you might want to soften the accusation by saying "your company" or "your organization."

7. What's the tone?

Some degree of irritation may be expected, but it's generally a good idea to assume, at first, that your audience will be reasonable and accommodate you. Probably not a place for humor.

8. How does it vary?

Many complaints about goods and services now take place on the Internet; some companies don't read snail mail or don't even have a mailing address. But whether you're writing a three-page rant. or just filling in the boxes of a form, the same principles apply: you need to include every fact and detail you can. While you're on the website, collect contact information, and be ready to call if you don't get a response to your complaint in a week or so.

Suggested Moves for Writing a Gripe Letter

I. Discover.

Most gripe letters are motivated by a desire to do something about a particular issue NOW so that the writer feels better about it. It might take some **Brainstorming** ➡69 to think of all the ways that the airline's losing your bag affected you, or all the kinds of pain that the bad implant cost you. If you're doing a gripe letter for an assignment, list the products that have gone bad on you recently or the things that have made you mad.

2. Develop.

Make sure you include all the details. **Answer the journalist's questions** ➡87, but there's no need to write much more than the facts. You might **Expand** ➡92 on the consequences of whatever you're complaining about.

3. Gather.

You just need names, dates, receipts, previous correspondence. If this is a serious complaint that might involve lawyers or large sums, **Keep a log** ➡105 of everything that goes on. If you have the time, you might consider doing a **Survey** ➡115 of all of the company's customers you know.

4. Integrate.

A quotation from the company's own literature might spice up your letter. **Integrate sources** ➡133.

5. Focus.

If you've been treated badly, you may need to focus your anger. Write down everything you're angry about, then decide which is the most aggravating and see if you can relate the others to it, so it becomes one gripe with many examples. **Find the problem/tension/conflict** ➡145.

6. Organize.

You have more freedom in a gripe letter than in other types of business letters; you're playing the role of aggrieved customer or client, not perfectionist professional. One easy approach is to summarize the situation, detail the problem, then sketch out your solution. Such an organization is likely to mirror that of **Answering the readers' questions** ➡159.

7. Revise.

Proofread well. If they can reject your claim because you were one digit off, they will.

8. Present.

Don't let them dismiss you because you're sloppy or careless.

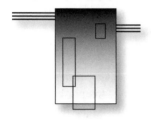

Literary 9 Analysis

EXAMPLE: **Undressing King Lear, Diantha Smith**

King Lear begins the play fully clothed, not only in a crown and robes, but also with power and respect. Throughout the play, Lear's mental and emotional states are reflected by his change in clothing. As he loses more and more control—first of the kingdom and then of his own mind—his body also becomes more exposed. At his greatest points of self-realization Lear says: "unbutton here" (III.iv.109) and "Pray you undo this button" (V.iii.310). The audience may literally see more of King Lear's body as he sees and understands more of his true self. His loss of clothing and sanity reveal a lot about human frailty and help make *King Lear* one of Shakespeare's most intimate tragedies.

The first item of clothing King Lear gives up is his crown and the Fool warns Lear, "Fathers that wear rags / Do make their children blind / But fathers that bear bags / Shall see their children kind" (II.iii.48–51). Lear soon realizes that his Fool is right—at least as far as his eldest daughters are concerned. Like the king in Hans Christian Andersen's tale of *The Emperor's New*

Clothes, Lear allows flattery to get the best of him and ends up losing not only his clothes, but his dignity as well. Ironically, as long as he wore the crown, Lear couldn't see the true nature of those around him, but as soon as he takes it off he begins to understand who truly loves him.

The next major loss of clothing occurs when Lear is thrown out by Regan and Goneril and left out of doors during a tempest. This night is the first time King Lear has ever been exposed to harsh elements and he considers the poorest in his kingdom, saying, "Poor naked wretches . . . O, I have ta'en / Too little care of this! Take physic, pomp, / Expose thyself to feel what wretches feel" (III.iv.28, 32–34). His realization of how his robes of state have blinded him is complete when he sees Edgar, almost completely naked, and says, "Thou art the thing itself; unaccommodated man is no more but such a poor, bare, fork'd / animal as thou art. Off, off you lendings! Come / unbutton here" (III.iv.106–109). The king takes off his clothes and puts them on "Poor Tom," foreshadowing Edgar's return to power (which seems to change hands just as easily as men change clothes). More importantly, however, we have evidence that Lear is fully aware of how shallow his life is. Without the warmth of love and kindness, all of his possessions—even the silks and furs—offer no real comfort unless they are shared with others.

Though Cordelia gives King Lear new hope and new garments when she finally finds him again, his return to comfort does not last long. The web of betrayal has already been spread and by the end of the play every member of Lear's immediate family is dead. For Lear, losing Cordelia is equivalent to losing any hope of redemption or future happiness. When he realizes that her life is over he symbolically pleads, "Pray you undo this button. . . . Do you see this? Look on her! Look her lips, / Look there, look there!" (V.iii.310–11). These final lines represent the final undressing of Lear as his spirit leaves his body, but the reference to "her lips" also tells us that Lear may have finally understood why Cordelia's silence was better evidence of her love than any words.

If this play has a moral, perhaps it is that we must be careful how we judge, especially when it comes to outward appearances. We may realize, as Lear did, that: "Through tatter'd clothes [small] vices do appear; / Robes and furr'd gowns hide all" (IV.vi.163–64). All of us hide behind appearances in some form or another. Though facing adversity is painful, it is usually when we are "unbuttoned" that we can see things most clearly.

EXAMPLE: **Luke Skywalker vs. Dracula: Gothic Elements in *Star Wars*, Benedek Nyikos**

The original *Star Wars* movies seem like an unlikely place to find Gothic elements. After all, they are all about spaceships, laser swords, and teddy bear creatures that can destroy elite military troops. On closer inspection, however, *Star Wars* turns out to be full of Gothic themes. Darth Vader is an obvious instance of a dark villain wielding mysterious powers much as the title vampire does in *Dracula*, and Princess Leia is a damsel who, like Mina, needs to be rescued, in Leia's case from the Death Star (though she repays the favor by rescuing Han Solo from Jabba). There are some less apparent but equally interesting Gothic elements in *Star Wars* as well, such as the theme of main characters losing control over themselves, swept along by forces outside their control.

The most overarching force that controls destinies in *Star Wars* is the aptly named Force. In the *Star Wars* universe, the Force is held to control people's destinies, as revealed in *Star Wars* by Han Solo, who comments, "There's no mystical energy field that controls my destiny." Though Solo may deny it, his affirmation of the existence of such a belief informs the viewer of this aspect of the Force. Of course, Luke Skywalker has the most important destiny, as revealed to him by Obi-Wan Kenobi. When Kenobi leaves Skywalker with Han Solo and Chewbacca in a Death Star room, Kenobi says, "Your destiny lies along a different path." Kenobi believes that Luke's story has been written for him, and Kenobi is confident enough in this belief to tell Luke what he should and should not do based on his destiny. Even villains inform Luke of his destiny, as when, in *The Empire Strikes Back*, Darth Vader tells Luke, "You can destroy the Emperor. He has foreseen this." Though Vader is trying to use the Emperor's vision to convince Luke to join Vader against the Emperor, the fact that the Emperor has foreseen Luke's ability to destroy him takes the event out of Luke's hands.

Of course, the Emperor has a different view of his foreknowledge. His most sinister line from *Return of the Jedi* is "Everything is proceeding as I have foreseen." When he later tells Vader that "I have foreseen it. His compassion for you will be his undoing. He will come to you and then you will bring him before me," the viewer knows that things will happen in exactly this way. The film does not give an opportunity for the viewer to doubt at this point that things will turn out this way, as they do. The climax of the series is based on the idea of breaking free from forces beyond the hero's control. When the Emperor tells Luke, "By now your father can never be turned from the Dark Side. So shall it be with you," he mirrors the ominous proclamation from *Dracula* when Dracula says, "Your girls that you all love are mine already; and through them you and others shall be mine—my creatures, to do my bidding and to be my jackals when I want to feed" (370). The menace in both these cases comes from the villain telling the hero that the hero has already lost, and the only thing that remains is for things to play out as the villain knows they will. Of course, both the Emperor and Dracula are mistaken, and the heroes end up destroying them in the end.

Neither the Emperor nor Dracula places his trust entirely in destiny to fulfill his diabolical plans. Both of them attempt to capture the heroes at some point.

Dracula locks Harker in his room, and when Dracula allows Harker out, he still cannot access the outside of the castle. Dracula's imprisoning influence also works to cause Lucy and Mina to stay indoors, either because of their ill health stemming from the vampire's bite or from fear of the vampire himself. In *Star Wars*, Vader imprisons Princess Leia in a cellblock awaiting execution. In *The Empire Strikes Back*, Han Solo is locked in carbonite and Luke almost shares his fate. In *Return of the Jedi*, Luke finds himself locked in a pit with a monstrous rancor, while Han, freed from the carbonite, is kept in a jail cell with his Wookiee friend Chewbacca.

As the finest trilogy in cinema, the original *Star Wars* trilogy has become a cultural icon. Every aspect of our culture has felt its influence, but in its day other sources heavily influenced it in turn. One of these sources was the Gothic tradition, which supplies, among other things, a fear of losing control as a major theme. Whether that control is metaphysical or practical, it allows the villains to manipulate the heroes right up until the end.

Questions about the examples:

1. Do you see any similarities between the two examples, despite their radically different subject matter?
2. Can you see how each example could teach a reader or viewer something new?
3. What purpose does either one serve?
4. If you know the pieces discussed (*King Lear*, *Dracula*, and the *Star Wars* movies), did you find the writers accurate? If you don't know them, did the essays make you interested to see them?

Questions about Literary Analysis

1. What are its purposes?

For years, English teachers have assigned students to write literary analyses in the hopes that learning to analyze a short story or poem will help the student to analyze other non-literary subjects. Literary analysis skills that will serve you well in a variety of thinking and writing tasks include the following:

- Close reading. Most poems require careful reading with a dictionary in hand and knowledgeable friends to consult. Housing contracts, tax forms, and a host of other documents deserve the same scrutiny. If you become skilled at wringing all possible meanings from a text, at paying attention to details, you will find that skill serves you well in situations where the right words really matter.
- Using your head and your heart. Some think of analysis as purely rational, left-brain thinking. But if the analyst doesn't really care about the subject, has not gotten close enough to form an opinion, the analysis is

likely to seem lifeless. Often good literary analysis uses the language of logic to try to explain a pre-logical, gut reaction. Many people need to learn to listen to all their strong reactions and see if they can make sense of them.

- Making connections. Anyone with hard work and perseverance can make a list, but it takes a spark of genius to make a good connection, see a relationship that others haven't seen. Literary analysis often connects particular details with larger themes in the work. But you can make connections involving genre, the author's biography, place and time of writing or setting, the music or metaphors of the language . . . The possibilities are almost endless. Literary analysis can be a treasure hunt. Get used to being the person who sees the meaning in the minor detail. That's a skill crucial to everything from research science to human resources.

- Developing meaning. By making connections, consciously and unconsciously, readers make meaning as they read, drawing on a wide range of information from linguistics to grammar to previous experiences. A good literary critic sees meaning where others see chaos.

- Making a difference. Eventually, every responder to a literary work needs to ask "What is the purpose of my response? Who cares?" Readers will care if your response illuminates the work: if readers read your paper, then reread the work, they should see more and appreciate more because of having read your paper. The reader of your paper cares because he or she wants to understand the work better and get more pleasure from it. How can you satisfy such an eager reader? Every discipline has its own process of making meaning out of details, often with the input of others. The more practice you can get in such processes, the more versatile your writing can be.

Can you identify these kinds of thinking in our example essays?

2. Who are its audiences?

One crucial question to ask anyone who assigns literary analysis is whether you should assume that your reader has read the text you're examining. Some literary critics write primarily for other critics and specialists. Others try to help the general public appreciate literary works. Some literary analysis transcends the boundaries of the genre and takes on qualities of the personal essay.

3. What's the typical content?

The analysis focuses on a particular element of the work—setting, language, character, history, etc.—and usually connects that element to another either inside or outside the work. We see in our example papers that Diantha Smith links the gradual loss of King Lear's clothing to his loss of power and mind, while Benedek Nyikos helps make sense of *Star Wars* by showing how it borrows some elements from *Dracula*.

4. How long is it?

I hope someone has given you instructions about this, because a literary analysis could be a short paragraph that a national magazine might publish or a book longer than the original text.

5. How is it arranged on the page?

Traditionally, literary analysis was written in long, full paragraphs, but the lessons of highlighting and bullets have affected many literary critics. Assume that you're writing for a conservative audience. Or find a blog that you might contribute to, and format your analysis for that blog.

6. What pronouns are used?

Practitioners disagree. There is a school of autobiographical criticism that's happy with "I" and a school that would prefer to think of literary analysis as similar to a science and critics as self-effacing scientists. No "I" for them. If possible, ask your audience.

7. What's the tone?

Some literary critics who reach an audience outside academia do so by being funny or caustic. Mark Twain's ever-popular "Fenimore Cooper's Literary Offenses" is both. More commonly, literary critics need to establish their authority by writing reasoned, judicious prose.

8. How does it vary?

Audience, of course, is crucial. If you're writing for a book-reading group, your analysis will likely be quite different from a paper you'd write for a class full of English majors. How formal does it need to be? Do you need in-text citations and a works cited (or references) page? The goal of most literary analysis is to illuminate the text, shed some new light on it so that others can appreciate it more. But if you're writing for a class, it may be even more important to show that you have a good grasp of the text and its context.

Suggested Moves for Writing a Literary Analysis

1. Discover.

First, **Ask your teacher or boss** ➡48 and **Write down your gut feelings** ➡67. You may need to **Shut up the critic** ➡47. **Brainstorm** ➡69 a list of everything that interested you in the work. **Look for what's valuable** ➡52. Choose one idea or image that most intrigues you and **Map** ➡73. If you're not coming up with anything, **Think like Zippy the Pinhead** ➡74.

2. Develop.

Adjust distance ➡85 and **Find the one detail that best speaks for your subject** ➡88. Save that detail. It might become part of a lead or end, or possibly you could organize your whole paper around it. Now **Brainstorm a list of contexts** ➡89. **Explain your code words** ➡93. **Define** ➡94. **Develop a thesis** ➡97.

3. Gather.

As you read, **Annotate** ➡104, then **Transcribe and explain** ➡107, and if you're working in a group, **Use group members' strengths** ➡118.

4. Integrate.

Does your professor or boss want you to integrate ideas and quotations from other people, or are you supposed to just come up with your own ideas? **Probe attitudes about integrating sources** ➡119.

5. Focus.

Focus with freewriting ➡140 about all the ideas you've had so far. **Find a focusing detail** ➡146.

6. Organize.

Weave your theme ➡164. **Try standard organizing patterns** ➡166. **Sketch the organization of your paper** ➡167.

7. Revise.

Make ends meet ➡197.

8. Present.

Is there a conference or a student magazine where you could present your paper?

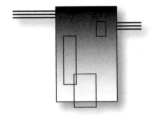

10

Literature Review

EXAMPLE: **Not Milk?, Anne Wilcken**

Milk has long been hailed as a healthy, comforting, and even essential drink by the American people. However, recent research suggests that regular consumption of cows' milk might actually be dangerous to human health. Those who oppose milk drinking claim that milk is composed of a cocktail of antibiotics, growth hormone, cholesterol, and bacteria. Most people are unaware of these claimed dangers of milk. Despite belief and evidence that milk is good for our bodies, research and the current health problems of America suggest that milk is actually unhealthy and does not provide the health benefits claimed.

Based on our planet's many species and what we know about nature, it is unnatural for humans to drink cow's milk, according to Dr. Robert Kradjian. Dr. Kradjian explains in his "Milk Letter," that we are the only species on Earth that drinks milk from another species, and that milk drinking after infancy is unnatural as well. He even goes on to compare the human's selection of a cow to get milk from to selecting a rat or dog for their milk (Kradjian 2009).

In her book *Nature's Perfect Food: How Milk Became America's Drink*, E. Melanie Dupuis, PhD makes a similar claim, "Milk drinking was an extremely minor aspect of the human diet until modern times" (2002, 4).

So how did milk become America's drink and why is it so widely accepted as healthy and essential for our bodies? Dupuis explains that milk drinking began as a breast-milk substitute for infants in the mid-nineteenth century. By the 1880s milk drinking expanded to children and adults (5–6). Dupuis suggests that the reason Americans drink milk is that "milk is more than a food, it is an embodiment of the politics of American identity over the last 150 years . . . a product of a particular social and political history" (8).

Robert Cohen explains an additional reason for the prevalence of milk drinking in American society: milk is heavily influenced and regulated by the government because it is a large industry. Recent concerns about food safety with milk have been dismissed by the FDA. For example, Cohen cites the instance where the use of rBGH (recombinant bovine growth hormone used to increase milk production in cows) has been endorsed by the FDA as not posing health risks to humans, despite concerns expressed by consumers and other groups (1998, 166).

Both Cohen and Kradjian agree that rBGH is indeed a dangerous part of milk and that it, along with other milk ingredients, is contributing to a vast array of common health problems in the United States. One of these major health issues is heart disease, which is America's number one killer (cholesterol in milk and dairy products contributes to heart disease). Other diseases associated with milk consumption include breast cancer, leukemia and diabetes (Cohen 5, 70, 166, 246–247; Kradjian).

Cohen and Kradjian also agree that most of the world's population is intolerant to milk, and that milk drinking is primarily done by Caucasians who seem to have kept at bay the genetic milk allergy. Even so, many Caucasians develop a milk allergy with age. Cohen and Kradjian use this wide-spread allergy of milk to conclude even further that milk is unnatural for our bodies (Cohen 259–261; Kradjian).

The common belief that milk is the best source of calcium and is essential to developing and maintaining bone density is challenged by Cohen. He makes the fundamental point that with large amounts of protein intake, calcium absorption is inhibited and is actually excreted in urine; milk contains significant amounts of protein and, therefore, is not the best source of calcium (266). Likewise a study on the effects of increased milk intake along with exercise on bone density concluded that "extensive milk intake reduces the bone density of women" (Yoshii 2007). Interestingly, this study also found that while milk intake did not increase bone density, exercise did (Yoshii). Scientists researching increased milk intake along with calcium-rich foods and the incidence of osteoporosis-related fractures concluded, "The study found no evidence that higher intakes of milk or calcium from food sources reduce fracture incidence"

(Freskanich 1997). The Harvard School of Public Health agrees that greater milk intake does not mean stronger bones. However, supplemental vitamin D does decrease fracture risk (Harvard School of Public Health 2009).

The traditional American conception of milk as a healthy and bone-strengthening essential drink is being challenged by scientific studies on milk consumption's relationship to disease and bone density. Through my research I have found sources that will help me to explore the reasons researchers are now questioning milk's health benefits, Americans' motives for drinking milk, and whether Americans should limit milk consumption to increase their health.

Works Cited

Cohen, Robert. *Milk: The Deadly Poison*. New Jersey: ARGUS Publishing, Inc., 1998. Print.

Dupuis, E. Melanie. *Nature's Perfect Food: How Milk Became America's Drink*. New York: New York University Press, 2002. Print.

Feskanich, Diane, et al. "Milk, Dietary Calcium, and Bone Fractures in Women: A 12-Year Prospective Study." *American Journal of Public Health* 87.6 (1997): 992–997. EBSCO Host. Web. 20 Oct. 2009.

Harvard School of Public Health. "Calcium and Milk: What's Best for Your Bones and Health?" *The Nutrition Source*. Web. 24 October 2009.

Kradjian, Robert M., MD. "The Milk Letter: A Message to my Patients." Courtesy of afpafitness.com, n.d.: n.p. Web. 6 Oct. 2009. http://www.not-milk
.com/kradjian.html.

Yoshii, Setsuko, et al. "Cross-Sectional Survey on the Relationship between Dairy Product Intake and Bone Density among Adult Women and High School Students." *Nutrition Research* 27 (2007): 618–624. Web. 28 Oct. 2009.

Anne Wilcken's literature review was written as one of the preliminary steps toward a persuasive researched paper, the major work of the writing course she was taking. In Wilcken's hands, a lit review comes to resemble a small persuasive essay. The assignment description asked students to "discuss five of the most relevant sources in your research." It explains, "a literature review lets the reader know that you have done your research—that you have looked carefully at the experts in the field and their varying opinions on your topic."

Questions about the example:
1. How does Wilcken demonstrate that she has done her research?
2. How is this literature review similar to and different from an annotated bibliography? In what circumstances would you choose one over the other?
3. Wilcken has definitely taken a side in the issue she's studying. Does that

make her paper more or less useful for other researchers?

4. What elements of the review make you interested in reading the full paper?

To see how a literature review fits in the context of a larger work, see the second example in chapter 14: Proposal.

Questions about the Literature Review

1. What are its purposes?

The literature review sketches the intellectual context in which a writer intends to establish his or her own terrain. It bolsters the writer's authority by showing that the writer knows the field. And it is a boon to readers interested in tracking the history of a particular issue or line of thought.

How does Wilcken's review establish her authority?

2. Who are its audiences?

Generally the lit review is part of a larger work like a thesis or dissertation, so the audience would be that of the longer work. Researchers you'll never meet or know about would be another audience.

3. What's the typical content?

Theoretically, the lit review surveys all the literature—books and articles—most relevant to the longer work that follows the review. "Relevant" is of course a subjective term, and sometimes the lit review will take on the character of an essay in its own right, focusing on only one aspect of the relevant literature. In general, a summary summarizes and a literature review synthesizes.

Does Wilcken's review seem balanced or focused on one side?

4. How long is it?

In some dissertations, the literature review can go on for chapters, so important is it for the writers to situate themselves in the ongoing conversations in their fields. Even in short articles, the lit review is usually at least a paragraph long.

5. How is it arranged on the page?

Often the pieces under review will be listed at the beginning. Otherwise, it looks much like an essay.

6. What pronouns are used?

Generally there's more of a pretense to objectivity than there is in reviewing movies or CDs, and perhaps less use of "I" and "you."

7. What's the tone?

Normally fairly distant, objective, perhaps dry.

8. How does it vary?

Some literature reviews are strictly informative, providing context for new work, with the writer being as objective as possible. Other reviews are persuasive: the writer takes a stand and arranges discussions of the works under review to make his or her point. Special considerations include whether the writer knows any of the authors under review and whether the audience is likely to agree with the thrust of the review. If the audience is likely to disagree, the writer should probably withhold an opinion and build inductively to a conclusion.

Suggested Moves for Writing a Literature Review

1. Discover.

You probably don't have to discover a subject; either the lit review will be part of a larger work with its own focus, or you will do it on something you've recently researched. **Ask your teacher or boss** ➥48 about the focus and limitations of the review. In some disciplines, the literature review could take up half of the total space. In others, the writer mentions two names and is done. If you're beginning to write a literature review, I hope you've done your homework—I hope you've been active as you read the texts, **Annotating** ➥104, **Keeping a log** ➥105, or using a **Double-entry journal** ➥106. Discovering should be a relatively enjoyable task of combing your notes for what joins the various texts and what makes them distinct.

2. Develop.

Spend some time listing sources and drawing connections between them, noting parallels and overlaps. A good lit review develops one heading under which all the sources fit, so be on the lookout for that heading, that overarching concept, as you make specific connections between items on your list. **Find the overlap** ➥86.

3. Gather.

Don't just read; use the gathering-with-reading moves in chapter 25. If your sources are books, chances are other people have written about them, and you can probably find review online. You shouldn't plagiarize, of course, or even necessarily quote from them, but other reviewers will see things in a different way than you did and may perhaps help you make the connections that will hold your review together.

4. Integrate.

A literature review is all about integrating at least the names of your sources into a larger whole that you construct. The major difference between a literature review and an annotated bibliography is that a lit review doesn't just summarize, it **Synthesizes** ➥126. Can you write about two or more of your sources in the same sentence? **Explain to integrate** ➥127.

5. Focus.

Some lit reviews are simply a survey, with no attempt to make order or meaning out of the variety: "Here's what's going on in this field at the moment." Other reviews make a point of ordering the chaos, unifying the variety: "The field is moving in THIS direction." Which tack did Wilcken take? **Summarize** ➥125 all the material you've read. **Brainstorm titles** ➥142 as a way of seeing for yourself where various focuses might lead. **Expand then choose** ➥152; don't try to be brief from the start.

6. Organize.

Your content will likely dictate your organization: if you have an organizing concept, you'll probably want to lay it out in the first paragraph, then present the sources as supporting evidence. **Weave your theme** ➥164.

7. Revise.

As is true anytime you're dealing with bibliographic information, little mistakes may easily creep into your work. Some people photocopy the copyright page of every source so they can refer back to it while proofreading.

8. Present.

Usually the literature review is presented as part of a longer unit, labeled "literature review" in a particularly long piece.

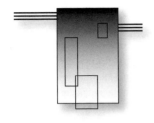

Op-Ed Essay

EXAMPLE: **The Importance of Writing Badly, Bruce Ballenger**

I was grading papers in the waiting room of my doctor's office the other day, and he said, "It must be pretty eye-opening reading that stuff. Can you believe those students had four years of high school and still can't write?"

I've heard that before. I hear it almost every time I tell a stranger that I teach writing at a university.

I also hear it from colleagues brandishing red pens who hover over their students' papers like Huey helicopters waiting to flush the enemy from the tall grass, waiting for a comma splice or a vague pronoun reference or a misspelled word to break cover.

I have another problem: getting my students to write badly.

Most of us have lurking in our past some high priest of good grammar whose angry scribbling occupied the margins of our papers. Mine was Mrs. O'Neill, an eighth grade teacher with a good heart but no patience for the bad sentence. Her favorite comment on my writing was "awk," which now sounds to me like the grunt of a large bird, but back then meant "awkward." She didn't think much of my sentences.

I find some people who reminisce fondly about their own Mrs. O'Neill, usually an English teacher who terrorized them into worshiping the error-free sentence. In some cases the terror paid off when it was finally transformed into an appreciation for the music a well-made sentence can make.

But it didn't work that way with me. I was driven into silence, losing faith that I could ever pick up the pen without breaking the rules or drawing another "awk" from a doubting reader. For years I wrote only when forced to, and when I did it was never good enough.

Many of my students come to me similarly voiceless, dreading the first writing assignment because they mistakenly believe that how they say it matters more than discovering what they have to say.

The night before the essay is due they pace their rooms like expectant fathers, waiting to deliver the perfect beginning. They wait and they wait and they wait. It's no wonder the waiting often turns to hating what they have written when they finally get it down. Many pledge to steer clear of English classes, or any class that demands much writing.

My doctor would say that my students' failure to make words march down the page with military precision is another example of a failed education system. The criticism sometimes takes on political overtones. On my campus, for example, the right-wing student newspaper demanded an entire semester of Freshman English be devoted to teaching students the rules of punctuation.

There is, I think, a hint of elitism among those who are so quick to decry the sorry state of the sentence in the hands of student writers. A colleague of mine, an Ivy League graduate, is among the self–appointed grammar police, complaining often about the dumb mistakes his students make in their papers. I don't remember him ever talking about what his students are trying to say in those papers. I have a feeling he's really not that interested.

Concise, clear writing matters, of course, and I have a responsibility to demand it from students. But first I am far more interested in encouraging thinking than error-free sentences. That's where bad writing comes in.

When I give my students permission to write badly, to suspend their compulsive need to find the "perfect way of saying it," often something miraculous happens: Words that used to trickle forth come gushing to the page. The students quickly find their voices again, and even more important, they are surprised by what they have to say. They can worry later about fixing awkward sentences. First, they need to make a mess.

It's harder to write badly than you might think. Haunted by their Mrs. O'Neill, some students can't overlook the sloppiness of their sentences or their lack of eloquence, and quickly stall out and stop writing. When writing stops, so does the thinking.

The greatest reward in allowing students to write badly is that they learn that language can lead them to meaning, that words can be a means for finding out what they didn't know they knew. It usually happens when the words rush to the page, however awkwardly.

I don't mean to excuse bad grammar. But I cringe at conservative educational reformers who believe writing instruction should return to primarily teaching how to punctuate a sentence and use Roget's Thesaurus. If policing student papers for mistakes means alienating young writers from the language we expect them to master, then the exercise is self-defeating.

It is more important to allow students to first experience how language can be a vehicle for discovering how they see the world. And what matters in the journey--at least initially--is not what kind of car you're driving, but where you end up.

EXAMPLE: **What Is a Practical Education? Donald M. Murray**

A university education is becoming more practical each semester. Our students are increasingly better prepared to go to work in a specific job the Monday after graduation—and that is just the problem. The better prepared they are for the Monday after graduation, the less prepared they may be for a lifetime of work in a society where change is the only certainty.

Few of us are doing the same job in the same way and in the same place that we were ten, five, or even two years ago. There is precious little security these days in being able to do a specific task for a particular organization. The successful survivors are those who can learn new jobs in a hurry. And the university has traditionally trained people who are prepared to learn and relearn as need or opportunity arises.

In recent years, however, there has been an enormous, understandable pressure from employers, parents and students to deemphasize those courses of study in the liberal arts and theoretical sciences that appear theoretical, impractical, and frivolous and to emphasize those courses that are pragmatic and vocational.

This conflict between general or liberal education and more vocational courses of study has always existed within the state university. It is a natural condition of schools that originally taught the agricultural and mechanical arts before becoming universities. Both strands must exist within the land grant university, but increasingly the forces within universities across the country that speak out for specific education and oppose general education have become stronger. Last year there was discussion of a new general education proposal on the campus in Durham, and some of the academic debate ranged from acrimonious to just plain nasty. This spring the issue of general education will come before the university again.

I may seem a strange supporter of general education, since I teach "vocational" courses in journalism. I do think such courses belong in the university—in moderation. We do *not* have a journalism major. We think that the best prepared journalists are those who have a few skills courses and many general courses.

Students with a university education should have breadth. Our society is increasingly complex. Our students should be able to put their job, their evolving beliefs, their votes in context. We need university-educated leaders who can see their decisions as part of an historical, sociological, political, aesthetic, scientific, philosophical context.

A student with a university education needs not only skills but theory. The student needs to know *why* as much as *what*, the reasons that lie below the tasks of the daily job.

Above all, university students need to know how to deal with change. They must be educated so that they are not frightened by change, but capable of absorbing and making use of it. The university, if it provides a good general education, challenges the student and forces the student to think about uncomfortable ideas, unexpected concepts, frightening theories, puzzling problems. The university prepares the student for a life of productive discomfort in which the student can deal with ideas and points of view that are not the student's own.

The university must be an uncomfortable place, a threatening place, a challenging place, a place that does not prepare the students just for a specific job, but for the many different jobs the student does not expect to hold.

I went to the University of New Hampshire as a student, knowing I would never teach, and came back 15 years later as a professor. I have taught engineers who have become editors, journalists who have become judges, foresters who have become writers, reporters who have become real-estate developers. We must educate our students for the lives they do not expect to lead.

We in the university, and those of you outside the university, must make sure that our universities, in a time of economic stress, do not become so practical that our students are cheated of the education they will need in a society that will certainly change in ways we cannot predict. We must make sure our students are given the practical advantages of an impractical education.

EXAMPLE: **Soap Box: All in a Day's Work, Jennifer Sinor**

That there was a skunk scuttling about on the side of the road yesterday morning as I ran did not surprise me. I have seen a lot of skunks on my running route in the past few years and have come to expect them at certain moments: near the fields, when it's warm, often halfway into my route.

I think I noticed this skunk only because it seemed so friendly. It didn't dart back into the long grasses but rather rambled along the edge of the road, as if enjoying the morning light, taking in the air.

I was thinking of how much this skunk looked like my cat, Este, and how lucky I am to live in a place where I meet with skunks on my morning runs, when a small truck pulled up alongside me. If it had been darker or if I was living somewhere besides Whitney, Idaho, I might have worried that a pickup truck was slowing down. In this case, though, I just kept running, leaving the skunk and the truck, wondering if perhaps the skunk was a pet and its owners had finally found it, or if they were there to work on the electric cables or the water lines, or if they, too, were surprised at the friendliness of this skunk and stopped to look.

I was a hundred yards away when I heard the gunshots: four of them, disrupting the morning stillness. I stopped and turned to look back but could see little. Two men had gotten out of the truck and were on the side of the road, but the truck's headlights made it difficult to see much else.

I debated about what to do. I was tired. I only had a mile and a half to go. More importantly, I wasn't sure I wanted to know what was happening back at the truck. It seemed easier just to ignore the situation, mind my own business, pretend that gun shots punctuated all my runs. Perhaps because I had only moments ago been thinking how happy that skunk made me, perhaps because the skunk reminded me of all that I love about living here, or perhaps because I had to, I ran back.

By the time I got back to the truck, the two men were already inside the cab and starting to drive away. I stood in the middle of the road, hoping they would stop. In my running shorts and t-shirt, I felt small and exposed and for a moment second guessed my decision.

"What are you doing?" I asked when the truck slowed to a stop.

"Did you know a skunk was chasing you?" the driver said, laughing like it was all a big joke. They were large men, barely fitting the cab. I looked around for the gun.

"I saw the skunk. He wasn't chasing me" I said. How dare he, I thought, make this about me, about what I needed, about my safety. "Did you shoot it?"

This is when the other man spoke, the passenger, or laughed really, like a crazy person might. "Yeah, we killed it," he said, grinning madly.

The driver, though, knew I was angry and shot his friend a look to silence him. "No," he said, "We just scared it away."

"But why?" I asked, "Was the skunk harming anyone?"

"Those people," he answered, and pointed to the two still-dark houses down the road. "If we didn't shoot it, a car would have hit it, and then it would have smelled. Do you know how bad they smell?" He paused, a smug look on his face. "We saved it from getting hit by a car."

By killing it, I thought. You saved it by killing it.

The men drove away. Our conversation was over.

What happens that two people are driving to work one morning and decide along the way to kill something? Yes, a skunk, I know, not a person, not even a dog. A skunk is a nuisance, or commonly thought to be one. But they kill it nonetheless. They take a life along with their coffee and the morning news. What happens when killing is that easy? What happens when you approach the drive to work, as you must your life and the world, in terms of exterminating all that threatens you?

The answer, sadly, is right in front of us. We are fighting a war that was initiated by the US as a preemptive strike, as a defense against the future. I often cannot understand how we can justify the assurance of violence as a means of preventing the possibility of violence. Then I watch two men kill a skunk for no reason, and I understand all too well.

How we live our daily lives is how we live our national one. I am reminded of Jane Tompkins who writes that genocide begins at home. In fact, it begins in a small town on the southeastern edge of Idaho, early in the morning as a skunk meanders out from the field.

I see no difference between the actions of those two men and those of our country. It's only a matter of scale. The little acts of violence we commit every day make possible the destruction of another country, of a people. Even when—and especially when—we carry out that violence under the banner of saving others.

What is the number of people who must be killed in order to assure that the Trade Center disaster will never happen again? How many people must die for us to feel "safe"? Genocide most certainly begins at home. What decisions will I make—will you make—on the drive to work this morning?

Questions about the examples:

1. The examples vary in many ways. What makes them similar? From this limited evidence, what conclusions would you draw about the op-ed essay?
2. How does Murray use readers' expectations to make his point?
3. Why does Sinor choose a skunk to be a focus of her essay?
4. How would you describe the voices of the three writers? Do you prefer one over the others?
5. Could these examples also be called "personal essays"?
6. Did Ballenger convince you about writing badly?

Questions about the Op-Ed Essay

I. What are its purposes?

"Op-ed" means "opposite the editorial page" though it could just as well mean "opinion-editorial." It's the page that many newspapers devote to opinion essays written (and signed) by people not on the paper's editorial board. (Usually the paper's own editorials, written by the paper's editorial staff, are not signed.) Sometimes famous people or experts in a subject use op-ed essays to get their opinions across, but most newspapers will also print well-written essays on currently relevant subjects from anyone.

Donald Murray, a journalist and English professor, wrote his piece for the op-ed page of *Foster's Daily Democrat*, a newspaper in Dover, New Hampshire. What were Murray's purposes? The essay is thirty years old. Has it lost its relevance?

2. Who are its audiences?

As is true for many writing projects, op-ed essays must appeal to at least two different audiences: the newspaper's editors and readers (and, if it's a school assignment, the teacher as well).

Do any of them aim for particular audiences?

3. What's the typical content?

The op-ed essay usually conveys a new, strong, or unusual opinion about a topic of current interest to the newspaper's readers. The content therefore varies as much as do the stories on the newspaper's front page.

How do our writers choose content for broad appeal?

4. How long is it?

Shoot for five to eight hundred words, two to three typewritten pages. If you're hoping to publish in a particular newspaper, see how long its op-ed essays are (and notice what they're about and what kind of tone they use as well).

5. How is it arranged on the page?

The newspaper will put it into columns and perhaps trim it to fit. You just need to present it as you would any other essay, with your name, the date, and a title at the top.

6. What pronouns are used?

Again, look for models in your target newspaper, but assume readers are expecting "I."

7. What's the tone?

It varies from impassioned and personal to more objective and distant, but all op-ed essays convey an opinion, so they're not as objective and impersonal as a news story would be.

8. How does it vary?

Each newspaper is slightly different, so you'd be wise to read a week's worth of editorial pages to get a sense of the acceptable length, whether the opinion essays are somehow linked to the rest of the editorial content, whether the paper uses essays from readers or only from syndicated columnists, whether it publishes only essays consistent with its editorial stance, or whether it welcomes alternative opinions.

Suggested Moves for Writing an Op-Ed Essay

1. Discover.

This is a crucial step for an op-ed essay because you need to find a subject and a perspective that both you and potential readers care about and are interested in. Start by doing inventories of **Authority** ➥62, **Strong feelings** ➥65, and **Territories** ➥66. Once you have a possible idea, **Dig into contexts and connections** ➥51. And before you get very far, **Tell your story** ➥78 and get some initial feedback.

2. Develop.

Answer the journalist's questions ➥87 to make sure you include all the basic information. Your essay needs to be tight, without holes (**Freewrite on what's missing** ➥83), and it probably needs to acknowledge and somehow deal with opposing viewpoints—**Take the other side** ➥82. Keep your eye open for **The detail that speaks for your subject** ➥88, and once you have a draft, circle and explain any **Code words** ➥93.

3. Gather.

It may help you to remember how your opinion on this subject formed. **Reflect** ➥102 on the origins and evolution of your ideas. One of the great challenges for an op-ed essayist is establishing credibility and authority, so ask yourself what sort of information might help you do that—facts, data, quotations from experts, references to other authorities. **Skim** ➥103 your sources looking for convincing material.

4. Integrate.

You may need to **Synthesize** ➥126 what others have said and integrate **Voices** ➥132 and **Sources** ➥133. Integration is a particularly important step for op-ed essays because establishing your authority is so crucial. See if you've used **Showing and telling** ➥134 and ***Pathos, logos,* and *ethos*** ➥135 to best effect, and **Check the flow** ➥139 with others.

5. Focus.

You'll almost certainly want to write more than your word limit, then boil it down to what's crucial: **Expand then choose** ➥152. Make sure you **Ask yourself the "So what?" question** ➥156. Readers will expect the essay to be all of one piece and easy to read, so **Brainstorm leads** ➥143 to find the best way to draw readers in.

6. Organize.

If you've brainstormed leads, choose the most likely one and expand it into a draft, trying to make your voice as strong as possible. Then **Outline your draft** ➥ 160. It would be smart to **Find a model** ➥ 163 essay in the newspaper you're writing for and see if you can imitate its organization. Get some help **Analyzing your thesis** ➥ 169.

7. Revise.

Editors will expect your essay to be tight and direct; **Polish out your weaknesses and build on your strengths** ➥ 201. Use as many of the revision moves as possible and get lots of **Feedback** ➥ 220.

8. Present.

There's nothing special about presenting an op-ed essay, but just for fun you might want to make it into columns to turn in for your class.

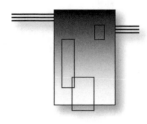

Personal Essay

EXAMPLE: **Everybody's Gotta Jump, Sam Abbott**

When I met poverty I wasn't prepared. I was 19 and hadn't left home more than a handful of times. And now, more than two years later, my mind still won't let go of that word or of the meaning I saw behind it. It seems to press on me, pushing me, prodding me. The seven letters that spell poverty bring me the same guilt a boy who's just peed in his pants feels. The word evokes a duty or responsibility that can't be shirked once it's heard. Meeting poverty is like jumping off a winter cliff into a frigid lake in Utah. The rush of the fall is exhilarating. The impact as you hit the water is shocking and painful. It's nothing you can imagine before you are in it. Everything around you is different and threatening. You learn and experience things for the first time that are frightening and cold, and you have no other options because once you leave the cliff you can't get back onto the dry ground. I experienced this jump. Here's how I met poverty in Visak, a small coastal city in Southeast India.

The first time I visited the Dola family—Prasad the father, Lakshmi the mother, and their teenage children Ganesh, Ramakrishna, and Dwarka—I walked to the edge of the cliff and looked over. All five of the family members worked overtime, 7 days a week. Ganesh and his father delivered steel rebar to construction sites, Dwarka ironed clothing at a shop across town, Lakshmi cleaned and cooked for a middle class family, and Ramakrishna sold vegetables in the local market. They each walked 45 minutes or more across their dark, crowded, sweaty city to get home every night. I met Lakshmi often as she traveled home and even though she looked worn and damp, she answered my "How are you?" with a simple "Happy, very happy." She was short and round. She was personable and outgoing. She smiled easily and often. She was totally contagious.

The Dolas lived in a cold cement shack smaller than most janitorial closets. When it rained the tin roof rattled like loose change down a stainless steel staircase. Nights without rain were spent sleeping on the dirt outside. Ramakrishna always said with an ivory grin, "It's nicer sleeping outside . . . less hot and more stars." He didn't speak much English. He was the older of the two brothers and worked hard to earn his father's respect. I never saw Ramakrishna with a shirt on except at church. His bare feet were flat and cracked from walking for years without shoes. He laughed at everything.

Dwarka was the youngest. She turned fourteen the fall I was in Visak. She had an optimistic attitude that didn't match her dilapidated, dirty clothing. I played an unnamed game with her, where we would try to spot each other first as I approached her home. She won every time. After she saw me, I would run up to her and shout a cheesy "Hello Family!!!" or a badly pronounced Telugu greeting, "Bangunnava!" Dwarka would always attract street dogs and give them celebrity names. She never touched them or fed them, but would tease them with her dress or a stick, or if she was lucky enough to find a ball she'd throw it for them to chase. She smiled like her mom. It was impossible, however, to ignore the brown color of her stained teeth. She chewed on a stick each day to clean her teeth - toothbrushes were not an option for the family. Whenever I left she would shout out the same thing. "Ok, Tata, Bye-bye, See-you!!!" And I'd yell it right back as loud as I could.

Ganesh was always rowdy. He got scolded often by his worrying mother and nagging sister. His favorite words were "Abbott, you're looking ugly. Why so ugly ra?" He snuck into movie theaters to watch Bollywood films he couldn't understand, and always commented on how pretty the actresses were. He didn't eat very much. He had a desire to protect his family, and eating less rice meant more for his mom and sister. I never told him I knew he was hungry.

The day I first greeted Ganesh and felt how hard and calloused his hands were was the day I jumped from the cliff. I never imagined a human hand could feel like rough granite. They were hard and bent from his rebar job. I didn't speak for several minutes. I felt my words couldn't approach him. My life felt so thin and vague in comparison to his. I hit the water and realized how cold and terrifying it was, and I wasn't sure I'd ever be the same. He questioned me about my strange reaction but I said it was nothing.

Prasad, the father, was different from the rest of them. He was like tough beef jerky. Like tough, silent, beef jerky. He communicated without words. I would see him smile, but when he did it was tired and fleeting. He asked nothing of those around him. He provided what he could for his family. He hurt deeply when his family didn't have food or when they were cold. He taught me what it means to be a father.

The Dola family didn't allow their poverty to govern the way they lived. They didn't know what the word even meant. They wouldn't allow the world to tell them how to feel. They were happy. But they affected me terribly. When I began to watch them and experience this word, it was as if I burst to the surface of that frigid lake gasping for air. Life became fragile and important. I thought about the things I owned and what was important to me.

My truck is huge, and uses gasoline faster than a toilet flushes. I have an iPod that fits in my mouth and holds a million cyber songs to soothe me when I'm lonely. My sleeping bag cost fifty dollars, and I want to spend more for the one that looks fancier. I own a computer and an Xbox. My house has three floors full of empty rooms.

I struggle to sleep because these thoughts still pound my head two years later. The names and faces are now etched in my life. I heard the word, jumped, crashed into a different world, and I can never make it back onto the dry ground of ignorance. I've got to tread water shouting until my voice fails. I've got to get others to jump in. That's the only way I can repay the Dola family for what they gave me.

This is how I met poverty. I didn't expect to be so changed by it. I've been shocked by how powerful the word is. It's not easy to meditate upon this one. It's not pleasant or simple, or even totally understandable. But until I felt the hands of a man who worked so hard for a family he loved so much, I didn't know life. Until I felt pure love from a family with nothing, I couldn't love. Now I invite people to come see the cliff for themselves.

EXAMPLE: **Music in the Milking Barn, Jeffrey Howard**

The music came on. He raised his clenched fists to ear-level, closed his eyes tightly, and started to sway. Right there in his dirty work jeans, stained T-shirt, and crap-covered irrigation boots. Back and forth. Right. Left. Over and over. Like he had gone to a place that no one else could follow.

I was embarrassed. *He* embarrassed me.

When Dad decided he'd had enough of milking other people's cows and bought his own back in 1989, some people made fun of his decision. After all, he'd been paid fairly well to work for his former employer, at least well enough to take care of his family and put away some money for retirement. After choosing to try it on his own, he became the only dairyman in the Tri-Cities, Washington area who milked Jerseys instead of Holsteins. I was only four years old at the time, but I remember my dad's old boss helping unload the cows from the cattle trucks and laughing about how small the animals were. My dad certainly never took that ridiculing seriously, though. Over the years, he just did what he knew how to do: twice a day, he went out to the milking barn, turned on the radio, and milked those little brown Jerseys. And he was content.

Dad went through radios for the milking barn like a chubby kid on a post-Easter candy binge goes through week-old Peeps. One after another. Now, he didn't enjoy having to buy new radios. Oh, no. Honestly, he only enjoyed *listening* to them. Unfortunately, he was often in need of another radio because they seemed to break down quickly in the barn. Every day, after all of the cows had been milked, I used the pressure-washer to clean the walls and floors and grates, and generally I managed to get at least a tiny bit—though generally more—of misting water on the radio speakers. Eventually, after continual moistening, the speakers would deteriorate, dominated by the hissing of static. So, as soon as one radio had passed on, Dad would then shop around at local thrift stores in order to find a decent replacement. He needed his music.

Of course, I can't say that I blame him for wanting music in the barn. Milking cows twice a day for two-and-a-half hours at a time with nothing to listen to but the beating pulsation of the milk pumps and the sucking noise of the milking machines slipping over a cow's teats can be, among other things, monotonous. Consequently, music was nigh essential to his sanity, as well as to mine and to my brother's because one of us—and sometimes both—was often in the barn helping Dad.

We only had one oldies' station in our area, but it was all Dad needed. He liked listening to the old songs, like Gary Puckett and the Union Gap's "Young Girl," Don Maclean's "American Pie," and many others. I was only ten years old at the time, but I could appreciate the old music, even though the musical groups on that station, like most of the people who still listened to them (my dad included), had long ceased to be popular and cool. But that didn't matter to me.

Something else did matter, though. At least, I thought it mattered back then.

My dad's favorite song in those days was—and, actually, I believe still is— "Nights in White Satin" by the Moody Blues. Whenever that song came on the radio, my dad did the same thing, regardless of how occupied he was at the time. Whether he was trying to push a new milk cow into the barn, stripping pus out of cow's infected teat, or angrily beating a cow's leg because she had dared to kick him when he had tried to put the milking machine on her, he automatically stopped what he was doing.

And he would dance.

That silly dance. His dance.

Now, I never would have had a problem with his dancing if he hadn't done it in front of me. My cheeks would color when the words "Nights in white satin / Never reaching the end" began (Hayward), because I knew he was about to start swaying on the rubber-matted cement floor in the milking parlor. Many thoughts came to me, but for the most part I just thought about what people would say if they saw him doing . . . that. It frustrated me that my dad acted that way. I tried to make him stop, but it only made him smile and rock more deliberately, as if he realized how his behavior tortured me and really wanted to make it sting.

Because the Moody Blues did not tend to come on the airwaves more than once or twice in a fortnight, I could have dealt with his occasional lapses in judgment and his obliviousness. But, no, he had plenty of other musical groups and songs to dance to in the absence of the Moody Blues. Roger Miller's songs "You Can't Roller Skate in a Buffalo Herd" and "King of the Road" were among the favored. He not only insisted on dancing to them, but he also sang along: "But you can be happy if you've a mind to. / All you got to do is put your mind to it / Knuckle down / Buckle down / Do it, do it, do it" (Miller). And he certainly did it. With eyes shut tighter than a monkey fist over a handful of nuts and a big smile on his sun-beaten face. In spite of my dismay and blood-filled cheeks. I'm not certain how many years he went on like that, but I know it was the same amount of time I spent being embarrassed and frustrated by his antics.

Almost a decade later and five thousand miles away, I sat down on my unmade bed in a small apartment in Brindisi, Italy and opened a letter I had just received from my mom. She explained that, because of economic difficulties and physical and mental strain, my dad had sold the cows and the dairy. I had known that selling the cows was a possibility for some time. Though Dad had never written to tell me how hard it had been to keep the dairy going productively after my brother and I had left, I knew the truth. And I could only imagine what my dad must have felt upon selling everything.

When I came back to the United States, my parents still lived in the same house that I had spent nine years of my life in, but the corrals around the old place were vacant. At seven in the morning and seven at night, I still expected to hear the milk pumps switch on and the strains of sweet, old-timey tunes coming from the barn with accompanying static. They never did, though. Not anymore. The radio had long since ceased playing, its intoxicating tunes crowded out by the static and fuzz of a hollowed-out reality.

Dad ended up finding a warehouse position, a job unlike the one he had had during the long decades before, and certainly not a job he enjoyed. It was a job. Nothing more. He still works there, too, working as hard as he always has to support our family. But if anyone happens to mention the dairy and the cows, it becomes instantly obvious that he still feels their distinct and deeply felt absence, like a kid whose favorite baseball has rolled beneath the couch to the only spot his short arms and stubby fingers can't reach. The worst part: he doesn't dance anymore.

In my mind, I can still look down the length of the narrow milking barn as though it were eternally present. The silence echoes. Then, from some place I cannot touch, the music starts again: "Nights in white satin / never reaching the end." And I think of my dad's little dance. The thought brings color to my face as I mentally observe him sway to his songs. However, my embarrassment is no longer due to him or to his odd routine.

I am embarrassed at myself.

I understand now that whenever I saw him doing that, the only thing I thought of was the possibility of people seeing him act like a three-year-old in a Toys 'R Us, and their thoughts about my connection with that man and his dancing. I never thought once that maybe he did it because he was where he wanted to be, doing what he wanted to do, and it gave him joy to the point that he didn't give a damn either way what others thought about him. Yes, I am embarrassed. Embarrassed that I never understood the significance of that mortifying dance and the songs that incited it. Above all, I am embarrassed because it took me so long to understand why he did it, not to mention all the wasted years I spent judging him rather than emulating his attitude or even trying to understand the reason why he danced. It's different now, though.

I'm the guy who dances.

Now, I go to work every day, teaching kids to read and write and explore their own minds. Pedagogy is my music; the classroom is my rubber-matted floor. And all of the businessmen and scientists in the world can be embarrassed, ask me to stop what I'm doing, and give me all the right reasons for trading in my dry-erase markers and argyle sweaters for a "more profitable" vocation. But, as far as I'm concerned, no other career could be more profitable to me. So when *my* music comes on, I close my eyes, raise my fists to ear level, and sway back and forth to a tune only the truly fortunate can hear because I don't actually give a damn whether people respect what I do or not. Let the economists' and the engineers' cheeks fill with blood on my account; I'll dance anyway. I'll dance like my dad did.

Works Cited

Hayward, Justin. "Nights in White Satin." *Days of Future Passed.* Deram Records, 1967. LP.

Miller, Roger. "You Can't Roller Skate in a Buffalo Herd." *Best of Roger Miller: His Greatest Songs.* Curb Records, 1991. CD.

Questions about the examples:
1. Does each piece have a thesis? Where?
2. Why does Abbott profile the individual Dola family members rather than

discuss money, economics, and politics, all of which are important to his subject?

3. Nothing much happens in Howard's piece. Is that a problem in an essay?

4. Much good writing aims to touch the universal by focusing on the specific. Do these pieces do that?

5. Can you find similes or metaphors in these essays? Would they be appropriate in other genres of writing?

Questions about the Personal Essay

1. What are its purposes?

That's a harder question to answer for the personal essay than for most genres. The essay is a literary form and for years a popular school form, practiced professionally by *New Yorker* writers like E. B. White and unprofessionally by millions of schoolchildren asked to write "themes" or "compositions." Like any literary form, then, the essay is at least in part aesthetic, admired for its beautiful images or precise phrasing. Most essays are also expressive, detailing the feelings or ideas of the author. And many current essays, especially those called "creative nonfiction," are informative as well, bringing the reader into a world and making that world real.

What do you think our authors' purposes are?

2. Who are its audiences?

For years, some English teachers acted as though the personal essay was a universal form, but now we have to admit that though the essay shares features with many other more businesslike genres, it's best used for personal and literary ends and read by people who enjoy good writing and deep thinking.

Who were Abbott and Howard writing for?

3. What's the typical content?

Anything that a writer might get interested in, which is to say anything at all. Get together with two or three classmates and spend five minutes brainstorming questions and meaningful contexts for the dullest object you can find—a pencil, a pebble, a piece of chalk. Did you come up with anything worth pursuing? Any subject is interesting when looked at the right way. And in personal essays, the writer and the writer's thoughts take center stage more often than in most other genres.

4. How long is it?

Five double-spaced pages seems to have become the default college essay length, but I have a feeling that has more to do with our liking to think in fives than it does with fifteen hundred words being an ideal essay length.

5. How is it arranged on the page?

Simply. It needs a title and has paragraph breaks. Otherwise, it tends to be straight text.

6. What pronouns are used?

Most personal essays have a first-person feel, whether or not "I" is actually used.

7. What's the tone?

Often reflective.

8. How does it vary?

What ten or fifteen years ago might have been called "essay" now appears in a blog or a wiki. We use "essay" loosely to mean any writing in which the writer grapples with a subject to figure it out or illuminate it. The original *essai* meant something like *sally forth* into the subject. Writers have done that in an almost infinite number of ways. And the Internet has opened up the possibilities for showing essays off to the world.

Suggested Moves for Writing a Personal Essay

I. Discover.

Perfect for getting started on a personal essay are all the moves that ask the writer to think on paper and dig into memories—**Freewriting** ➡72, **Brainstorming** ➡69, **Inventories** ➡61–68. You could productively spend an hour sampling moves from chapter 23 and you'd almost certainly come up with multiple essay topics.

2. Develop.

Choose the most interesting and surprising ideas from your first step and expand them—**Explain your code words** ➡93, **Play with time** ➡84, **Adjust distance** ➡85. Writing a personal essay is often somewhat self-indulgent, so be ready to revel in yourself without feeling too guilty about it. It's part of the assignment!

3. Gather.

If you haven't fixed on a subject yet, it's time to choose. And if you have a subject but are unsure of where you want to go with it, maybe you should focus before you start gathering. Few personal essays are weighted with extensive citations, but it gives the essay breadth and weight if researched information can match the personal. So once you have a direction, start reading and Googling . . . and use the **Memory joggers** ➡100.

4. Integrate.

Dialogue plays an important role in many essays. Everyone knows you can't remember exactly what someone said, but perhaps you can capture a person or moment by inventing something they might have said. If you're pulling in outside information, try to do so naturally, as though you were mentioning something in conversation, without footnotes or citations. **Check the flow** ➥139.

5. Focus.

Writers debate about how directly a personal essay should state its point, how narrow its focus should be, how direct its statement of purpose. Do you feel most comfortable with a clear thesis, or do you prefer to let readers come to their own conclusions? **Brainstorm leads** ➥143, as many as you can, and then **Find the problem/tension/conflict** ➥145 or **Find a focusing detail** ➥146. Personal details often echo through personal essays.

6. Organize.

Essays use all the **Standard organizing patterns** ➥166 sketched in chapter 28. Some build on a definition; some probe an event to determine its causes; some draw parallels between two things to learn from them both. Some tell a story like a piece of fiction; others are self-consciously poetic and organized by association. **Try an alternative thesis approach** ➥98.

7. Revise.

Because of their literary heritage, essayists are allowed a certain amount of poetic license by their readers. You can probably get away with made-up words or unusual punctuation better in an essay than in a memo or report. But that's no excuse for neglecting to make sure that everything's exactly the way you want it to be.

8. Present.

Most likely, you wrote your personal essay for a class, and "presenting" involves simply turning it in to the teacher. If you get a chance, read your essay aloud. Reading aloud a meaningful personal essay can be a moving experience for both reader and listeners.

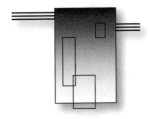

Profile 13

EXAMPLE: **Stephen Laurent, Brock Dethier**

Stephen Laurent, Abenaki, is bringing back New Hampshire's lost first language by preserving the Abenaki language. Since 1965, he has spent countless hours translating the first written records of the Abenaki. The work, which led to a recently completed Abenaki-English dictionary, required both a speaker's and a scholar's knowledge of French, English, Abenaki, and Latin.

In addition to his written translation, Laurent is taping his pronunciations of Abenaki words. These tapes are an important part of his work, since most English speakers would be baffled trying to pronounce long, complex Abenaki words, which bear no resemblance to those of Indo-European languages.

Laurent was born at the reserve now called Odanak, on the St. Francis River in Quebec Province. The reserve is one of the last surviving settlements of the tribe, which figured prominently in New England colonial history. The village of St. Francis has been inhabited by the Abenakis for three hundred years, and approximately one hundred fifty people live on the reservation today.

Questions about the example:

1. This profile appeared in *Native Peoples* magazine (Spring 1996). How can you tell from the writing that the author was assuming his readers would know something about Native Americans?
2. What do you think of the balance in emphasis between Laurent himself and his work?
3. Where have you seen short, focused profiles similar to this one?
4. Do you admire people who dedicate themselves tirelessly to one pursuit? Reading about such people is one of the joys of reading profiles.

EXAMPLE: What I Really Wanted: In Search of Authentic Experience, Michelle Theriault Boots

You can tour almost anything.

There are slum tours in Mumbai, culinary tours of Italy, tours of the Great Wall of China, tours of pristine glacier-fed bays in Alaska. You can pay to swim with dolphins, trek to remote villages in Thailand or sample the finest marijuana in Amsterdam. If there is an experience on earth that is sublime, chances are someone has turned it into a tour.

And yet, tours are almost universally disappointing.

Tour groups crowd special places, are humiliatingly obvious (ever tried walking through Paris with a group of people wearing matching name tags?) and have a way of making even the most miraculous place feel somehow tawdry and a little bit sad.

There are few sights as poignant as that of a tour bus full of Texan retirees in Alaska, hands and faces pressed against the unopenable windows of a sixty-seat coach bus with a soft upholstered interior, roof-mounted air-conditioning and a four-stroke turbocharged engine, craning their necks to catch a glimpse of a roadside moose stumbling through the willow trees.

So what is it that passes for a real, authentic experience these days?

And how do you know if you're having one?

If you can find him, I'd suggest asking a man from Seoul, South Korea, named Dong-Sun.

I met him on a three-day organized safari of the Sossusvlei Dunes of Namibia, a sparsely populated former German colony in Southwestern Africa. The brochure described the tour using Meaningful Capitalization. Our tour company would drive us in a Specially Equipped Safari Vehicle to the Namib Desert, a harsh and lonely landscape of dry riverbeds and red dunes that can rise to 1,000 feet high. The Stunning Landscapes of the Sossusvlei Dunes would Overwhelm us with their Timeless Beauty and Grandeur. We each paid $325 and dutifully packed warm clothes for camping in the desert, sturdy shoes for hiking and a water bottle.

There were nine of us in the tour group: Some severe Dutch couples in matching wire-rimmed glasses, a chain-smoking German woman, a couple of affable, hung-over Australians, plus Dong-Sun and I.

We were ready to have Incredible Experiences.

There's a line of thinking among sociologists that goes like this: Going on a tour is the modern remake of the original pilgrimage, a quest for a pure, pristine experience that is uncluttered with the hubris and debris of everyday life.

If you're a tourist, you're attempting to experience something that can't be found in normal space of life.

That's why the brochure for the Three-Day Sossusvlei Explorer Adventure described every experience—camping under the desert stars, hiking the dunes—as "Magical."

And a lot of it was, technically.

We watched the sun rise from a perfectly sculpted apricot dune, in the company of seventy to eighty others. We clucked our tongues at a rowdy young group of Irish students on a package tour, who somebody said were "horsing around" at the top of the dune during the most photogenic moment of luminous golden dawn. (Bastards!) This was the very dune, it was explained, where a pregnant Angelina Jolie and her partner Brad Pitt had posed for a Vanity Fair photo shoot.

Soon, we had devolved into our national stereotypes.

The Dutch couple dutifully recorded each awe-inspiring sight with an expensive arsenal of camera equipment. The Australians punctuated sentences with the phrase "could go for a beer right now." The German girl chain-smoked, applied eyeliner and summed up most experiences with a curt "I did not like it."

Dong-Sun was quiet. For most of our tour, he was so glum that he posed for pictures making the face of a sad blowfish: cheeks puffed out, eyebrows furrowed, as if punctuating his disappointment. He had come all the way from Korea because, as he said in halting English, there was something he "really wanted," in Namibia. He didn't say what that was, but it was clear that he hadn't found it.

Something he really wanted?

The tour meandered on. We walked, en masse, through a landscape that could have stood in for Mars, with dunes that coiled like snakes or curved like a woman's body. The air was prickly and the sun seemed to throb like a beating heart.

Mostly we complained—the sand in our shoes! The heat! Did our guide know where we were going? And what about lunch? Scorpions?

Sometime in mid-afternoon, we walked up a dune so high that there was nothing but sky and shifting sand.

I could go for a beer, said one of the Australians.

At the top, we looked out to see an ocean of sand and a flat, cracked white salt plain—the remnants of an old river that had long since changed its course. It was studded with the blackened skeletons of 500-year-old Acacia trees, dead but preserved in this dry place. The scene looked like an abstract expressionist painting: bleached-bone earth, walls of fire-colored sand, blue sky and slashes of black.

Dong-Sun went soft-eyed and looked stunned. He paused a moment.

"This is it!" he yelled. His eyes went wide. "This is what I really wanted!"

He tore down the dune, sinking into the flour-like sand.

For the next half-hour the rest of us wandered around doing what tourists do: posing for pictures, exclaiming and complaining.

I watched as Dong-Sun wandered around alone, sometimes laughing, pressing his face to the ground to smell it.

This is what I really wanted, he kept saying to himself, to the bleached-bone earth, the walls of fire-colored sand, the ancient fossilized trees, the blue sky, Namibia.

Dong-Sun was no tourist. He was a pilgrim.

This is what I really wanted.

Questions about the Profile

This selection was published as an essay in the journal *Etude*, which features "new voices in literary nonfiction." In what ways is it a profile? What does it offer a reader? Why might a reader seek out either kind of example profile? Which is more fun to read? Which is more informative?

1. What are its purposes?

Think of the metaphor behind the word "profile" used to describe a writing genre: the profile of a person or other shape, the outline of the face, very individual to the person but not providing the depth that a full portrait would provide. Most profiles are of people, though you can write a profile of a company. A profile gives the strongest possible outline to an individual without going into great depth.

Can you imagine why I wrote the profile of Stephen Laurent? What were Boots's purposes?

2. Who are its audiences?

Many readers know the profile as a journalist's genre, but it is now often highly literary, appreciated for its writing as much as its characterization of its subject. The audience depends almost entirely on the subject of the profile. A profile of the upstart candidate for mayor in Smalltown might be read avidly by the citizens of Smalltown but ignored by everyone else in the world. Profiles of media stars fill glossy magazines and TV shows. So we're all the audience for the next profile of Madonna, whether or not we want to be.

Who do you think read my profile?

3. What's the typical content?

Like an essay, a profile generally has some kind of hook in the lead, a quirk or habit or look of the person. Readers expect at least a brief summary of the subject's life and background, and eventually an answer to the question "Why should I care about this person?" The profile may touch lightly on all aspects of a person's life, or it may concentrate on the subject's background and stance on certain issues—the Smalltown dump, for instance, or what the profiled star thinks of the prospects of finding another husband. Most profiles are inherently laudatory and therefore tend to focus on the positive, though it is certainly possible to profile the crime boss.

Why did our authors choose these particular details and emphases? Why did Boots spend so little time on Dong-Sun?

4. How long is it?

Among the most famous American profiles were those written by President John F. Kennedy in the book *Profiles in Courage*, which briefly inspired a TV show. Some of Kennedy's profiles were twenty pages long. On the other extreme, many newspapers run miniature one-paragraph profiles of people being hired or recognized at local businesses. The length depends on the purpose.

5. How is it arranged on the page?

A profile looks like any other essay except that ideally the profile will be spiced with pictures of the subject or of scenes from the subject's life.

6. What pronouns are used?

The full range.

7. What's the tone?

The tone can range from flattering to objective and distanced to the slightly belligerent tone of a probing investigative reporter. But most often the tone is upbeat and admiring.

8. How does it vary?

Our examples give some sense of the range of the profile, but you'll see profiles much less thorough than either one in newspapers and trade journals and company newsletters, as well as in social media. If you have a boss, editor, website, or relative asking you to write a profile, ask "Why?" as many times as is necessary for you to understand what kind of work is expected. Obituaries could be considered a kind of profile, as is, after-all, a drawing of a sideways-facing subject.

Suggested Moves for Writing a Profile

1. Discover.

A profile depends very much on its subject, so you're smart to spend some time finding the best possible subject. **Brainstorm** ➥69 a list of "remarkable" people that you know or have had some contact with. "Remarkable" could mean anything from "has lived 99 years" to "carves ships out of potatoes" to "was a voice of Daffy Duck." Narrow your choices by thinking about which people you could actually get an interview with and which would appeal to the widest audience or to the specific audience you're targeting. **Analyze your purposes** ➥55. Are you celebrating someone's life or explaining someone's importance or writing an essay that just uses someone as a jumping-off point?

2. Develop.

Freewrite ➥72 on your choice—your associations with him or her, why he or she was on the list in the first place. Give yourself plenty of time to think about everything that makes your person remarkable. **Dig into contexts and connections** ➥51.

3. Gather.

You'll almost certainly need to use a variety of gathering techniques. An **Interview** ➥113 or series of interviews often provides the core of the profile, but do your homework before you interview your subject. Talk to family members, co-workers, friends of the subject. Research in the library and on the Internet. Perhaps **Brainstorm leads** ➥143 before you do the big interview, so you can get a sense of where the piece might take you and therefore what you should ask about. Consider **Interviewing like a folklorist** ➥114.

4. Integrate.

When very skilled writers create a profile, they often use the techniques of fiction or essay writing to draw the reader in with plot or theme, informing the audience about the profile subject while still telling an interesting story. To achieve that effect, try **Integrate voices** ➥132, and **Integrate showing and telling** ➥134.

5. Focus.

Inherent in all profiles is the claim "This person is interesting." Especially if your subject is someone well-known, you may feel that the subject's inherent interest will keep the reader attentive, and all you have to do is present the facts of the subject's life. But most profiles focus on some aspect of the subject's life or character, so finding your focus can be as important in writing a profile as in doing other kinds of writing. Play with perspective, jotting down all the people and institutions that have some connection with your subject.

Try **Frame it** ➡151, **Find the problem/tension/conflict** ➡145, and **Find a focusing detail** ➡146.

6. Organize.

Use headings and subheadings, even if you decide to take them out later. A person's life is likely to have many facets, and sometimes giving each facet a heading works better than forcing a number of transitions in the text. Also, **Answer readers' questions** ➡159, starting with "Who is this person?" and "Why should I care?" You might try writing a first draft, however it comes, and then **Outline your draft** ➡160. An organizing principle may emerge as the outline shows you where your emphasis is.

7. Revise.

You want to make doubly sure that you get the details of your subject's life right. If possible, share your draft with the people you've quoted or who would know the facts.

8. Present.

Profiles can take many different forms—eulogies for the dead, "roasts" of someone being celebrated at a club, the starlet stories of Sunday magazine sections, stories about Michelle Obama and the kids. All share many elements with profiles. If you're not presenting your profile, you should strongly consider at least "publishing" it to the subject and other people who might be interested. Many publications publish profiles, from company newsletters to local newspapers to national magazines, so if you get excited by them, there's no telling where your work might end up.

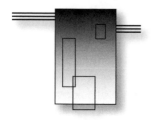

Proposal

EXAMPLE: **Undergraduate Research Grant Proposal**

ABSTRACT: I request an Undergraduate Research Grant to pursue my study of the water chemistry of Ridler Creek. By testing the creek at several points and over several weeks' time, we can determine what effect campus has on the water in the Creek.

LITERATURE REVIEW: With my literature review I can establish the validity of my sampling methods (references X, Y, and Z). I can mention some standard water chemistry books (references A and B). And I can list the literature most specific to small creek water chemistry (references Q and R).

RESEARCH OBJECTIVES[1]: Careful, frequent sampling over an extended period of time will provide a strong empirical basis for my study's conclusions.

RESEARCH METHODS: Using the methods outlined in References, and in consultation with my faculty advisor, I will take three samples from each of three places on Ridler Creek at 3 pm each day for three weeks. I will analyze each sample for presence of *E. coli* bacteria.

OUTCOMES: I will establish either that the Creek picks up *E. coli* pollution as it flows through campus or that it doesn't.

SIGNIFICANCE AND INNOVATION[2]: This work will be significant to me, since it will give me practice in the lab and in the field. And it will be significant to the University, as it should either confirm or quiet rumors that the University's antiquated sewer system is in trouble.

PUBLIC PRESENTATION OF RESULTS[3]: I will present my results in a poster and written report that will be part of the URG "Showcase" on December 10.

TIMELINE: August 1—Proposal accepted
Sept. 1—Begin sampling
Sept. 22—End sampling
Oct. 30—End analysis
Nov. 15—first draft of report
Dec. 10—Present report and poster

BUDGET: Including all expenses related to the project and noting any other funding sources.

REFERENCES: All the sources I've mentioned in the proposal and perhaps a few more to show breadth of knowledge.

About the numbered items in the example:
1. You could also say "aims," "goals," or "hypothesis" here.
2. A similar heading is "benefit of research." Somewhere you need to tell the grantor how someone will benefit.
3. If you're asking for public money, you can count on giving a public presentation when you're done.

EXAMPLE: The Impact that Level of Physical Activity Has on the Relationship between Eating Disorder Risk and Emotion Regulation in Female College Students, Alyson Bernhisel and Kendra Homan

Abstract
Research has demonstrated a strong link between emotion regulation and eating disorders. Driven physical activity has also been described as a prominent feature of eating disorders, yet its association with emotion regulation is unclear. While some studies have found physical activity to be a protective factor for emotion regulation difficulties, other investigations have found high levels of physical activity are associated with higher levels of emotion dysregulation. The purpose of the proposed study is to examine the impact that level of physical activity has on the relationship between eating disorder risk and ER difficulties.

Introduction and Literature Review: Eating disorders are severe psychological illnesses associated with a host of adverse medical morbidities, negative psychological sequelae, and significant reductions in quality of life (*e.g.*, Blinder, Cumella, and Sanathara 2006; Nielsen 2003; Rome and Ammerman 2003). *The Diagnostic and Statistical Manual of Mental Disorders* (4th ed., text rev.; DSM-IV-TR; American Psychiatric Association 2000) recognizes two distinct types of eating disorders, anorexia nervosa (AN) and bulimia nervosa (BN). AN is characterized by a refusal to maintain a normal body weight and a corresponding fear of weight gain or becoming fat, a disturbance in body image, and amenorrhea in postmenarcheal females. BN is characterized by recurring episodes of binge eating accompanied by a subjective experience of loss of control over one's eating, inappropriate compensatory methods to prevent weight gain, and undue emphasis of weight and shape in their self-evaluation (American Psychiatric Association 2000). Prominent in clinical descriptions of AN and BN are references to difficulties in identifying and expressing strong, negative emotions (Harrison, Sullivan, Tchanturia, and Treasure 2010; Hayaki 2009; Sim and Zeman 2004). These emotion regulation problems are often considered important factors in the development of both AN and BN, and emerging research indicates that these problems may even contribute to the maintenance of eating disorder symptoms (Fairburn et al. 2003; Gilboa-Schechtman, Avnon, Zubery, and Jeczmien 2006).

In addition to the aforementioned emotion regulation difficulties, it has been well documented that individuals with eating disorders engage in high levels of compulsive exercise and physical activity (*e.g.*, Davis, Kaptein, Kaplan, Olmsted and Woodside 1998; Touyz, Beumont, and Hoek 1987) and that these behaviors are also judged to be important factors in the development and maintenance of these disorders (Davis et al. 1998; Epling and Pierce 1996). Research indicates that females who participate in both non-organized exercise (*e.g.*, Levitt 2008) and competitive athletics (*e.g.*, Greenleaf, Petrie, Carter, and Reel 2009; Torstveit, Rosenvinge, and Sundgot-Borgen 2008) are at a greater risk than females in the general population for developing clinical eating disorders and are more likely to engage in pathological weight control behaviors such as vomiting, misuse of laxatives/diuretics, and/or fasting. When exercise occurs for reasons beyond the desire to gain and/or boost performance, it becomes excessive and is described in the literature as driven physical activity (Davis and Claridge 1998; Sundgot-Borgen and Klungland Torsteit 2003). Thus, in considering some of the factors that may contribute to the development of eating disorders, it seems clear that separate lines of research have examined emotion regulation and levels of physical activity independently. A reasonable assumption, however, is that they may interact in contributing to the development of eating disorders and the maintenance of symptoms.

Research Objectives: Current research shows a relationship between eating disorders and emotion regulation difficulties, and eating disorders and compulsive exercise have been well documented in the literature. However, the question of whether an association exists between the two and eating disorders has not been evaluated. The purpose of the proposed study is to examine the impact that level of physical activity has on the relationship between eating disorder risk and emotion regulation difficulties.

Methods

Participants: Female college students from USU will be invited to participate in this study. Students will be drawn from both undergraduate and graduate programs. The participants will complete one comprehensive measure of eating disorder symptoms, three measures of emotion regulation, and one inventory assessing physical activity as described below. Three measures of emotion regulation will be used because no single measure has to date covered all of the domains of emotion regulation adequately. Participation in this study will be voluntary and all procedures will be in accordance with state and federal guidelines for the protection of human participants.

Measures: *General Demographic and Background Information*. General demographic and background information measures include general demographic questions concerning age and ethnicity/race. Additionally, participants will answer questions concerning the amount of physical activity and exercise patterns.

Eating Disorder Inventory-3. The Eating Disorder Inventory-3 (EDI-3; Garner 2004) is a 91-item self-report measure used to assess eating disorder symptomology and psychological characteristics associated with the development and maintenance of AN and BN. Individuals are scored on a 6-point forced-choice Likert scale ranging from *always* to *never* with higher scores indicating a greater severity of eating disorder symptoms and increased psychological maladjustment.

Difficulties in Emotional Regulation Scale. The Difficulties in Emotional Regulation Scale (DERS; Gratz and Roemer 2004) consists of 36 self-report items that assess individuals' complaints about emotional regulation problems. The DERS includes six subscales: Nonacceptance of Emotional Response Scale; Failure to Engage in Goal-Directed Behavior; Impulse Control Difficulty; Lack of Emotional Awareness; Limited Access to Emotion Regulation Strategies; and Lack of Emotional Clarity.

Cognitive Emotion Regulation Questionnaire. The Cognitive Emotion Regulation Questionnaire (CERQ; Garnefski, Kraaij, and Spinhoven 2002) is the multidimensional, self-report questionnaire designed to assess individuals' cognitive coping processes in affect regulation. The questionnaire consists of 36 items and 9 subscales. Each subscale consists of four items. The subscales appear to be roughly divided among cognitive strategies that are generally considered to be either adaptive or maladaptive: Self-blame; Acceptance; Rumination; Positive Refocusing; Refocusing on

Planning; Positive Reappraisal; Putting into Perspective; Catastrophizing; and Other-blame.

Toronto Alexithymia Scale. The Toronto Alexithymia Scale (TAS-20; Bagby, Taylor, and Parker 1994) is a self-report measure that consists of 20 items (5-point Likert Scale) with three subscales that assess a general lack of emotion regulation coping strategies. The three subscales reflect the general, theoretical construct of alexithymia. The three subscales relevant to emotion regulation are: Difficulty Identifying Feelings and distinguishing them from the bodily sensations of emotion; Difficulty Describing Emotions to others; and Externally Orientated Thinking style.

International Physical Activity Questionnaire. The International Physical Activity Questionnaire (IPAQ; Booth 2000; Craig, Marshall, Sjostrom, Bauman, Booth, Aisworth, Pratt, Ekelund, Yngve, Sallis, and Pekka 2003) is a self-report measure that assesses physical activity within the last 7 days (hours per day, hours per week) through 26-items arranged in 4 domains: job-related physical activity, transportation physical activity, housework, house maintenance, and caring for family, and recreation, sport, and leisure-time physical activity.

Procedures: After agreeing to participate in the study, participants will be provided with the informed consent for their review and signature. The participants will then complete the general demographic and background information sheet, EDI-3, DERS, CERQ, and TAS-20. Following the completion of the measures, information regarding appropriate professional referral sources will be provided to all participants in the event that completing the questionnaire elicits concern that they might have mental health problems.

Outcomes: Eating disorders is a very serious health problem due to the fact that it has the highest mortality rate of any mental health issues, greater than 10% (Keel, Dorer, Eddy, Franko, Charatan, and Herzog 2003). The study will allow us to examine the separate (main) effects and joint effects of emotion regulation and physical activity on the severity of eating disorder symptomology. Results of the study will have important implications for eating disorder prevention and education programs, as well as treatment, particularly if it is found that these two constructs jointly impact the severity of case symptoms. I have a keen interest in health psychology treatments for illnesses such as eating disorders and this research project will help me establish expertise in this field and the research skills I will need to pursue graduate training. I plan on submitting the results of this research to the Utah Conference on Undergraduate Research and the Academy of Eating Disorder Conference.

Budget

Monies Required:

2 SPSS Site Licenses @ $65.00 each	$130.00
Survey Software	$200.00
Eating Disorder Inventory Manual and Inventories	$415.00

Reproduction for Public Domain Inventories	$75.00
Office Supplies	$25.00
Student Research Office Printer	$155.00
Total Budget Requested for Project	$1000.00

Sources Monies Requested From:
$500.00 requested from URCO
$500.00 match requested from the Psychology Department

Budget Justification:
Site licenses for data analysis. Survey software is for use for administration of self-report inventories. Cost of the Eating Disorder Inventory Manual and Inventories are costs charged by commercial vendor for use. Reproduction for Public Domain Inventories will be needed for the reproduction of self-report inventories administered. Office supplies and printer will be necessary for reproduction of library research materials, long-distance contact with off-campus students, and materials needed for manuscript preparation.

References

American Psychiatric Association. (2000). *Diagnostic and statistical manual of mental disorders* (4th ed., text revised). Washington, DC: Author.

Bagby, R. M., Parker, J. D.A., and Taylor, G. J. (1992). The twenty-item Toronto Alexithymia Scale-I: Item selection and cross-validation of the factor structure. *Journal of Psychosomatic Research, 38,* 23–32.

Blinder, B. J., Cumella, E. J., and Sanathara, V. A. (2006). Psychiatric comorbidities of female in patients with eating disorders. *Psychosomatic Medicine, 68,* 454–462.

Booth, M. (2000). Assessment of physical activity: An international perspective. *Research Quarterly for Exercise and Sport, 71,* 2, 114–120.

Craig, C. L., Marshall, A. J., Sjostrom, M., Bauman, A. E., Booth, M. L., Aisworth, B. E., Pratt, M., Ekelund, U., Yngve, A., Sallis, J. F., and Pekka, O. J. A. (2003). International physical activity questionnaire: 12-country reliability and validity. *Medicine and Science in Sports and Exercise, 35,* 8, 1381–1395.

Davis, C., and Claridge, G. (1998). The eating disorders as addiction: A psychobiological perspective. *Addictive Behaviors, 23,* 463–475.

Davis, C., Kaptein, S., Kaplan, A. S., Olmsted, M. P., and Woodside, D. B. (1998). Obsessionality in anorexia nervosa: The moderating influence of exercise. *Psychosom Med, 60,* 192–197.

Epling, W.F., and Pierce, W. D. (1996) An overview of activity anorexia. In Epling WF, Pierce WD, editors. Activity Anorexia Theory, Research and Treatment. Hillsdale, NJ: Erlbaum.

Fairburn, C. G., Stice, E., Cooper, Z., Doll, H. A., Norman, P. A., and O'Connor, M. E. (2003). Understanding persistence in bulimia nervosa: A 5-year naturalistic study. *Journal of Consulting and Clinical Psychology, 71,* 103–109.

Garnefski, N., Kraaij, V., and Spinhoven, P. (2002). *Manual for the use of the cognitive emotion, regulation questionnaire: A questionnaire measuring cognitive coping strategies,* DATEC: Leiderdorp, the Netherlands.

Garner, D. M. (2004). *Eating Disorder Inventory–3: Professional Manual*. Lutz, FL: Psychological Assessment Resources, Inc.

Gratz, K. L., and Roemer, L. (2004). Multidimensional assessment of emotion regulation and dysregulation: Development, factor structure, and initial validation and difficulties in emotion regulation scale. *Journal of Psychopathology and Behavioral Assessment, 26*, 41–54.

Gilboa-Schechtman, E., Avnon, L., Zubery, E., and Jeczmien, P. (2006). Emotional Processing in eating disorders: Specific impairment or general distress related deficiency?. *Depression and Anxiety, 23*, 331–339.

Greenleaf, C., Petrie, T. A., Carter, J., and Reel, J. J. (2009).Female collegiate athletes: Prevalence of eating disorders and disordered eating behaviors. *Journal of American College of Health, 57*, 489–495.

Harrison, A. A., Sullivan, S. S., Tchanturia, K. K., and Treasure, J. J. (2010). Emotional functioning in eating disorders: Attentional bias, emotion recognition and emotion regulation. *Psychological Medicine, 40*, 1887–1897.

Hayaki, J. (2009). Negative reinforcement eating expectancies, emotion dysregulation, and symptoms of bulimia nervosa. *International Journal of Eating Disorders, 42*, 552–556.

Keel, P K., Dorer, D. J., Eddy, K. T., Franko, D., Charatan, D. L., and Herzog, D. B. (2003) Predictors of mortality in eating disorders. *Archives of General Psychiatry, 60*, 179–183.

Levitt, D. H. (2008). Participation in athletic activities and eating disordered behavior. *Eating Disorders, 16*, 393–404.

Nielsen, S. (2003) Standardized mortality ratio in bulimia nervosa. *Archives of General Psychiatry, 60*, 851.

Rome, E. S., and Ammerman, S. (2003). Medical complications of eating disorders: An Update. *Journal of Adolescent Health, 33*, 418–426.

Sim, L., and Zeman, J. (2006). The Contribution of Emotion Regulation to Body Dissatisfaction and Disordered Eating in Early Adolescent Girls. *Journal of Youth and Adolescence, 35*, 219–228.

Sundgot-Borgen, J, and Klungland Torsteit, M. (2003). Prevalence of eating disorders in elite athletes is higher in the general population. *Clinical Journal Sport Medicine, 14*, 25–32.

Torstveit, M. K., Rosenvinge, J. H., and Sundgot-Borgen, J. (2008). Prevalence of eating disorders and the predictive power of risk models in female elite athletes: A controlled study. *Scandinavian Journal of Medicine and Science in Sports, 18*, 108–118.

Touyz, S. W., Beumont, P. J. V., and Hoek, S. Exercise anorexia: A new dimension in anorexia nervosa? In Beumont PJV, Burrows GD.

Questions about the example:

1. How closely does this actual, successful proposal follow the outline of the first example?
2. How do Bernhisel and Homan use sources to establish their credibility?
3. Does this proposed project have a legitimate research question that could yield interesting results?
4. Does your institution have internal grants or scholarships that encourage undergraduate writing and research?

Questions about the Proposal

1. What are its purposes?

There are almost as many kinds of proposals as there are letters. They're all similar in that they propose to take certain actions and need the help, cooperation, or approval of the addressee to act. So the purpose of the proposal is to secure that help.

2. Who are its audiences?

The audience for a proposal is often very small because one committee, perhaps even one person, will decide whether to accept the proposal. It can succeed or fail on the strength of the writer's ability to aim the proposal for that small group. When whole careers are on the line, as they are with National Science Foundation grants, the grant writers study past proposals and can get in touch with NSF administrators. It's smart to study the proposal audience, find out what kinds of proposals the committee has accepted in the past, see if you can get a sense of what they like.

3. What's the typical content?

There's a problem or need, a proposed action, the results and benefits of that action, and a request. The key may be demonstrating that the proposed action will improve upon current practice. Make sure to mention how you will measure the improvement. Does Bernhisel and Homan's proposal meet these criteria?

4. How long is it?

You should be able to make your case in a page or two. You can always tack on appendices of data and other relevant material.

5. How is it arranged on the page?

Most organizations have either a form or a required format for proposals they will consider. If you can't get one from the organization, use headings similar to those in our example, running the headings down the left.

6. What pronouns are used?

The first person is common in proposals, but the proposal should focus not on "I" but on the evidence that demonstrates why the proposal should be approved.

7. What's the tone?

Most proposals are formal, professional, and businesslike. Flattery and fawning will probably just hurt your cause. You want to appear confident about the importance of your proposal and your ability to accomplish what you're proposing, but not arrogant.

8. How does it vary?

Proposals vary in the levels of formality and detail expected. If you can't find models of past proposals, see if you can at least get a sense of expectations. Make yours a little more formal than you think it has to be, just in case.

Suggested Moves for Writing a Proposal

I. Discover.

Whether you're writing a proposal in school to practice the form or a real proposal for money or other support, you want to choose something that you know a lot about. You don't want to have to do too much research before writing the proposal, and good background knowledge in a subject helps you figure out where to go when you do need research. Make an **Authority list** ➡62 and a **Territories list** ➡66. If they don't suggest any good avenues, make a list of problems that you're familiar with and think you might be able to solve. Better to spend some time finding the right subject rather than deciding to use the first thought and then discovering you have nothing to say about it. Also, if you haven't already done so, **Analyze your audiences** ➡56. Who has the power and authority to grant what you're asking for in your proposal? Find out as much as you can about this person or organization so that you can make sure that what you're asking for falls within the area of interest of the individual or the mission of the organization.

2. Develop.

A proposal is part summary, part argument, so I'd recommend working on the **Accordion principle** ➡152, developing and gathering as much good material as you can find, then trimming it down to essentials. Try **Answering the journalist's questions** ➡87 and make sure you work the answers into your proposal. Then become your own probing journalist to think about how your audience might be resistant or skeptical about your proposal. Finally, **Adjust distance** ➡85—a proposal needs both the close-up, to show what you're actually doing, and the big picture, to show the significance of the project.

3. Gather.

One of the tricky things about writing a proposal is that in order to make a convincing case, you may need to do much of the research that your proposal is proposing. You need to find the best examples and arguments to make your case, and **Keep a log** ➡105 so that you don't have to repeat the process if your proposal is accepted. Statistics may be particularly persuasive in a short proposal. See if you can **Interview** ➡113 an expert in the subject to find out about the latest thinking and trends. If possible, you want to propose something related to cutting-edge ideas about your subject, something that hasn't been done hundreds of times before.

4. Integrate.

As always when you read, keep an eye out for a particularly relevant quote or statistic that might establish the need for or the importance of your project. You need to establish your authority and the value of your project quickly in a proposal.

5. Focus.

In something as short as a proposal, you need to make sure that your writing is focused on the key concern. Use **Fill in the blanks** ➡141 to probe your own thinking and feeling about the issue. Then try **Find the tension/problem/conflict** ➡145 to make sure that you've focused on a problem that your audience will think is worth solving. Finally **Brainstorm titles** ➡142 for the project as a whole. Make sure your audience knows exactly what you're asking for and how your proposed actions will benefit them.

6. Organize.

The organization you're applying to may have guidelines about what should come where in the body of your proposal. Be sure to **Find a model** ➡163 and analyze it. Starting with your title, **Answer readers' questions** ➡159 and see if your answers create an organizational scheme. You almost certainly want to **Use headings and subheadings** ➡165. You probably don't need a full-fledged outline, but a brief sketch might keep you on track.

7. Revise.

The success of your proposal may well depend on how perfect you can make it, so **Get some feedback** ➡220 and **Revise for meaning, coherence, language** ➡203.

8. Present.

You may get a chance to present your proposal in person, in which case you probably want to use some visuals not in the proposal itself. More likely, you'll hand or send the proposal to an organization and hope. If you haven't already done so, share the final copy of your proposal with someone who will tell you if things don't make sense or are incomplete. If you don't yet have an audience for your proposal, consider posting it on the Internet as a website or on a blog. Doing so opens up a whole realm of possibilities for using multimedia materials.

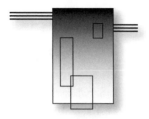

15

Reflection

EXAMPLE: **Reflection, Emmie Harmon**

When I was young I had a strong interest in writing. My mother encouraged this passion. I have stories that I wrote as a young child about ants and a little girl named Molly and princesses that lived in forests. I had a big imagination and I loved to write my ideas down. As I got older my creative works subsided but I started to keep a journal and I wrote in that faithfully. I wrote about my life and feelings and concerns and I wrote down poems and scriptures that were interesting to me. I have continued to do so ever since and writing in my journal has gotten me through some of the most trying times of my life. While writing papers in my first college English class I have noticed that I am pretty good at making my papers sound personal and putting my own voice in them. I think that this is in part due to all the time I spent writing for fun as I grew up.

This semester I have written a paper about sappy songs, a personal essay about death, a movie review, and a research paper on the history of nursing. I liked writing the review because it was something new to me. Although time consuming, the research paper was also interesting because I learned new information. I would probably choose a different topic for my personal essay if I could go back because I lost interest in the topic after the first or second draft. The essay was about a friend of mine that had passed away and after writing the paper I had no desire to look at it anymore because I wanted to resolve the pain that I had felt and move on with my life.

I think it was valuable to do the assignment analysis because it made me really think about what the instructor is asking for instead of just quickly reading through the instructions. I learned that it is wise to read through the instructions a while before the paper is due so if anything is ambiguous one has time to ask the instructor questions about the assignment before it is due.

I want to remember what I have learned this semester about focusing papers and making them have a general question instead of being "all over the place," as my papers often are. I want to remember the importance of revising and perfecting papers. I learned that it helps a lot to get a second opinion on your papers and I learned to appreciate close friends and my professor who were willing to read through my papers and give me feedback on my writing.

Questions about Reflection

1. What are its purposes?

Reflecting back on a semester or a lifetime of writing can help us realize what we've learned, how we've improved, and what we want to remember for the future. In all its forms, reflection assists memory and comprehension. So someone asking you to write a reflection paper is probably most interested in advancing your education, though they may hope that your reflection yields other benefits. My students' reflection papers help me adjust my teaching for next semester. What do you think Harmon got out of writing this paper?

2. Who are its audiences?

Some successful personal essays are largely reflective, so sometimes reflection has a wide audience. More often, the person reflecting is the main beneficiary of the reflection. If one of your purposes in reflecting is to remember the most important features of an event, you may want to address your paper to your future self, who could make use of the insights you write down today.

3. What's the typical content?

You may be asked to reflect on specific things: how you learned to get along with your roommate, how you've used writing in the past month, how to figure out what the calculus teacher was talking about. Or you may reflect on a particular time period or the results of a particular class or event. In general, you'll write about the ideas in your head, without using outside sources. I always ask my students to include their strengths as writers in any reflection paper.

4. How long is it?

Most school reflection papers are one to five pages long, but a reflection can grow into a book-length memoir.

5. How is it arranged on the page?

Like a traditional essay or book, though there's no reason a reflective writer couldn't bullet a series of insights or changes.

6. What pronouns are used?

Even the most conservative readers would agree that "I" is the pronoun of reflection.

7. What's the tone?

Readers of reflective pieces are prepared for nostalgia, reminiscence, and perhaps regret or self-congratulation.

8. How does it vary?

Reflections vary as much as their relative, the journal: there are no limits on form and the subject can span the spectrum of human existence. Any time you're asked to look back and learn—doing your own performance appraisal, for instance, or summing up your learning from a class—you're reflecting. The key question: Is the reflection for you or for someone appraising you?

Suggested Moves for Writing a Reflection

1. Discover.

First, **Ask your teacher or boss** ➜48 and **Freewrite** ➜72 about the class or the period or the ideas you're supposed to reflect on. **Analyze your strengths as a writer** ➜57 if that's one of the issues you're supposed to cover. **Analyze your "cultural eye"** ➜58 to see what you can learn by focusing on the view through a particular lens. **Brainstorm** ➜69—get a list of everything you want to cover in your reflection.

2. Develop.

Change perspective ➜81 to fill out your memories, **Play with time** ➜84 to get both a broad and a narrow picture, and be sure to **Talk** ➜3 to others about your reflections and how you're going to focus them.

3. Gather.

To make sure you're not forgetting anything important, try some **Memory joggers** ➜100 and **Reflect** ➜102. Experiment with **a double-entry journal** ➜106, writing down what you remember on one page and what it means on the other.

4. Integrate.

In your reflection, you will likely move from past to present, from reflection to speculation, from observation to memory. **Integrate your own ideas** ➥131. It may be a challenge to say everything you want to say without leaving your readers behind. Try to **Integrate showing and telling** ➥134 and **Check the flow** ➥139 with others.

5. Focus.

Some reflections meander and remain unfocused, but they're more effective and more interesting if they cohere around a central point. **Focus with free-writing** ➥140 to try to find the center of gravity of your subject, and **Fill in the blanks** ➥141 if no one thing is standing out above others. Try to **Expand then choose: The Accordion Principle** ➥152, so you at least consider a large amount of memory and detail.

6. Organize.

As you start to organize your draft, you might want to think about the need to **Write reader-based prose** ➥158. Chances are the first draft of your reflection is written in writer-based prose. Can you re-aim for a reader? Once you have a number of items to work with, **Group them, find labels for the groups, and order them** ➥162.

7. Revise.

With something as personal as a reflection, it's particularly important to **Read aloud** ➥189, **Revise for voice** ➥191, and **Listen to the draft** ➥192.

8. Present.

Who might want to read your reflection paper besides your teacher?

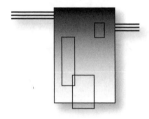

Report

EXAMPLE: **Report Headings**

ABSRACT: See chapter 1. This may be the only section that some people read, so make sure it represents the whole thing.

TABLE OF CONTENTS: The longer the report, the more important this page is. Make it easy to understand at a glance, which generally means using dot leaders between the contents and the page number. See the table of contents for this book.

LIST OF FIGURES AND TABLES: Now we're getting really technical . . . but if you've got figures and tables, list them.

FOREWORD AND/OR PREFACE: Either of these sections situates the report in context—why was it written, why is it significant, how does it relate to other works in the field? Forewords are usually written by someone other than the report's author, preferably an expert in the field whose name will lend the report some authority. The preface is written by the report's author(s) and may acknowledge support and help received.

LIST OF ABBREVIATIONS AND SYMBOLS: Only if you're using ones that readers won't understand.

EXECUTIVE SUMMARY: This is the first part of the body of the report. Longer (up to 10 percent the length of the report) and more complete than the abstract, the executive summary includes the project's purpose, background, methods, findings, and recommendations. It needs to make sense on its own, in case it's the only part of the report that someone reads.

INTRODUCTION: If you include all these parts of the report, you're going to end up repeating yourself—the introduction is likely to contain some of the same material as the preface and executive summary. The introduction should orient the reader to the general content of the report, why it was written, and how it will be presented. None of these introductory sections should mention specific findings, recommendations, or tables and figures.

THE TEXT ITSELF: This may be the most familiar part of the report for someone who has written other papers and essays, but the style of the text or "body" should be consistent with the rest of the report: lots of headings and subheadings, white space, and sign posts to help the reader along. If you haven't had much experience with headings, you may find they're a little trickier than they appear. You need to make sure that headings on the same level use the same kind of font and indentation and are grammatically parallel. A reader should be able to skim your report, reading just the headings, and get a pretty good sense of what the whole report is about. Figures and tables should be numbered and given a title, and the text should refer to them by number. Sometimes they are placed in the text as soon after they're mentioned as possible, and sometimes reserved for an appendix. See if your organization has a standard method of handling figures and tables, as well as explanatory notes. Generally, the closer such things are to the text that refers to them, the more likely they are to be read.

CONCLUSIONS AND RECOMMENDATIONS: In a longer report, these should be separate sections. The conclusions should grow naturally out of the text and should be consistent with the scope and focus of the project laid out in the introduction. Not every report will make recommendations; the report may not be conclusive enough for the author to recommend what should happen next.

WORKS CITED / REFERENCES: As is true for any academic paper, a report must list the sources referred to, or quoted from, usually on a page at the end of the body, labeled "Works Cited" by those following MLA guidelines, "References" by writers using APA.

BIBLIOGRAPHY: If the report's author consulted sources not listed in the Works Cited or References section, those sources can be included in a more-inclusive bibliography, the first section in the "back matter."

APPENDICES: Sometimes the appendix is longer than the body of the report, as it may contain technical details for several of the report's audiences. Figures and tables, as well as such things as sample surveys, may be included in the appendix. Try to work anything important to all your readers into the body of the report; reserve appendices for information that will interest only some readers.

GLOSSARY: If the report uses technical terminology not explained within the body, it should include a glossary of definitions, arranged alphabetically.

INDEX: An index can be very helpful for readers of a long report. It is an alphabetical list of key subjects, followed by page numbers of important references to the subjects. Don't bother trying to create an index until you have stable page numbers, when you've completed the rest of the report.

Questions about the example:

1. Most readers would insist that the report have a title. Why?
2. What are the advantages and disadvantages of having so many headings?
3. How could you figure out which headings your institution wants?
4. If you've ever written a report, did you use these kinds of headings? Would they have been useful to you?

Questions about the Report

1. What are its purposes?

A report is the conclusion and culmination of a project. A student or employee is assigned to research, analyze, or test something and "reports back" in written form.

2. Who are its audiences?

Reports can be difficult to write because they often have a wide range of audiences—executives who just need to see the budget numbers or conclusions to write their own reports, managers who may need to hire or reassign employees as a result of the report, technical staff who may need to find ways to implement the report's specific recommendations. I think of reports with an odd image. You know those dolls that come apart in the middle, revealing a smaller (and smaller and smaller) doll inside? Well, imagine that, magically, the doll sizes could be reversed, so that inside each small doll there's a bigger one. That's the way a report should work. Everyone sees the initial small doll—the abstract or executive summary. Those who need more detail open doll after doll, getting the body of the report and eventually even the appendices, which may include detailed instructions or crucial numbers.

3. What's the typical content?

Most reports answer questions: How feasible is the Wilton Park Proposal? What would it cost to switch the company to a four-day workweek? Should the homeowners' association try to restore the pH balance in the lake? Reports are usually accompanied by a letter or memo that explains what the report is about and why it's being sent to this particular person or group, highlights important findings, and closes with something equivalent to "I'm glad to assist further or to answer questions."

4. How long is it?

Reports can be from a few to a few thousand pages long. Generally something that can be handled in two or three pages would call for a memo, not a report. There's no particular value in making a report longer than it needs to be; you just need to answer the key questions for your various audiences. Some parts of the report, especially the abstract and executive summary, will repeat other parts of the report, like the conclusions and recommendations.

5. How is it arranged on the page?

Most reports use headings, bullets, lists, whitespace, typography, and other clues to allow readers to skim quickly and find the material most relevant to them.

6. What pronouns are used?

Often reports are written by more than one person, so "we" would be more appropriate than "I." Sometimes, especially in the sciences, report writers avoid the first person altogether, saying "the researchers" if they need to refer to themselves, removing the human element as much as possible.

7. What's the tone?

Reports can be either formal or informal. A formal report will have most of the sections listed above and will be consistently professional and businesslike. Any report likely to be passed up or down the institutional hierarchy or provided to people outside of the organization should be formal, because you never know whose hands it might fall into and how they might react to informality. A strictly in-house report, however, might be slightly less formal, with more room for humor. Adjust your tone based on your understanding of how the report will be used and who will see it.

8. How does it vary?

"Book report" is the first genre many of us learned in elementary school. So while the headings in our example may seem foreign to you, you're familiar with the idea of "reporting back" to some group about something. What do they want to hear, and how do they want to hear it? The response to those two questions results in much of the variation in reports.

Suggested Moves for Writing a Report

I. Discover.

The many headings used in most reports can simplify, to some degree, the process of writing the report. So as part of your initial work, find examples of how reports are organized in your organization. Try to go through the whole list of questions to **Ask your teacher or boss** ➡️48. Check the report headings and see which ones you have trouble filling in. Chances are the toughest parts are the conclusions and recommendations. **Brainstorm** ➡️69 the things you want to put in those two categories, perhaps using **Mapping** ➡️73 so you'll see the whole network of conclusions and recommendations. If you were given a central question to answer, return to it and make sure you answer it as directly as possible.

2. Develop.

Remember the dolls-inside-dolls. Think about your different audiences. You may already know what you need to say in your executive summary—what happened and what you recommend. But developing the body and the appendices so that they answer all the potential questions of your most technical readers is another story. You might want to start by **Freewriting** ➡️72 about the issues most important to your various audiences. **Use a tree diagram** ➡️99, starting with the most important question the report was to answer.

3. Gather.

If you're working on a serious report, you may have been "gathering" for weeks or months, and what you really need to do is focus. **Reflect** ➡️102 on the work you've been doing. Perhaps do an informal **Survey** ➡️115 of others connected to the project. They may have their own ideas about what's important to put into the recommendations, and it would be to your advantage to hear and deal with their ideas now, when they'd be suggestions, rather than after the report is finished, when they could be criticisms.

4. Integrate.

There are two common integrating challenges with a report: creating and successfully **Integrating text and visuals** ➡️137, especially charts and graphs, so that they will communicate their message most efficiently, and **Integrating sources** ➡️133 so that you give proper credit and create a research trail without pages of citations.

5. Focus.

What's your central question? What's the answer to **"So what?"** ➡️156? What did the person who assigned the project want you to figure out? Go through **Focusing questions** ➡️155 to see if they help put the project into perspective.

Although it makes some sense to leave the abstract and/or executive summary until the end, you might try drafting them now. Boiling your thinking down to a page or less can force you to articulate a focus that's consistent with what you've done and that answers the assigner's questions.

6. Organize.

The headings commonly used in reports do much of your organizing for you, but you still have to order the body of the report. **Answer readers' questions** ➥159. Decide who your most important audience is and try to address that audience's questions. Try some **Standard organizing patterns** ➥166. If your audience isn't likely to be shocked by or resistant to your recommendations, try starting with the most important and working your way down to the least important issue. If the audience is likely to disagree with what you're saying, try starting with evidence and building your way toward your most radical ideas. You're trying to save your audience time and effort, to deliver to them the information they need just when they need it.

7. Revise.

Reports usually reflect the work of many people, so even if you're the one assigned to write the report, use the others; try all the **Share moves** ➥219–221 in chapter 30.

8. Present.

If you're going to give an oral report as well as hand in your written report, you may want to ignore what you've written while you brainstorm what you should say. Go back to your notes for **Answer readers' questions** ➥159 and see if you can answer those questions orally with some well-placed visuals. Don't read the report aloud. Cover the highlights as quickly as you can without rushing, and leave time for questions. Don't expect that your audience has read your report, even if they've had time to; answer their questions and refer them to the relevant sections in the written report.

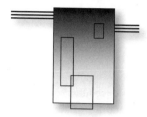

17

Response to Reading

EXAMPLE: **Respose to Marvin Swift's "Clear Writing Means Clear Thinking Means . . . ," B. Stihl**

Marvin Swift's article proves the power of example. You can talk all day about how important writing is, and how writing IS thinking, but until you actually see someone revise their thinking as they revise their writing, you won't really be convinced. That's what's magical about the article—Swift transports us inside the writing/thinking head. Swift takes as example a minor issue—use of the copy machine—and shows how the issue could turn into either a big problem for the company or a chance for management to bond with employees, depending on how the boss writes a quick memo. Seeing how something so small could have such large consequences encourages readers of Swift's article to take care with all their word choices.

Questions about the example:

1. A response to a reading can go on for volumes—think about the books that respond to the Bible—or be just a few incisive words, like the response to

the prose of Henry James: He chewed more than he bit off. What would be the value of a response this long?

2. What are the strengths and weaknesses of this response? What question(s) does it seem to be answering?
3. Have you ever been asked to write a reading response like this? What function did it serve?
4. At what point does this response go beyond simple summary?
5. What questions does this response leave you asking?

Other examples: Other responses to readings include the annotated bibliography in chapter 2, the literary analyses in chapter 9, the literature review in chapter 10, and the rhetorical analyses in chapter 20.

Questions about the Response to Reading

1. What are its purposes?

In school, a response to the reading assignment is likely to have many purposes: checking to see if students have done the reading, preparing them for a class discussion, helping them think more deeply about something they're likely to have skimmed over. The mini-response above was to a five-minute prompt "Write about one thing that interested you in one of the readings for today."

On the job, you might be asked to respond to a reading for a specific reason—to see if the boss should read it, to help build a strategy against it, to prepare for the changes it foresees.

2. Who are its audiences?

You might turn your reading response into a full-blown paper, but initially most responses are directed toward the professor who assigned them. You should find out whether you're supposed to write for readers who have read the text under discussion or for people trying to decide whether to read it.

3. What's the typical content?

All reading responses are based on the text, but the audience may want anything from a just-the-facts summary of the main points to a personal narrative for which the reading is a springboard.

4. How long is it?

Response articles can be substantial in scope, length, and depth, but most reading responses in school are short, a page or two.

5. How is it arranged on the page?

No special requirements except that you need the name and information of the text you're responding to somewhere prominent.

6. What pronouns are used?

In all informal and most formal situations, "I" would be appropriate and natural, since you're writing about your own responses and opinions. Find out how your response will be used.

7. What's the tone?

Even some high-brow reviews in elite journals can be playful, humorous, satiric, even mocking at times. For student writers, an open and honest stance toward the subject is probably best. Attempts at tones like sarcasm often go awry.

8. How does it vary?

If you're not given any directions on how to respond, you've got a tough job to do, because your response could be analytical (you take one part and assert its relation to the whole), evaluative (you assess and judge something), descriptive (you describe something in the reading), personal (you connect a personal experience or opinion to the reading), or creative (you write something inspired by or in the same form as the reading).

Suggested Moves for Response to Reading

1. Discover.

Your teacher or boss may have told you what important things to look for in your reading—"find all the allusions to other works" or "note all the references to our competitors." If you don't have such clear instructions, base your responses on your feelings; try to discover why you reacted as you did and build your response on those reactions. You might want to do some **Focused freewriting** ➡140 on "Why did I feel that way?"

2. Develop.

Analyze what you did in "Discover" for **Code words** ➡93 or phrases that you can **Expand** ➡92.

3. Gather.

Unless you're doing just a quick in-class response, you'll need to write down the full bibliographic information for the reading and any other sources. **Skim** ➡103, **Annotate** ➡104, **Transcribe and explain** ➡107 to help wring ideas from what you've read.

4. Integrate.

To show your understanding of the reading and your ability to make sense of its ideas, you may want to quote from the reading, perhaps more than once. See **Integrate voices** ➡132.

5. Focus.

Details can offer great focusing possibilities for any response to reading. What one line, fact, number, image caught you as you read? How can you relate that detail to your overall feeling about the reading or one of its aspects? **Find a focusing detail** ➡146.

6. Organize.

Fairly early in the response, you need to mention what you're responding to. After that, any kind of **Outline** ➡95 will probably help.

7. Revise.

Pay particular attention to your quotations, making sure you have punctuated them right.

8. Present.

Often a teacher requires a reading response mainly to see if the student did the reading and understood some of it. But sometimes you *can* present your response in creative ways—by creating an image for the cover of the book, for instance, or by taking part in a debate based on your initial reaction. Exchanging responses with others will almost certainly help you think more deeply about the material.

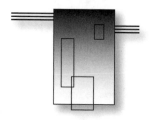

Resume

EXAMPLE: **Sample Resume**

Johnathan B. Goode
120 Easy Street
New Orleans, LA XXXXX
Phone
johnnybgoode@geemail.com[1]

OBJECTIVE: To be the leader of a big old band.[2]

QUALIFICATIONS:
- Can play a guitar just like ringing a bell
- Have been a band leader for two years
- Have played since I was two[3]

EXPERIENCE:
- 2009–2010: Band leader, "Johnny's Brawlers," Memphis, TN
- 2008–2009: Guitar Tutor, Gunnysack Music, Memphis, TN
- 2006–2007: Lead guitarist, May Bulleen High School Jazz Band[4]

EDUCATION: 2003–2007 May Bulleen High School

COMMUNITY SERVICE: Played at the Tinytown Skate Park Benefit

About the numbered items in the example:

1. Someone using a layout program can do startling and creative things with your basic information. But centering works fine.
2. Be succinct. You'll probably have to adjust this for different applications.
3. What are the three or four best reasons someone should choose you for the specific job?
4. If your education is particularly impressive or you're applying for an academic job, you might put education before experience.

EXAMPLE: **A "Real" Resume**

Alyson Frederick

P.O. Box 1234

Wellsville, UT 80000

algae@utah.gov

435-555-0000-Home

435-555-0000-Cell

EDUCATION

B.S. Family, Consumer, and Human Development,
    December 2009, cum laude
Family and Community Services Emphasis
Utah State University, Logan, UT

- Dean's List, Fall 2008 and Spring 2009
- Gerontology Certificate

ACADEMIC AWARDS

- Joan F. Budge Scholarship: 2008–2009
- Simmons Single Parent Scholarship: 2008–2009 and 2009–2010
- Women's Center Scholarships: 2005–2006, 2006–2007, and 2007–2008

RELEVANT WORK EXPERIENCE

BEAR RIVER AREA AGENCY ON AGING
Case Manager for Caregiver Clients: April 2009–Present

- Assessed the needs of clients, prepared plans, and contacted service providers
- Maintained client files and tracked case progress
- Developed and enhanced my ability to communicate with the elderly population

- Effectively ran activity groups for individuals with memory loss
- Worked closely with co-workers to problem solve
- Effectively worked with co-worker to teach a class entitled "Maintain Your Brain"

WILLIAMSBURG RETIREMENT COMMUNITY

Recreational Therapist Assistant: April 2009–August 2009

- Effectively planned and implemented activities for residents
- Contacted community organizations for information regarding activities and their cost
- Worked closely with supervisor in order to plan the most beneficial activities for the elderly
- Communicated and worked effectively with the elderly population
- Assisted residents with activities of daily living

IRS

Data Entry: Tax season 1998

- Transcribed selected fields from individual tax returns into the data base
- Trained in confidentiality policies and procedures

SPECIAL SKILLS

- Prepared and presented a group policy on child visitation rights
- Administered the DENVER PRE-SCREENING and THE HOME visit
- Planned and implemented age appropriate activities for two-year-olds
- Prepared and presented a self-esteem workshop to various audiences

VOLUNTEER EXPERIENCE

- President of the Student Gerontology Association
- Organized, planned, and conducted Gerontology Association meetings
- Contacted agencies about students helping in the community
- Organized students to help serve at Caregiver Recognition night
- Activity coordinator and planner for senior citizens
- Assisted USU's Women's Center with the Clothes Line Project to bring awareness about domestic violence to the community

REFERENCES

Questions about the example:

1. In what situations do you think Frederick should put work experience before education?

2. Why include volunteer experience?

3. What single detail would most make you want to hire her?

Questions about the Resume

1. What are its purposes?

A resume and the longer, more academic curriculum vitae (CV) are intended to summarize in a short space the parts of your life relevant to a prospective employer or other interested person. As http://jobstar.org/tools/resume/index.php puts it, "The resume is a **selling tool** outlining your skills and experience so an employer can see, at a glance, how you can contribute to the employer's workplace."

2. Who are its audiences?

People who are serious about a job application will often custom-create a different resume for each new job application. Therefore, the audience for any one resume may be just one person or human resources department. But most people like to have a standard resume ready to modify for specific jobs and for less important purposes.

3. What's the typical content?

You need to find and focus on anything about you that makes you look well-suited for the job. The employer wants to know what you can contribute to the employer's organization. Most often, you can convey that information with the headings used in our model: Objective, Qualifications, Experience, Education, and Community Service. But if your advisor's name is likely to open doors for you, you might want to have a "References" section. If your participation in a professional organization might establish a link with the employer, add "Professional Organizations."

4. How long is it?

Some job ads will specify: for example, "one-page resume." If you have enough legitimate accomplishments and experiences to merit a second page, include them. But a clean, well-highlighted single page is more impressive than a padded two pages.

5. How is it arranged on the page?

You'll see endless variations, but the simplest way is just to center your contact information at the top, then use bolded headings down the left side. Microsoft Word and other word-processing programs offer a number of resume templates.

6. What pronouns are used?

Often the resume is written in telegraphic style, with an understood "I": "Organized groups for the retreat . . . Wrote software documentation . . . Responsible for balancing the books." Avoid "you."

7. What's the tone?

Try to imagine a proud parent or teacher asked to write a totally objective summary of your life. They might manage to avoid verbal judgments, but all the evidence they bring forth, all the arguments they make, all the assumptions they base their judgments on will show their pride in you. Don't sing your own praises, but try to make the objective facts sing for you.

8. How does it vary?

"Resume types" include chronological, functional, combination, and targeted, says the first hit on Google (jobsearch.about.com/od/resumes/p /resumetypes.htm). Resume examples on the Internet are certainly worth mining for good ideas, but your goal should be not finding the right "type" but finding the best way to highlight your strengths. If you're strong on education but weak on experience, devote most of your space to your schoolwork. If your on-the-job skills are your big selling point, start with your most recent job and its responsibilities. If the job ad asks for a specific skill, get that out front. It's worth working up the energy to craft a new resume for each new job or type of job you're applying for.

Suggested Moves for Writing a Resume

1. Discover.

Formulating an objective and defining your best qualifications tend to be the most difficult parts of writing a resume. So **Freewrite** ➡72 on your objective—what would you LIKE to be doing?—and **Brainstorm** ➡69 a list of your qualifications. Don't edit yourself!

2. Develop.

Most people have a difficult time coming up with much to say about their strengths. But it's now or never. **Brainstorm** ➡69 a list of experiences and abilities that have relevance to the job. Get trivial! If you remember to brush your teeth most mornings before you go to work, write it down. Two or three other trivial details like that might convince you to include in your resume "reliable" or "pays attention to detail."

3. Gather.

It's worth spending some time gathering information about the intended recipients of your resume. Read about the organization you're applying to. Maybe one of their buzzwords could end up in your resume's "objective."

4. Integrate.

You probably won't be integrating outside material into your resume.

5. Focus.

Some people have strong enough credentials in such a wide range of areas that they can legitimately focus their resumes to highlight their strengths in a number of different roles—writer, tutor, teacher, editor, researcher. Younger people need to focus by keeping their eyes on the job description. Do some **Focused freewriting** ➡ 140 on what you think the organization wants.

6. Organize.

You want to figure out a way to put your strongest material first; that could mean starting with experience or education or qualifications. Much of a "functional" resume is built around important skills or functions that the resume writer can demonstrate. Most traditional resumes use an order similar to that of our models.

7. Revise.

Make sure to get someone else to proofread. Little mistakes on a resume are particularly embarrassing.

8. Present.

Some people like to get their resumes printed on fancy paper.

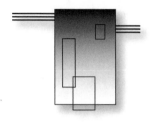

Review

EXAMPLE: **Kamin Thai Cuisine: A Cache County "Must Try,"
Whitney Olsen**

For a small Utah college town, Logan seems quite opposite of a place that would have a wonderful, exotic restaurant like Kamin Thai Cuisine. It is everything a restaurant should be—appetizing, accessible, attentive, attractive, and affordable. It has a menu that pleases both the adventure-phobe and the investigative palate. The restaurant is easy to get to from anywhere in Logan and surrounding areas. Kamin's staff members are polite and helpful, and the location is cozy, clean, stylish, and comfortable. On top of it all, the menu items are both generously portioned and modestly priced.

Appetizing: The Cuisine

Kamin has delicious, beautifully-presented food. The restaurant serves a wide variety of tasty, traditional Thai dishes. I've experienced firsthand that almost anyone, picky or not, can find something amenable to their tastes at Kamin. From sweet to spicy, light to hearty, the cuisine suits many appetites. There are plenty of appetizers (from spring rolls to calamari), drinks both familiar and exotic (from Pepsi products to Lychee juice and hot Thai tea), exotic salads, unique soups, lots of entrees, and typical Thai desserts. Any dish can be customized; a choice of meat is offered for most entrees, as is a choice of spice level—mild, medium, or spicy.

The menu features a number of delectable noodle dishes. Kamin has a delightfully wide selection, from Pad Thai (rice noodles with a bright orange, sweet and tangy sauce), a better-known Thai dish, to Pad Woon Sen (cellophane noodles with garlic). A number of varieties of fried rice are available too, like the tangy Phuket Pineapple Fried Rice or the spicy Basil Fried Rice. Noodles and rice dishes are served with a choice of beef, pork, chicken, shrimp, or tofu so the dish can be customized for both mood and taste.

Don't think that dining at Kamin has to mean light entrées. For heartier meals, Kamin offers many meat dishes like Med Ma Muang and Pad Preaw Wan (the Thai versions of cashew stir-fry and sweet and sour, respectively). Kamin's Thai curries are heavenly, awash with clean, fresh flavors like basil and coconut in contrast to the more common but heavier Middle Eastern and Indian curries. The restaurant's rendition of the traditional massaman curry is a classic and delicious blend of coconut milk, tender potatoes, meat, and Thai spices.

The menu can appeal to anyone, from the gourmet chef to the wary Thai restaurant first-timer. For palates like mine, which seek fresh combinations of flavors and a variety of carefully-prepared cuisines, Kamin is a perfect solution to my small-town-restaurant blues. Their chefs use all the requisite ethnic ingredients like basil, tamarind, lemongrass, garlic, scallions, fish sauce, coconut milk, Thai chilies, and tofu. The meats are tender, the noodles are cooked al dente, and the sauces are neither too thick nor too thin. From visit to visit, I can easily find a new blend of flavors to appeal to what my palate is searching for, or order my standby favorites like Pad Thai and the massaman curry.

Accessible: Getting There, Staying There

Located at 51 West 200 South, Kamin is just half a block off of Main Street, so it is easy to get to from anywhere in Logan, Providence, Smithfield, and is even a worthwhile drive from farther locations like Richmond and Hyrum. A sign on Main Street, on the corner near the Best Western Baugh Motel says "Kamin Thai Cuisine" and points west—that road is 200 South. The restaurant has its own small parking area, a bonus given the crowded parking conditions at numerous other restaurants, even in Logan. There is also plenty of room out on 200 South to park. Kamin has very usual hours for a restaurant: 11:00 a.m. to 3:00 p.m. and 5:00 p.m. to 9:30 p.m. Monday through Thursday, and 11:00 a.m. to 10:00 p.m. on Friday and Saturday. Kamin is also easily accessible by bus. Cache Valley Transit District has a bus stop just half a block west of the restaurant at 100 West 200 South.

Attentive: Kamin's Service

I'll admit it: if we visit Kamin on a slow night, we sometimes have to wait a few minutes for the host or hostess (who also functions as a server) to return to the podium. Most of the time, the host or hostess is ready and waiting near the waiting area to seat us. There is infrequently a wait, and we have always been seated at clean, set tables.

Kamin's servers are generally knowledgeable and attentive, and if they're not sure about something, they will promptly find the person who is, as with my gluten-intolerant guest Jen. When we arrived after speaking with the owner on the phone and asked our server about gluten-free options, she made arrangements for us to speak with members of the management again to make sure our experience was a good one.

Admittedly, at times my water glass has gone almost empty, in part due to the small size of Kamin's stemmed water glasses, but also because the servers sometimes seemed to forget about refilling. Getting the check sometimes becomes a longer ordeal than necessary, but I find it's a nice opportunity to catch up on chatting that got lost while eating and enjoy the pleasant after-effects. In all, I have always felt well taken care of at Kamin.

Attractive: The Ambience

Kamin is no hole-in-the-wall; the restaurant is beautiful inside and out. It is a quaint building that was probably once a house. It has a small patio with outdoor seating, and a large grassy yard bordered with planted gardens and trees. The waiting area just inside the front doors is calming and beautiful. A water fountain decorated with colored glass and flowers bubbles on the floor. Several Asian-style benches with red cushions stand nearby in case of a wait. In true Thai style, the walls are painted bright goldenrod and canary and hung with stylized Asian pictures and ornamental hangings. Soothing ambient music is always playing, from instrumental renditions of popular songs to Thai string solos.

In the sunroom, in the northeast corner of the restaurant, the maroon and gold wallpaper actually has ornate patterns of Buddha in it, only visible when we sit very near it. It is a tasteful addition that highlights the attention to detail of the restaurant's designers. Everything works together to create a charming and exotic ambience. The combination of the bold colors of the walls is warm, welcoming, and refreshing. The colors are vivid without being overwhelming. The restaurant mercifully lacks walls crowded with memorabilia and tacky artwork. The clean, bright, simple colors and moderate decorating create a tasteful environment for a tasty meal.

Affordable: The Cost

When all is said and done, the check will come—breathe. Kamin is moderately priced, especially for the exquisite, exotic cuisine they serve; their pricing is actually competitive with other Logan restaurants like Chili's and Olive Garden, averaging at least a dollar less per entrée than either restaurant. Even customizing an order to include seafood makes the most expensive entrées at Kamin a modest $14.99, a price that falls in the middle range of menu items at Chili's, and the low range of menu items at Olive Garden. The difference? Chili's and Olive Garden are chain restaurants, while Kamin is privately owned, making their modest pricing even more admirable—Kamin has higher-quality cuisine for better prices than the local turn-and-burn chain restaurants.

My husband and I can dine at Kamin for under $25.00, including the tip. We typically get ice water with our meals, so after tax and tip, we come away from a pleasant, delicious meal for a very good price, plus two boxes of leftovers for lunch the next day! The portions are large enough to fill up on sharing a single entrée, if we need to. Even if we order drinks, two entrées, and share dessert, the tab still stays under $35.00 with tax and tip, no mean feat for eating out! We like Kamin because we get it all in that reasonably-priced check: wonderful food, an easy location to get to, good service, and a lovely, comfortable ambience in which to enjoy it all.

Questions about the example:

1. Does this review provide enough details to allow you to make up your own mind about the restaurant?
2. Are the reviewer's criteria clear?
3. What detail would most affect your decision about whether to go to this restaurant?
4. What else would you want to know about? What does Olsen not cover?

EXAMPLE: **Not a Hard Decision, Emilio Zamudio**

Nike Mercurial Vapor V FG is the official name. I have used a number of soccer cleats so far in my life and although I have had many positive experiences with others, this is by far the one that I would definitely recommend. Everything from the extreme colors to the fit on your foot to even its special features makes this the best shoe to use. I feel the pros far outweigh any complaints customers may report.

APPEARANCE: any soccer player can agree that the appearance of your shoes can say a lot about you and where your skill level is at. The Mercurial Vapor comes in some extreme colors that are sure to turn heads. Colors such as max orange, obsidian blue, abyss, and vibrant yellow, give you a one-of-a-kind look when compared to the traditional colors such as black and white shoes. This can also provide a sense of intimidation from opponents when they see you step onto the field with a pair of Mercurial Vapors.

WEIGHT: At only 8 oz. (230 grams), these extremely lightweight shoes were created to make a player faster and they do just that. Its sleek design helps keep the weight of the shoe down along with the thin material that surrounds your foot. The lightweight feel of the shoes helps you become more agile and gives you added quickness. This is especially important when it comes to getting away from and even past defenders.

CONS: These shoes retail for somewhere around $239 and that can make quite a hole in anyone's pocket, especially for one pair of shoes. The narrowness of the shoe improves the feel and can also improve your touch on the ball. However, anyone with a wider foot has always found these very uncomfortable and that has resulted in some bad blisters and small cuts. These shoes have also been known to be hard to tighten since two-thirds of the shoelaces are being hidden by an immovable lace cover.

PROS TO THE CONS: As I have previously stated, I feel the pros outweigh the cons because there is a positive side to any of the cons previously mentioned. The retail value of $239 makes the shoe very hard to find cheaper than that. In this case, cost comes along with quality. I used these shoes for almost two years and I've played in over one hundred games and even more practices than that. Your $239 is guaranteed to go a really long way. Even if they fall apart for some reason, the shoe comes with a two year guarantee from Nike that promises to replace your shoe if any such problems/complaints should arise. In other words, you have nothing to lose.

NARROWNESS: The narrow fitting shoe might make anyone with a wider foot uncomfortable, but the Mercurial Vapors were made for speed and a perfect fit. That is why they must be made narrower. Being narrower, it provides a better touch on the ball and improves your acceleration and sprint speed. The narrow fit also molds the shoe to the shape of your foot allowing for a custom fit and providing more comfort and support as you play.

SPECIAL FEATURES: The lace covering that prevents you from tightening your shoes from the very bottom by the toes is also a unique feature. The covering covers the laces and provides a clean strike zone so that your shots go exactly where you intend them to. This also is designed to give you a more powerful shot. The outsole/studs on the outsole of the shoe provide really great traction and also make it easier for turning and quickly changing directions. These studs don't wear down very easily if used on appropriate playing fields. The laces are made from a string-like material that makes it almost impossible to become undone when tightened. I have never had a problem with the shoe coming untied in the middle of a game.

DURABILITY: There are also a number of factors that customers should take caution in when purchasing these soccer cleats. The number of times you use them will greatly affect how long these shoes will last. Someone using these shoes only for games instead of both practice and games may find that the shoe will last you even beyond the two year guaranteed lifespan that Nike promises. However, using them in both games and practices will still outlast other shoes' durability. This is one pair of shoes that can endure any beating that comes from playing soccer.

ADVERSE CONDITIONS: These shoes are meant to be played on firm ground. Meaning, any other type of field use will cause your shoes to take a beating and/or prevent you from performing at your top level. Firm surfaces help extend the life of your shoes and also make it more comfortable to wear. Conditions such as rain, snow, hot weather, will also affect your performance. The Mercurial Vapors become very heavy when water gets inside them, adding resistance to any movement you want to make with or without the ball, defeating the purpose of using lightweight shoes. Snow also makes your shoes very heavy and your toes are not very well insulated causing them to become very cold. The opposite is also true; the synthetic leather absorbs extreme heat and may cause a burning sensation on your feet. Not fun.

These shoes are the best around and are highly recommended for anyone looking to improve on their soccer abilities. They won't make you a better soccer player simply by wearing them, but will definitely help you become the better player you want to be. Many world class athletes rely on the Mercurial Vapors to upgrade their game and it's easy to see why. These shoes won't disappoint and you can expect everything previously mentioned when you lace up in these shoes.

Questions about the example:

1. Did you find the headings useful or annoying? The author found the headings helped him organize his material.
2. What details are particularly convincing? How could the author have made a stronger case?
3. A college class may never ask you to review soccer shoes or Thai restaurants, but how might this kind of organization help you in other papers?

Questions about the Review

1. What are its purposes?

The reviewer's job is complex: he or she must first interest the reader in the subject, quickly establish enough credibility so that readers will take the review seriously, and present enough evidence and convincing argument to bring the reader around to the reviewer's perspective. Readers read reviews in order to make decisions. Reviews often include brief summaries because just knowing that the movie is science fiction or the restaurant is Tex-Mex may be all a reader needs. Readers expect to learn a reviewer's opinion in a review, but most readers don't want to be badgered with a too-strident opinion, so when and how to reveal an opinion is one of the reviewer's most difficult tasks.

How do our authors reveal their opinions in our example reviews? Would you like to have heard more or less of it?

2. Who are its audiences?

You've probably read dozens of reviews, so it may be helpful to imagine that you're writing for someone like you. The subject of the review often determines the audience—the audience of a review of a new role-playing game may be totally different from that for a review of a retirement facility. So to a large extent you can gear your review to the people interested in your subject. In what ways is Zamudio's review aimed specifically at soccer players?

3. What's the typical content?

Readers come to the review for information as well as opinion, so the reviewer normally includes as much information as possible, **Answering the journalist's questions** ➥87 and including such relevant information as actors' names, recipe ingredients, and price at discount stores. The reviewer's criteria should be evident in the review, even if they're not stated directly; they add to the information a reader can gather. A cookie reviewer might criticize a particular cookie because of its texture, for instance. If the reviewer reveals that she favors crispy cookies and the reader prefers soft ones, then the reader knows to ignore the reviewer's opinion on that issue.

You may want to follow our authors' lead and make your criteria, or the factors you're judging, into headings, as they did.

4. How long is it?

Most reviews of a single product or book are perhaps three or four pages long, but some reviewers include a number of products and expand the review to be a kind of personal essay. Readers read reviews to get their questions answered, so they probably aren't interested in pages of description.

5. How is it arranged on the page?

Get the basic information out first, often with the name of the subject of the review in the title: "Barney's Breakfast Barn: The World's Freshest Eggs." In a long review, headings may be helpful.

6. What pronouns are used?

"I" seems appropriate and natural, since you're writing about your own responses and opinions. But the clever review writer stays in the background and presents information that will lead the reader to share the writer's conclusion, even if it hasn't been stated.

7. What's the tone?

The reviewer's many purposes can make the selection of tones tricky. The review needs to be serious enough to establish credibility and professionalism, but it may need some humor or cleverly selected details or a controlling metaphor to keep readers reading. Some reviewers develop a reputation for being nasty and hard-to-please, but it's hard to attract readers to Mr. or Ms. Negative. Be sure to **Play the believing game** ➡ 38 at some point, no matter what you're reviewing.

Do you find Olsen's or Zamudio's tone appealing? Whose judgment do you trust more? Why?

8. How does it vary?

The Internet has led to an explosion in reviews and reviewers, giving some of them singular power. Your critical review of the latest computer game may at best provoke response from the game's defenders, but your two-sentence comment about the motel's thin walls or bedbugs could ruin an already-shaky business. Reviewers traditionally attempted to be objective or even-handed, but today many commentators freely admit their biases.

Suggested Moves for Writing a Review

I. Discover.

To find an appropriate subject, compile an **Authority** ➡ 62 list or a **Strong feelings** ➡ 65 list. The reviewer needs to look both outward, at the subject, with moves like **Explore with your senses** ➡ 49 or **Look for what's valuable** ➡ 52, and inward, at opinions and values, with moves like **Analyze your tastes** ➡ 59 or **Write down your gut feelings** ➡ 67. Perhaps most important, reviewers need to open their minds. I don't want to read a review by someone whose mind was made up long ago.

2. Develop.

Fairly early in the process, the reviewer needs to start listing criteria with **Focused brainstorming** ➡ 70. What would the attributes be of the ideal movie, CD, or restaurant? Remember, when you add your criteria to your opinions you give your reader information. Be sure to **Take the other side** ➡ 82 at some point, so your review won't be one-sided. And as soon as a judgment starts to form in your head, explore it with **Explain your code words** ➡ 93.

3. Gather.

Your exploration in the discovering stage should have helped you gather lots of details, but you'll want to return and make sure that you got the movie quotation right or that the restaurant really did set each place with three forks. Can you include others' opinions, using **Interviews** ➡ 113 or **Surveys** ➡ 115? **Use a double-entry journal** ➡ 106 to take notes and think through your observations.

4. Integrate.

You'll definitely want to **Integrate showing and telling** ➡ 134 and **Integrate** *pathos,* *logos,* **and** *ethos* ➡ 135. If you've talked to others about their opinions, you'll also need to **Integrate voices** ➡ 132 and **Integrate sources** ➡ 133. A review is a kind of argument for the validity of the reviewer's opinions, so ideally it should be as tightly constructed as a debater's spiel.

5. Focus.

The reviewer's opinion can be all the focus that a review needs: "Bad, bad, bad, that's all you need to know about the new Gut Punch movie." But providing a detail to exemplify the opinion can make the review more interesting and convincing: **Find a focusing detail** ➡ 146. As is so often the case, coming up with a variety of openers can help you see what you're thinking and what's most important: **Brainstorm leads** ➡ 143.

6. Organize.

This would be a good time to remember what it means to **Write reader-based prose** ➡ 158. Ponder what readers need and want to hear, not necessarily what excited or appalled you. Would it make sense to **Use headings and subheadings** ➡ 165, perhaps making each factor or criterion a heading?

7. Revise.

Almost certainly, you need to **Revise for voice** ➡ 191, preferably after you **Talk . . . and listen** ➡ 157. It's difficult to negotiate the tricky tone of a review without enlisting other ears.

8. Present.

You don't have to be a newspaper food columnist to find an audience for your review. Simply trading reviews with classmates can teach you about the genre. If you enjoy having people respond to your opinions, think about writing for or creating a blog. A good review saves readers time and money, so good reviewers are cherished.

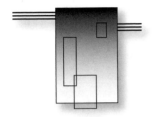

20

Rhetorical Analysis

EXAMPLE: **The Trade of Scavenging, Greg Geddes**

In Lars Eighner's essay "On Dumpster Diving," he discusses the formalities of what it takes to become a master in the art of digging through garbage. He tells his own personal story of how he became involved with dumpster diving. His story outlines everything he has learned as a scavenger and presents the information in a way that would help train someone to begin searching through what most people call garbage. His use of rhetoric in the essay enables the reader to see dumpster diving from his point of view. Lars Eighner proposes that dumpster diving is a reasonable way to acquire necessary goods.

This essay appeals to two different audiences: (1) People who are interested in dumpster diving or are already involved in it, and (2) people who are wasteful. Readers interested in dumpster diving may find this essay as a useful "how to" guide. After reading the essay, the reader will gain an understanding of dumpster diving along with a knowledge of what to expect while digging through junk. To people who are wasteful this essay will serve as a wakeup call. The author assumes that the audience already has an attitude towards dumpster diving, whether it be positive or negative.

Right after the opening paragraph of the essay, Eighner throws in a paragraph that is only eleven words long. It reads, "I began Dumpster diving about a year before I became homeless" (2). This sentence stands alone as its own paragraph in order to emphasize to the reader that Eighner chose to be a scavenger before he was left with no other choice. This demonstrates that from Eighner's point of view, dumpster diving is simply another occupation. The rest of the essay helps reemphasize that dumpster diving should not be looked at as something that only homeless people do, but rather be viewed as another way to acquire goods.

One of the highlights in the essay is Eighner's description of the "predictable series of stages a person goes through in learning to scavenge" (31). This section clearly depicts the author's view on homelessness. Eighner has recruited several people into the trade of scavenging, and as a result, he has seen the stages a person passes through before viewing dumpster diving as he does. At first, the new scavenger is ashamed of being seen by others, and will go to different lengths to protect his/her self-image (ducking behind things, digging through garbage at night, etc.). Eighner counters this by stating that most people instinctively look away from scavengers, and skulking around only draws attention and arouses suspicion. Also, it's obvious that diving at night is ineffective and messy. He then explains that the new scavenger has a hard time seeing garbage as being anything but garbage. "Every grain of rice seems to be a maggot. Everything seems to stink" (33). The use of the word "seems" in these sentences shows that Eighner looks past the negative attributes most people apply to junk. By doing so, he helps the reader to see that garbage is not junk, but rather just things. He shows that the negative mindset passes with experience. The new dumpster diver learns that people throw away perfectly good things. At this stage, the diver realizes that "those who disparage his profession are the fools, not he" (37).

After explaining how one can arrive at the top of the ranks in a dumpster diving career, Eighner shows the certain formalities involved in the profession. By explaining the common courtesies that are involved, *i.e.*, dumpster diving etiquette, Eighner portrays the art of dumpster diving as a normal way of life. Just as in other areas of life where one must practice proper etiquette and manners, so it is with dumpster diving. He explains how "can scroungers" lack respect for dumpster divers. Can scroungers are blind to everything in dumpsters except for cans. They look past all other articles present in a dumpster, and as a result end up making a complete mess out of a dumpster, leaving everything in disarray. This is a major inconvenience to frequent dumpster divers. Along those same lines, Eighner states that can scroungers go to extreme lengths to collect cans, *i.e.*, searching through garbage cans at residencies. The difference between foraging through a dumpster rather than a residential garbage can is that there is a personal kind of invasion. A dumpster contains excess from multiple people and places, whereas a residential garbage can comes from one home. Eighner expresses a manner of politeness in avoiding more personal scavenging.

In showing the different kinds of scavengers and the courtesies involved, Eighner successfully lays out the dumpster diving industry. Occupations are involved, new recruits are gathered in, and a sense of order is established.

Eighner appeals to *ethos* through his own personal dumpster diving experiences. He is an authority figure on the subject of dumpster diving. The way Eighner sets up this trust is by explaining that a depleting savings account made him look into other ways to acquire his daily necessities for many years. Credibility is also established when he describes how to tell when a found food is edible or not. His thorough description is proof that he is an expert in the field. The fact that he uses so much description to show whether certain foods are edible makes it more believable that he actually has to do that in order to survive.

Emotion plays into this essay in various parts to satisfy the rhetorical appeal of *pathos*. One of the main factors that elicits emotion is when he mentions that all his savings money is being put into rent. The reader then realizes that becoming homeless is inevitable. The reader feels sorry for him to a certain extent because he has no other means of obtaining the necessary things to live. However, this initial sad feeling is relieved when the reader learns everything Eighner is able to find dumpster diving. Eighner states that there is often an abundance of goods and he even gains weight while diving. Another area that appeals to emotion is the unsaid stories behind different items he comes across, *e.g.*, old teddy bears, shredded wedding books, a bag containing unused condoms and contraceptives, even pets. Some of these items he finds have sad stories behind them that speak for themselves. Although much of the essay is centered around feelings of sadness and sympathy, Eighner still lightens the mood with a bit of humor. He entertains the reader with the thought of his dog doing the Dance of a Zillion Fire Ants. He describes his dog Lizbeth doing a dance when she sees lots of fire ants. The image of his dog jumping around adds a bit of lightheartedness to the essay.

Logos is the rhetorical appeal most often used in this essay. He explains the process of finding out what food is safe to eat in an almost scientific way. His logical thinking is evident when he says, "Except for carbonated beverages, all canned goods should contain a slight vacuum and suck air when first punctured. Bulging, rusty, dented cans and cans that spew when punctured should be avoided, especially when the contents are not very acidic or syrupy" (11). He often banks on the importance of common sense. His reasoning in describing safe foods enables the reader to logically understand what is safe to eat and what is not.

Eighner does a great job in portraying his outlook on the dumpster diving lifestyle with the closing paragraph "I find my desire to grab for the gaudy bauble has been largely sated. I think this is an attitude I share with the very wealthy—we both know there is plenty more where what we have came from. Between us are the rat-race millions who nightly scavenge the cable channels looking for they know not what. I am sorry for them" (69). Most people will find his comparison between dumpster divers and the very wealthy outrageous. But he makes the point that he knows what he wants out of life, and he knows where to find it. The majority of everyone else is wandering aimlessly around because they don't know where to find what they want.

Work Cited

Eighner, Lars. "On Dumpster Diving." www1.broward.edu. n.p., n.d. Web. 2 Mar. 2010. http://producer.csi.edu/cdraney/archive-courses/fall07/engl102 /e-texts/eighner-dumpster.htm.

Questions about the example:

1. Do you feel that Geddes did a good job of explaining the rhetorical success of the dumpster diving article?
2. According to Geddes, how does Eighner convince readers to change their minds about dumpster diving?
3. What practical use might this kind of analysis have?

EXAMPLE: **Rhetorical Analysis Essay, Cambri McDonald**

In his letter to the *Statesman* editor, John Doe argues girls look "stupid" in knitted headbands because they cover "entire faces" and the "entire upper-half of [their] body." He also claims knitted headbands are unprofessional because girls would not wear them in a professional workplace.

The intended audience of the letter is not static. Doe begins by addressing "you girls," but digresses into a "we" narrative. The shift makes some sense as he uses "we" to encourage all college students to look more professional, though the change in narrative is still jarring. However, the use of "we" makes Doe seem hypocritical. He states that "head sweaters are a small representation of how sloppy we look as college students," suggesting that he is one of the sloppy college students. The next sentence takes this idea even farther as "we" changes into a feminine "we": "I could go on and on about how ridiculous it looks when we show up for class in sweats, slippers, and giant fake flowers in our hair." Doe seems to suggest that he also wears sweats, slippers, and giant fake flowers in his hair. Reverting back to a gender-neutral "we," he continues by saying girls persistently wear these headbands; however, in the last line he tells the audience to "Ditch the head sweaters," proof that he has yet again switched to a female-only audience.

Doe also makes numerous, faulty assumptions. He assumes knitted head-bands are solely functional and are a characteristic of twelve-year-olds. Beginning with the phrase "I'm positive," he assumes college students will never wear knitted headbands in a professional workplace. When he states "we are responsible for . . . acting the part of what we're working toward" he excludes certain endpoints that college students might desire. Fashion majors, art majors, and theatre majors might be striving for the very expressive creativity knitted headbands can, in a small way, provide. He also assumes college students want to be something different than what they currently are when he states "start representing the person you want to be." Is it not possible that at least one single college student at Utah State University *is* in fact currently representing who they want to be?

Though fluctuating and thoughtless assumptions hurt Doe's credibility, he does have one moment in which he doesn't undermine his own authority. He establishes in the introduction that clothing changes take place in the winter. Though this is a rather obvious fact, it does have the potential to be a good introduction to the topic; however, mechanical flaws undermine his authority as a writer.

Doe's word choice is inconsistent. The use of words such as "embark," "excluding," and "tenacity" seem misplaced in association with "stupid" and "things." Exaggerating the misplacement of this overly-formal language is the use of colloquial phrases, such as "last, but certainly not least" and "Dress for success."

Offensive language also undermines his authority. Statements such as "you few brave souls who have the tenacity to show off your frost-bitten toes to the rest of us" limit his potential audience because he offends this select group of readers. He also states "Girls, you look stupid," and then emphasizes this insult by adding "I meant that in the nicest way possible." Not only does such a statement cause his audience (or momentary audience) to become automatically defensive, but it also illustrates the limitations of his writing because such an offensive phrase is his best attempt at conveying a controversial opinion.

Additionally, grammatical errors damage his *ethos*. The first sentence is in the wrong verb tense. "I notice" should be "I have noticed" because the author realizes this each year, thus the "noticing" has happened in the past, not just the present. Because Doe mentions several patterns of fashion, "pattern" should be plural; the verb "sweep" agrees with "patterns" and can remain, though it did not agree with the original word "pattern." In the second sentence, "obvious" is the subject. What is an "obvious?" "Obvious" should be an adjective: "The obvious patterns of fashion . . ." Again, the subject did not originally agree with the verb. By making "obvious" an adjective for "patterns," however, the verb "are" can remain. The phrase "fewer flipflops are noticeable" does not make sense within the sentence. The sentence is a list beginning with the verb "are," so the use of "are" again is unnecessary and confusing. Also, "flip flops" are two words, not one. The sentence "Maybe, the majority of us are nowhere near graduating and about to embark . . ." does not make sense. The difference between "graduating" and "to embark" makes the reader think the "nowhere" only applies to "graduating" but that the majority are about to embark. The words should have the similar "-ing" ending. Such grammatical errors not only cripple Doe's authority, but also distract the reader and make the argument difficult to understand.

Doe fails to use any appeal to *pathos*. He attempts to use *logos* by providing a concession: knitted headbands may serve a functional purpose. Yet he ruins this logic with the hyperbole that follows. He also attempts to use a question to get the reader thinking. This attempt also fails though because the components of the question pose false alternatives, one of which is again a hyperbole.

There are multiple fallacies within the letter. A red herring occurs when Doe switches from trying to establish the use of the headbands to stating an irrelevant hyperbole. He makes a hasty generalization when he states "you girls refuse to take them off," assuming that all girls wear knitted headbands and all girls refuse to take them off. Non sequitur occurs when he states "it's difficult to identify their use," "This makes me question their use after all," and then "I do not understand the purpose of the head sweater": How can he question a use he cannot identify or understand? He explicitly states his purpose as wanting to "point out" that he does not understand the purpose of the knitted head bands and to say "Girls, you look stupid." His actual purpose, however, is to encourage girls to dress more professionally by not wearing knitted head bands. He also states "we are college students, and we are responsible for looking professional." The association between being a college student and looking professional also seems to be a non sequitur because the definition of a college student does not necessarily include professionalism. He presents false alternatives by asserting that head bands are either functional or fashionable, though headbands can plausibly be both. The argument that girls should not wear knitted headbands because they cannot wear them to work is an irrelevance fallacy. One would not say that pajamas should never be worn because you cannot wear them to work. Thus Doe's approach to encouraging professionalism fails. Finally, the claim "everybody knows" knitted headbands are ridiculous is an argumentum ad populum fallacy.

In sum, the letter is not persuasive. Fluctuating narratives, faulty assumptions, and multiple fallacies create instability, toppling any argument Doe might possibly have. The offensive language not only illustrates Doe's ignorance concerning persuasive techniques, but also shows how unprofessional and thus hypocritical he is.

Questions about the example:

1. McDonald has many criticisms of Doe's letter to the editor. Which do you find most effective?

2. You can imagine that McDonald read the letter to the editor and was irritated by it. Do you think it was more satisfying to write this analysis than to just gripe to friends about it? Why?

3. In what situations would this kind of analysis be useful to you?

Questions about Rhetorical Analysis

1. What are its purposes?

You analyze the rhetoric of a piece of writing or speech to understand it and perhaps prepare to counter it. "Rhetoric" refers to all the tools that a writer can use to influence a reader. A rhetorical analysis seeks to uncover all the ways that a text is achieving its goals—and where it's falling short. Various forms of rhetorical analysis serve a variety of purposes in educational settings. Analyzing one of Karl Marx's arguments can help an economics student understand the history of economic thought. Dissecting the rhetoric of a political speech can help a student of political science understand why the speech was effective. Understanding the logic of a debater's point can allow for an effective counterattack. The professional economist, politician, or lawyer has the same needs and the same uses for such analysis. A rhetorical analysis would seldom stand alone, but it can be part of many reports.

In "The Trade of Scavenging," Greg Geddes analyzes the rhetoric of an essay about dumpster diving in order to determine how author Lars Eighner "enables the reader to see dumpster diving from his point of view." How can the reader be persuaded to see dumpster diving as "a reasonable way to acquire necessary goods"?

What do you imagine Cambri McDonald's purposes were?

2. Who are its audiences?

The audience is the person who needs to understand the text or who can benefit from getting inside the writer's head. In college, a professor may assign a rhetorical analysis not to probe the text itself but to evaluate students' comprehension and ability to articulate their understanding.

Is either sample analysis useful to you?

3. What's the typical content?

The analyst will most often focus on how the delivery of the message affects its content, answering questions such as

- Who is the audience and what are the purposes of the message?
- How are certain issues made central—in the title, in the opening paragraph, in headings, with highlighting?
- What rhetorical moves does the arguer use—repetition, examples, argument from assumptions, appeals to authority?

- Where and how effectively does the arguer appeal to *logos*, *pathos*, and *ethos*? (See MOVE 135.)
- What undermines or contradicts the writer's points? Are there logical gaps or fallacies?
- What's the context in which the message was written? Is it part of an ongoing conversation?
- Do Geddes and McDonald touch every base here?

4. How long is it?

Length depends entirely on purpose. A rhetorical analysis could be a few words—"He emphasizes everything with caps and exclamation marks"—to a dissertation on why a Supreme Court judgment was wrong.

5. How is it arranged on the page?

Since the analysis is likely to be part of a larger piece, layout may not be an issue. Highlighting and bulleted or numbered lists are often appropriate.

6. What pronouns are used?

The purpose of the analysis and the analyst's relationship to the audience will determine the pronoun use. If the analysis is part of a longer formal report, use of "I" would probably be inappropriate, but if the assignment is to analyze and give a personal opinion, the audience may want to see "I."

7. What's the tone?

If the analysis is part of a report, it should be business-like and formal. But if just answering the question "What do you think of this approach?," an analysis could be relatively informal.

8. How does it vary?

Purpose is crucial. If you're trying to learn from a master, your analysis will be very different from the one you'd write on the opposition party's political candidate's speech. The questions of rhetorical analysis can be expanded to examine websites and in fact anything visual. Technical writers have made almost a science of analyzing web pages.

Suggested Moves for Writing a Rhetorical Analysis

1. Discover.

First, **Ask your teacher or boss** ➡48 and **Analyze your purposes** ➡55. As you read over the piece you're analyzing, **Write down your gut feelings** ➡67. To start making sense of the argument, **Dig into contexts and connections** ➡51.

2. Develop.

Sometime during your analysis, you should probably **Take the other side** ➥82, becoming an enthusiast if you tend to be skeptical, doubt if you're inclined to believe. Considering the other sides of an issue will almost certainly improve your understanding of it. Especially if you're trying to develop a compromise, a solution, **Find the overlap** ➥86. You might see if you can **Use a tree diagram** ➥99 to make sense of the argument's decision questions.

3. Gather.

You need to read the text you're analyzing many times. **Skim** ➥103 sometimes to get a sense of how the whole thing ties together, and **Annotate** ➥104 as you read. Consider **Using a double-entry journal** ➥106 to keep track of what you notice or observe in one column and how the observed feature functions rhetorically in the second column.

4. Integrate.

You probably won't want to bring a lot of outside information into your analysis, but you'll need to **Quote** ➥123 or **Paraphrase** ➥124 from the text, so that your readers know exactly what you're referring to.

5. Focus.

Find the problem/tension/conflict ➥145. It may not be obvious what the text is arguing, but locating the central conflict is crucial. Once you're reasonably sure what the central issue is, **Abstract** ➥150 it, then **Frame it** ➥151.

6. Organize.

Using your summary as a starting point, **Outline** ➥95 all the points that build up to the summary. Or try to **Answer readers' questions** ➥159 about the text and use your answers as an outline. If you seem to have more pieces than are manageable, **Group them, find labels for the groups, and order them** ➥162.

7. Revise.

As you revise your analysis, remember that you don't need to follow the order or organization of the text itself. **Start as close to the heart or climax as you can** ➥194. If you have trouble getting one of your summaries right, **Try rephrasing the idea in four or five different ways** ➥207. **Get some feedback** ➥220, if possible from your actual audience, and **Learn from feedback** ➥221, which is often a challenge in itself.

8. Present.

You probably will be told how to present your analysis. If you're to report orally, be ready to boil down all your thinking to a "yes" or "no," or to a single sentence of analysis or recommendation.

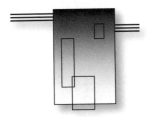

21 Wiki

EXAMPLE: **Wikipedia**

I can't explain on paper what a wiki is as well as a wiki can explain it on the web. On this subject, Wikipedia is authoritative: http://en.wikipedia.org/wiki/Wiki.

EXAMPLE: **Technical and Professional Writing Program Technology Wiki**

Wikipedia is the largest and best known wiki and therefore as good a "sample" as you'll find. Here's a screen shot of a very different wiki created by Rebecca Walton for her students to research and write about the technology useful to technical and professional writers.

You can see the rest of the page, and in fact the entire wiki, at http://engl4410.wikispaces.com.

Spend a few minutes looking at the wiki. Did you learn anything? (I learned how to use Jing.) Can you imagine writing for such a wiki? Certainly there are experts who could write more authoritative definitions, but contributing to

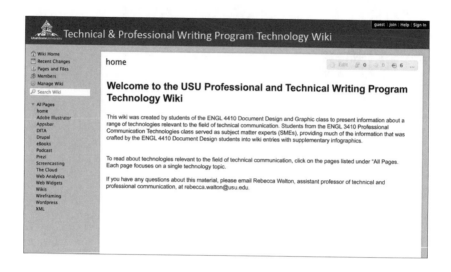

the wiki helps students learn and remember the concepts, and having all the definitions in one place is very convenient. It shows that you don't have to be a world authority to contribute to a wiki; you just need to do enough research to be able to add to the conversation.

Questions about Wikis

1. What are its purposes?

Wikis are most useful when a group of people needs to *collaborate*, the participants are geographically *spread out*, and the information the group studies tends to *change* quickly.

Professors may also use wikis to encourage individual work on a collaborative project.

2. Who are its audiences?

Audiences are as varied as wikis themselves. Many who at first scorned Wikipedia have now been won over to the concept, and a wiki has become the first stop on the research express.

3. What's the typical content?

Information. Readers go to blogs for opinions, wikis for facts. But they can be facts about anything. Readers of wikis—and other contributors—expect a high level of accuracy and integrity from all wiki entries. If you're contributing to a wiki, you're speaking for the wiki, not just for yourself. So the wiki writer needs to be especially careful to use source material ethically.

4. How long is it?

I doubt even Wikipedia's administrators know how "long" it is, since people are constantly adding content. Most wikis keep the opening page relatively short but link it to a wealth of other information.

5. How is it arranged on the page?

A wiki resembles a print dictionary or encyclopedia but of course it makes use of the Internet—many wiki entries are crammed with links, pictures, footnotes, and sources.

6. What pronouns are used?

"I" is not as common in wikis as in blogs; the writer generally tries to get out of the way of the information.

7. What's the tone?

Fairly formal, objective.

8. How does it vary?

Wikis are so new that it's possible by the time you read this that either they'll already be fading into technological history or they will be sweeping the Internet as Facebook did. Their variety is potentially unlimited.

Suggested Moves for Contributing to a Wiki

1. Discover.

Contributing to a wiki requires reading enough to know what has already been said and to figure out where and how you might contribute. **Inventory** ➡61–68, especially your territories and things you're an authority on. Your best contribution to a wiki may come from what seems to you a minor and idiosyncratic area of expertise but happens to be one not shared by any other contributors. Wikis require thinking about links as well as about a linear progression of ideas. To get a sense of where your subject fits into various matrices and to start making sense of the argument, **Dig into contexts and connections** ➡51.

2. Develop.

Change perspective ➡81 or **Take the other side** ➡82 should help you further understand your topic and give you a sense of how you want to approach it.

3. Gather.

You'll need to spend a good deal of time gathering all the information you can from the wiki itself. You'll need to know everything from contribution guidelines to what precisely has been said about your topic. Your own resources are likely to be extensive and scattered, so **Freewrite** ➡72 or **Brainstorm** ➡69 about all your potential sources and which are likely to be relevant. You'll be in good shape if you keep good reading logs.

4. Integrate.

Integrating your material into a wiki can be a challenge. Ideally, a wiki should sound as though it were all written by one person, so the first thing you need to do is read a lot of entries in the wiki, looking at such things as how and when the entries use footnotes and links, the length and complexity of sentences, and the amount of explanation. You'll want to **Probe attitudes about integrating sources** ➡119 and be very careful to **Leave a research trail** ➡121.

5. Focus.

Chances are, your entry will need to be tightly focused and not stray into anyone else's area of expertise or into another entry. What is the *essence* of what you have to report? Try **Fill in the blanks** ➡141 and **Find a focusing detail** ➡146.

6. Organize.

Look closely at the way other entries are organized. Do they for instance first define the term, give some history and examples, and then end with the way the concept is changing? Be sure to **Answer readers' questions** ➡159, and if you have a number of different points to make, **Group, label, and order** ➡162.

7. Revise.

Use other people involved in the wiki. **Get as much feedback** ➡219–221 as you can. More people may read your entry than anything else you've written. It deserves lots of close reading and revision.

8. Present.

Work with the wiki administrator to make sure you post your entry in the appropriate way.

PART II

Moves

You can *prepare* to write by analyzing and understanding the instructions you've been given, the models you've been shown, and the genre you're supposed to use. But understanding alone doesn't get any writing done. The next ten chapters offer 228 *moves* that actually DO get words on the page. About the only rule for using the moves is, *if it helps get the writing done, use it.*

How should you approach all these moves? If you're writing in a particular genre, try using the moves I suggest for that genre in Part I. If you're stuck in a particular stage of the writing process, read over the chapter titles to find a move targeted for your writing situation. Unless your writing process always goes smoothly, you might want to start by skimming chapter 22, "Solve Your Process Problems," which suggests solutions to such problems as procrastination and not caring about your writing. Or read the appendix which offers twenty "plays," each a series of moves, to help writers from start to finish.

The moves can be combined, modified, or reimagined. Try to approach them with a spirit of playfulness, and you may find that your writing is less stressful and more productive.

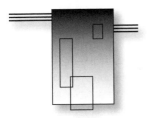

Solve Your Process Problems

22

This section is about process. My hope is to help you become confident using a variety of writing process moves so that you will be flexible as a writer and thinker, ready with your bag of process tricks to handle whatever writing projects and situations come your way. I've divided the moves into ten chapters that follow a typical writing process, from discovering to presenting. But first I want to concentrate on the psychological and emotional side of writing. If you had no writing history, you could probably try move after move without getting hung up, blocked, or traumatized. But everyone beyond grade school comes to writing with a history, and usually that history is marked with scars of frustrations and insults, leading to all manner of psychological tangles and unhelpful habits.

In this chapter, I suggest solutions for some of the most common process problems. If you're generally able to work your way through a writing assignment without crises of confidence or vast stretches of time-wasting frustration, skip this chapter. There's no point in wallowing in other people's problems. But if your writing process feels like a blindfolded obstacle race, read on. We'll try to take the blindfold off and suggest some ways to conquer those obstacles.

Finding an Idea

Even if your assignment is very specific—"Write about the practical consequences of this experiment," for instance—it almost certainly requires some choice on your part, a decision to write on A, not B. And that can be a very difficult choice. Nothing jumps out at you and says, "Write about me!" and you can't be sure you really know what the assignment requires and what the teacher or boss wants. Most of the moves in chapter 23, Discover, are intended to help you make these initial decisions. Here we'll take a slightly different approach.

First, one "DON'T"—DON'T sit in front of your computer and try to start writing a draft, at least not for very long. Spending an hour or two confronting blankness—of the screen, of a sheet of paper, of your brain—is demoralizing and will make it much harder to get going in any other way. There's no point in banging your head against a wall—the wall is always going to be harder than your head. Instead **Analyze the writing situation** (MOVE 1). Look at the key verbs in the assignment. Are you supposed to "summarize," "report," "choose," "prioritize," "compare"? The task may be simpler than you imagined it; we tend to read the assignment with our worst fears in mind. Maybe you're just supposed to compare the strengths and weaknesses of various options rather than choose among them, or to explore why a problem has arisen rather than solve it. Ponder what you know about the assigner and the general context of the assignment. If you're in a class, what have the focuses of the class been and how do they relate to the assignment of the moment? Perhaps you're writing a political science paper, for instance, and you know that the professor always sees things in economic terms. Is there some economic slant you can take on the assignment? If you're on the job, perhaps you know that the boss is looking for ways to expand the company and you can focus on expansion potential. Above all, think *audience, audience, audience*. Who will see your writing, and how can you be sure that you'll impress them in the right ways?

If you're lucky enough to be in communication with whoever gave you the assignment, **Ask the assigner for ideas** (MOVE 2). You don't need to be ashamed or see this as a sign of weakness; frame your query in terms of wanting to do the best job possible, making your paper perfectly fit the need. A two-person brainstorming session can be very productive—if you can come up with even an inkling of a specific angle or interest, chances are the assigner can suggest ways that you can build on that idea.

Talk (MOVE 3) to anyone about your task. Someone familiar with it can offer knowledgeable insights, but what you mostly need is someone to listen. Talking it out will help you see your own path into the assignment, even if you get no response from your listener. Finish the sentence "The only thing that interests me about this assignment is . . ."

Because the origins of great ideas are as diverse as the people who come up with them, it makes sense to **Look for help** (MOVE 4), for connections, anywhere you can find them—in newspaper and magazine stories, for instance.

A news item about the Anasazi might provide an interesting hook for your anthropology paper. Your utility bill could be a small piece of evidence in a paper about how we need to fight the energy crisis.

This one may make your inner perfectionist quail, but it's crucial if you hope to let any new ideas sneak into your brain. **Lower the bar** (MOVE 5). Accept that for half an hour you're going to write utter garbage, and then charge ahead into the next step. Later, when you go back to pick through the garbage for gems, you may find the whole thing is not that bad.

We ask too much of our ideas—we expect to greet them with an "oh wow!" response, to see immediately the grand oak that can grow from the acorn of inspiration. I find that the ideas that finally make their way into books or articles usually lurk at the edge of my consciousness for quite a while as sexier things drift by, until finally I pay attention to them. Your critic should be absent during this searching stage. What you need is an idea that you feel okay about and can grow into. Accept what your subconscious gives you.

Freewrite ➡72. Move your fingers as fast as you can with pen or keyboard. Your hand can never keep up with your mind, but if you forget all the things that slow you down—worrying about grammar, punctuation, making sense— you may write fast enough to trick your mind into revealing something that hasn't yet been processed by your conscious mind. Let yourself blather on, whine, complain if you want, but try to come back to the assignment and your free associations with it.

Read (MOVE 6). Nothing sparks good ideas more reliably than reading about other good ideas.

Many famous authors counsel keeping a regular appointment with the writing desk, even if you're "too busy," even if the words don't seem to come. I've tried it, and I like the romantic picture of the driven writer, bleary-eyed and empty-brained, confronting a blank screen at 5:30 every morning. I can't say I do this myself—I write any time of day. But if what you do isn't working for you, try it for a few weeks: **Sit** (MOVE 7) at your desk at the same time every day and **Wait** (MOVE 8). Franz Kafka, author of "The Metamorphosis" and other fictions that helped define the twentieth century, had a single word above his writing desk: *Wait.* My writing mentor, Donald Murray, said he always knew the best writers in a class because they were the ones staring out of the window after they'd been given a prompt or assignment. Sometimes we start writing too soon and would be better off letting our subconscious mull longer, doing some of our thinking for us. If you engage your brain with the subject as soon as possible, you'll give your brain the chance to do all this "free" thinking for you. Even if you feel you have nothing to say, make writing a habit.

If you enjoy your writing tools, you're going to get to the writing faster. **Play with your tools** (MOVE 9). Indulge yourself with fancy pens or a new laptop or a clip-on reading/writing light. Experiment with the features of your new word-processing program.

Write a silly email in between stretches of working on that big paper. If the surroundings are fun, the task won't be so onerous.

Caring

Some people—especially those who end up being ghost writers and technical writers—can write about almost anything, motivated by the challenge of turning dull material into lively prose. But other writers need to *care* about the subject they're writing on. You may have trouble coming up with an idea because you're aware that if you don't care about it, you'll get bored, you'll procrastinate, and the actual writing will be torture. Finding a topic that intrigues you is only one battle. The actual writing needs to focus on an angle that can sustain your interest.

Sometimes a seemingly selfish approach is the best. **Look for personal connection** (MOVE 10). If in some way you can link your past, present, or future to the subject you're writing on, you'll get more invested in it. Can you bring into your Great Depression paper the story of your great uncle who sold the family estate in 1940 to pay off his debts—or your cousin who did something similar in 2008? Can writing this paper be a first step or a doorway into an area that will be productive for your career? Once you've written on a subject—advantages of outsourcing for your company, say—you become the expert on the subject, and if the topic itself attracts more interest with time, your star will rise. Your "personal connection" may be more strategic than nostalgic.

Even if the topic has nothing to do with you personally, it has some relevance to a particular person. **Find a human face** (MOVE 11). If you want to care about a subject, write about it in human terms, even if the humans involved are strangers to you. If you're writing about DNA and falsely convicted prisoners, you need to tell the detailed story of a prisoner, not just convey numbers. Your passion about the need for a new university computer system will grow if you focus on a particular student whose academic career has been ruined by the computer.

"It's who you know" is even true, to some extent, in research. **Discover sources that you can exploit** (MOVE 12). Don't be bashful about calling your lawyer uncle Phil to ask him about the water rights case he's been working on or to use your friend's connection to the mayor's office when you're writing about city government. Having a good, easy source can be such an advantage that it's worth slanting your work so that you can make the most use of your best sources.

Don't hesitate to **Reward yourself** (MOVE 13). This may seem the most obvious or the most desperate of suggestions, but setting up an external reward system for getting writing done has worked in clinical trials. In one ingenious scheme, blocked writers had to write a check to an organization they hated—the Ku Klux Klan would work for me—and then if they didn't meet their productivity goals for the week, they had to send the check. The organizations didn't make much money.

Overcoming Procrastination

I don't crusade against procrastination because some people *do* write one-draft, last-minute marvels, though for most people procrastination is clearly self-defeating. I'll just make some suggestions. As usual, the first one is to analyze the existing situation: **Figure out why you're not writing** (MOVE 14). Some people procrastinate because they fear seeing how they would be judged if they really did their best work. By putting it off and not allowing enough time, we shield ourselves with the excuse "I didn't do it as well as I could have." (See Stuck and Reducing Writing Apprehension sections.)

Some people have worked out very elaborate justifications for procrastination, and they may find it difficult to **Challenge the justification "I write better under pressure"** (MOVE 15). I don't buy it; I think it's a rare person who enjoys the feeling of time running out and the inevitable less-than-enthusiastic responses to work done at the last minute. Wouldn't you really rather avoid that experience? Procrastination quickly becomes a vicious circle: procrastination leads to a weak paper and critical responses, which increase writing anxiety, which increases procrastination, which leads to a worse paper . . .

One valid defense of procrastination is that writers need to allow their subconscious minds to do as much work as possible. If you whip out your response to an assignment the minute you get it, you don't give the wheels in your brain time to turn; you don't get to "sleep on it." But while there can be value in waiting, can you distinguish between productive waiting and unproductive blocking? Most people need to **Write early in the process** (MOVE 16)—it's too easy to forget the brilliant approach we conjured up but couldn't write down during that long walk.

You may not be able to conquer procrastination in a single semester, but try anyway to **Take small steps** (MOVE 17). Every bit helps. If you normally don't write a word until the night before, try persuading yourself that "this is the night" twenty-four hours early. Then see how much happier you are with the work you do.

To kick the procrastination habit, **Set aside ten minutes a day** (MOVE 18) for as long before the deadline as possible to practice some of the moves I've described in this book. You don't have to think of it as writing.

Writer's block experts Mack and Skjei advise, "**Try deliberately inviting it [procrastination] into your writing schedule** (MOVE 19), planning for it but keeping a very tight rein on just how much dawdling you indulge in" (Mack and Skjei 1979, 58).

Getting Started

Although I've got many suggestions about how to change your writing process, I don't generally interfere in someone's process unless it's clearly not working for them or I'm asked for help. There is, most emphatically, no *right* writing process. And I would almost say there are no wrong processes. But the *perfect first paragraph syndrome* may be the single most destructive story that writers tell themselves. There *are* people who write great first paragraphs and then use them as springboards into fine pieces of writing. Much more common, however, are writers who THINK they need a perfect first paragraph before they can go on and get so hung up on doing the impossible that it destroys their whole writing process and leaves them blocked, frustrated, and down on themselves.

I don't discount the possibility that perfect-first-draft writers need to get something written in that first paragraph before they can venture further into the body. All I ask is that you try other possibilities. Might one of the focusing or ordering moves give you the sense of direction that you need? Could you get it from a good title, outline, detail, or quotation? Could a pretty good first paragraph give you enough momentum? Would it really hurt to plunge into a draft without a perfect opening?

What you need is a change in thinking. Rather than looking for, hoping for, waiting for the perfect, inspired springboard of a lead, try to get into the "sifting through garbage" mindset. Try **Brainstorming multiple leads** ➡ 143, something I discuss in greater length in chapter 27. Have no expectations. If you want, tell yourself that everything you're going to do will be crap. But then write them anyway—five, ten, fifteen leads. If you write fifteen, I can almost guarantee you that hidden among them, or in some conglomeration of them, is a lead that will work for you. Leads are probably best if they spring from your head, unprompted, and often I find the best leads are the ones that come a little more slowly, after four or five quick ones. But if you dry up completely and find that all you can write are variations on the same old ones, **Try these specific kinds of leads** (MOVE 20), most suggested by Donald Murray's *A Writer Teaches Writing* (2003):

1. *Direct statement*—State the main issue as simply and succinctly as you can.
2. *Anecdote*—Tell a quick story that either symbolizes or leads into your issue.
3. *Quotation*—Did one of your sources have something interesting to say that could start you off?
4. *News*—Is there some new information that will interest your readers?
5. *Informing detail*—Look for a single detail that encapsulates or symbolizes what you're interested in.
6. *Dialogue*—An overheard piece of conversation may intrigue a reader.
7. *Surprise*—What surprised you in your research? What might surprise a reader?
8. *Description*—What one aspect of setting or characters deserves to be in the lead?
9. *Mood*—Can you convey the atmosphere in which events take place?
10. *Find a human face*—➡ 11

11. *Scene*—Sometimes setting the scene can also convey some sense of why the scene matters.

12. *First person*—See how it feels to put yourself in the shoes of one of the characters.

13. *Third person*—Try a more distanced approach.

14. *Tension*—Can you reveal the central tension of the issue in the first few sentences?

15. *Problem*—Describe the problem in enough detail so that readers will get a sense of its difficulty and perhaps of how to solve it.

16. *Process*—Was the process of researching and writing revealing or instructive?

17. *Voice*—Sometimes you'll start writing about something and it will just *sound* right. If that ever happens to you, stick with that voice as long as you can, no matter where it leads.

18. *Statistics*—Readers like numbers. Do you have any that could lead readers in the right direction?

19. *Common ground*—What do you and readers agree on?

20. *Story*—Can you tell a story about your subject?

21. *Importance*—How can you establish the importance of your subject?

22. Revisit *purpose and audience*—Why exactly are you writing, and who are your readers? Spend five minutes defining each and see if something comes from bringing them together.

Quieting the Critic

Perhaps those monks who can sing two tones at once can gain control of their inner critic, but the rest of us mortals will always be plagued by a watcher at the gates, a critic on our shoulder, a grammar cop breathing down our neck, left brain criticizing right brain, ego berating id, call it what you will. If you are sincerely motivated to get the writing done, yet have serious problems getting going, your relationship with your inner critic almost certainly deserves some blame.

Relief may come not from ignoring the critic but from clarifying its function. **Recognize that we don't need the critic to create** (MOVE 21). We need the critic, of course, to help us revise and perfect, but when we're trying to get an idea into gear in the first place, somebody fighting with us for the gear shift is not helpful. It may not have occurred to you that it would be possible to separate the critical from the creative parts of yourself, to "turn off the critical voice" or "banish critical thoughts." And of course we always do have standards—we don't write pure gobbledygook, at least not for very long. But most successful writers—especially those who write over a long period of time and without the torment for which some writers are famed—find a way to get something down on paper, agreeing with their critic to improve it later.

Now we're getting really warm and fuzzy. But it might work. **Develop a mantra** (MOVE 22). It can't hurt. Use my "It's good enough for now" if you want. Like a toddler being ignored, your critic will protest any attempt to shut up that whining critical voice. You have to be persistent, and you probably have to believe in it. I sincerely think "It's good enough for now," and that means I seldom have to force myself to park my rear in the writing chair. I give the critic plenty of rein in later stages of the process.

Simple and effective: **Blindfold your critic** (MOVE 23). Your internal critic can't be nasty about what it can't see. Turn off your monitor so you can't see what you're writing. Yes, you'll probably write sloppily, but the sense of freedom you gain will make it worth the experiment.

You can take the previous moves a step further and **Find out what soothes your critic** (MOVE 24). For many people, it's a good night's sleep, and/or strong caffeine, and/or exercise. Try writing at various hours of the day and before and after various activities. Some people can only write with Uni-Ball Ultra Fine 0.03 pens on a yellow legal-sized lined pad in a crowded coffeehouse that sells beer. You probably know the histories of artists who found far more destructive ways to soothe their critics. Good luck with yours!

You've got to be honest with yourself and **Follow through on your promises** (MOVE 25). Don't make "It's good enough for now" a pretext for forgetting about revising altogether. The perfectionist tendency is really a glorious thing and should be nurtured—just in its own sweet time. If you don't give it that time on one project, it may demand it too early on the next.

Writing Too Slowly?

Most people feel that they write too slowly. If you compare your output to that of an incredibly prolific writer like Orson Scott Card, you're definitely going to look like a slug. I don't know of a reasonable way to measure writing speed. Some journalists can write an 800-word column in under an hour. Other writers spend all day writing one word and then crossing it out. The real issue, of course, is not how fast you write a draft, but how long it takes you from start to finish. And you can never ignore the stress factor—if slowing down would reduce your overall stress level, it might be worth it.

Let's ignore for the moment the question of whether you actually write more slowly than the next person and see if we can figure out ways to speed up your writing. I can't *prove* that making a number of my pre-draft moves would help a writer finish the task more quickly. They definitely prod writers to think through the subject more thoroughly and write with more ease than the get-it-right-in-one-draft writer, but who knows which approach takes longer?

So which parts of your process seem to go extra slowly? Can you distinguish periods of mental gathering and rehearsal from equally inactive periods that aren't productive at all? Altering your writing process is very tricky because what may look like block may actually be incubation. If it's slow because it's painful, then I suggest that you try some of the moves in the first few chapters of the book before you try to write a draft to see if the draft ends up being easier. One streamlined approach would be to brainstorm a page full of ideas, **Make a rough outline of the biggest ideas** ➥95, and **Write multiple leads** ➥143 before you start into a full-fledged draft.

Getting Unstuck

Everyone runs out of steam at some point, but if your steam runs out before you've gotten anywhere, or if you can't regain momentum after a break, try these steps.

- **Ask yourself if your brain is trying to tell you something** (MOVE 26), perhaps that you haven't sufficiently prepared to take the next step in your writing. Should you do some more thinking, discovering, or focusing activities? Should you take a walk? It does no good to get mad at yourself or down on yourself about getting stuck—try assuming that the block is meaningful, and figure out what it might mean. Do you secretly disagree with some of the conclusions you're about to draw? Is thinking about some other piece of writing or work distracting you? Did you end up at a dead end because you took a wrong turn a page or so ago?
- **Freewrite** ➥72. Freewriting can get you going again no matter where in the process your ship has broken down.
- **Change your tools or habits** (MOVE 27). If you usually do everything on a keyboard, try a pen and yellow pad. Or vice versa. If you think of yourself as a morning writer, try riding an after-dinner sugar buzz. Or think, what tools or habits have you been neglecting? Did something change at about the time you became stuck?
- **Write about the stuck place** (MOVE 28) in an email to a good friend—vent, but also explain in as much detail as you can the hurdle you're trying to get over. (The friend will understand . . .)
- **Outline/sketch** (MOVE 29). You need to know where the next few writing steps will go, and you can probably figure that out better on scrap paper than in front of a screen.
- Reread some of your most important source material.
- It might help you to back up a step and **Address your anxiety toward writing in general** (MOVE 30). See the next section.

Reducing Writing Apprehension

I try to reduce writing apprehension not just because it's an unpleasant feeling but because it can undermine all the skills and strengths a writer may have; it may be the single most important barrier between a writer and success. Writing apprehension limits lives: highly apprehensive writers avoid classes and even careers that require writing.

Apprehension can grow from many things—a writer may have a realistically low appraisal of his or her own writing, but it's just as likely that the writer is suffering from an insult that occurred half a lifetime ago or simply from the accumulated boredom of lots of uninspiring English classes. Regardless, writers who "hate English" and become anxious at just the thought of writing something are not going to produce their best work, and the most important thing such writers can do for their writing is to reduce that anxiety.

Discuss writing apprehension (MOVE 31) directly with anyone willing to talk about it. Where does the apprehension come from? What seem to be its effects on your writing and general state of mind? It's comforting to know that so many people are apprehensive about writing, but they keep writing nonetheless. And it may be heartening to know that at least some of us think there's something you can do about it. You're not weird or hopeless if writing makes you anxious—you're pretty much normal. To start doing something about your apprehension, you probably need to see that apprehension is widespread, debilitating, and unlikely to go away on its own.

Name your writing fears (MOVE 32). Researchers talk about "blank-page paralysis," "evaluation apprehension," "task avoidance," and "mechanical skills competence," but you can make up your own names. Researchers argue that simply applying a name to something you have struggled with is therapeutic (Riffe and Stacks 1992, 47). You may become less apprehensive through realizing that you're not alone in your writing hang-ups, that such hang-ups are not evidence of character flaws, and that you can target the particular source of your writing anxiety.

Understand how important writing is to your career (MOVE 33). You'll work harder to overcome your writing problems if you see writing as central to your life's work, not as something you will leave behind after school or after a particular job. If you're on the job, analyze how much writing you now do. And how much you'll be doing if you get a promotion. If you're in school, talk to people in your major or doing the job you'd like to do. How much do they write? Many people are surprised to learn how much writing is required by a wide array of jobs.

Banish the idea that good writers are just "gifted" (MOVE 34). People who believe that good writers are born, not made, tend to be fatalistic about their own writing and unwilling to invest the effort they need to improve (Palmquist and Young 1992). Most writers become good through hard work. Writer James Dickey: "I work on the process of refining low-grade ore. I get maybe a couple of nuggets of gold out of 50 tons of dirt." Theodor S. Geisel (Dr. Seuss): "To produce a 60-page book, I may easily write 1000 pages before I'm satisfied."

Reduce negative self-talk (MOVE 35), replacing it with positive mantras. A psychologist who has treated writer's block among faculty members finds this kind of self-talk key to changing writers' attitudes and productivity (Boice

1983). Tearing yourself down because you're stuck, or because you write more slowly than you'd like, may just make your creative side give up altogether.

Separate your creative and critical functions (MOVE 36). Writers who must always contend with harsh inner critics tend to get blocked and to hate writing. Such writers can learn to be more productive by being creative now, critical later. Promise your critic that you'll make it perfect eventually and firmly suggest that your critic take a vacation while you work on the first few drafts. See the Quieting the Critic section earlier in this chapter.

Challenge "rules" and myths about writing process (MOVE 37): "you have to outline" (or "outlines are useless"); "you've got to make all writing lively and interesting"; "you need your first paragraph perfect before you can go on"; "you must always follow certain steps in the writing process." All bunk. Writing processes are infinitely variable and idiosyncratic. A judgment that a process is "right" or "wrong" depends entirely on whether the process produces an acceptable product without causing the writer too much pain and trauma.

Learn to play "the believing game" (MOVE 38) with your own writing and with others'. We're all schooled in criticism but not in being supportive, finding the good elements, imagining what the ideal version of the text would look like. Stifle the urge to criticize heavily, and encourage your readers to do the same. Sure, you need to eliminate errors to improve the paper, but more importantly, you need to build on strengths. Ask your readers to help you decide what those strengths are.

Give up the romantic notion that only spontaneous, unconscious writing is worthwhile (MOVE 39). Novelist Joyce Carey says, "Inspiration is another name for knowing your job and getting down to it." Sinclair Lewis: "Writing is just work—there's no secret. If you dictate or use a pen or type or write with your toes—it is still just work." Virtually all writers testify to the importance not of spontaneous, automatic writing, but of revision. Ernest Hemingway: "I rewrote the ending to *Farewell to Arms*, the last page of it, thirty-nine times before I was satisfied."

Keep in mind that apprehension may be situation-specific (MOVE 40). Just because you're apprehensive in one writing situation doesn't mean you will be in the next. You may have an easy time writing a lab report in biology but get uptight about writing a history paper. See if you can figure out when and why writing is easier or harder for you and build future writing projects on those insights.

Knowing When to Stop

How do you know when a paper is done? This worry is more hypothetical than real, since for most of us the answer is the same: when the deadline arrives and we've run out of time. But sometimes you have the luxury of lots of time to revise. How often should you return to the same text? The question, to my mind, is whether you're doing something valuable with each pass—are you discovering new things or at least finding typos? Or do you put in a comma in the morning and erase it in the afternoon? Don't wait for a satisfied sense of "done, finished, perfect," before you submit your text. You may never get it. Time and experience will show you ways to improve almost everything.

Knowing How to Stop

There's nothing that tells me "this is done" more clearly than an end I'm happy with. But how do you find such an end? If one doesn't come to me the first time through a draft, I may return to the last section over and over, hoping that when I reread what's supposed to be the penultimate (second-to-last) paragraph, the kernel of the final paragraph will pop into my head. If that doesn't work, try these options.

Look back at your first paragraph (MOVE 41). If there's a question in that paragraph, could you answer it with your last sentence? Is there a detail you could return to or a conflict you could reflect back on? Readers expect beginning and end to "talk" to each other, so the opening is the logical place to find a closing.

If you've been puzzling about it for a while, **Ask yourself if you could end with your current last paragraph** (MOVE 42) . . . or possibly even cut that one. Sometimes we don't recognize when we're done and keep prattling on, not giving our big ideas a chance to reverberate in readers' minds.

Skim through your text (MOVE 43) looking for catchy details, quotes, implications and speculations, or conclusions that you could move to the end.

Change your perspective (MOVE 44). Obviously, one function of the end is to pull together or sum up what has come before, but many endings also contain a nugget of thought about the future, a twist on the line of reasoning.

Bring yourself back into it (MOVE 45). If you've been a presence in the text, would a return to "I" or your point of view help you wrap things up?

Easy Does It

I have limited patience with writers who complain about the torments of writing. If it's that bad, why not drive a truck? Writing shouldn't be something we fear or put off. It's a way of being and of becoming who we want to be—what else is life about?

Anyway, you should be able to provide yourself with the best advice about how to make it easiest for yourself. What moves, steps, approaches, have ever worked for you without trauma? For me, the answer is easy—if I can sit and jot down things on a clipboard, it's no sweat. So I try to organize my writing process in order to do as much as possible in jotting-on-clipboard mode. What's easy for you? **Go back through**—jotting on a pad—**the process you used to write a recent paper** (MOVE 46). Jot down everything you can remember doing, and indicate whether it was painful or easy. Any revelations? If you can't mark anything easy, **Try a different recording mode** ➡184. Get a recorder and give yourself some time to get used to it. Writers in all fields have used technology to get words down, at least since blind writer John Milton had to dictate *Paradise Lost* in the seventeenth century.

Try something in the Stuck section, or anything in chapter 23 ("Discover"). The first writing moves tend to be the easiest.

Conquering Process Problems—Communication

Communication professor Jack Lannamann is the first to admit that he's a neurotic writer, often blocked, often frustrated. He finds himself getting stuck because of the literature review. He feels that there is always more to read, he wants to give credit where it's due, he's fearful that he won't accurately summarize someone else's work, and he feels that he needs to tip his hat in all the appropriate directions before he can continue with his own ideas. Recently, however, he discovered a way to take an end run around his lit review problems. He took a personal tack to a professional paper, allowing himself "to write about something that made me shake," his background as a Christian Scientist. Beginning with the personal, instead of posing a problem and then doing a literature review, allowed his writing to flow, and he was able to integrate the literature review more naturally and organically.

The fiction writer Donald Barthelme may have been thinking of experiences like this when he said, "Write about what you fear most." Is there a personal, perhaps difficult or delicate, connection to your subject? Remember, you can always delete. You don't need to keep your scary, perhaps overly personal entry into your subject, or even show it to anyone. But if you have a breakthrough like Lannamann's, try to figure out what happened and if you can replicate it.

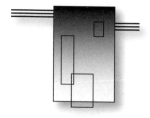

23

Discover

Writing, like life itself, is a voyage of discovery.

—Henry Miller

First you have an idea, a need, or an assignment . . . or a line or an image sticks in your head or two words butt up against each other in an interesting way. Every piece of writing has to start somewhere. We have to answer the question, What are we going to write about? A damaging writing myth says that great ideas appear full-blown in dreams or opium reveries like the one that supposedly inspired Samuel Taylor Coleridge to write his poem "Kubla Kahn." If you're lucky, you do get an "Aha!" moment in the shower or on the treadmill occasionally, a moment that leaves your head full of something that might turn into a piece of writing, if you can remember it until you get a chance to write it down. But you may never write a word if you passively wait for that light bulb to go on, illuminating a complete, brilliant idea.

No, you're not likely to write first draft "A" papers in college, even if you did so in high school. You may have to coax inspiration, sneak up on it with small steps, alert to the faint glimmer of an Aha! bulb, open to all the unlikely forms that good luck and good ideas can take. To engage in the process of discovering, you must be ready to see the story, the question, the answer, in the most unlikely places and at the most inconvenient times. Writers simply need to be more aware, more sensitive to details, than other people.

Most good writing results from a writer's desire to know, understand, or express. Writers thrive on more than just an assignment or other external motivation; most need to find a topic that *matters* to them, that's meaningful beyond class and school. What are the facts about adding fluoride to public water systems, as happened in the city where you grew up? Can you make sense of why you and your siblings responded so differently to your parents' divorce? What's the rationale for the math requirement that's giving you such trouble?

It's worth investigating any approach that will lead to a good idea. All the discovering moves in this chapter are low-cost, low-stress, low-expertise approaches that transfer to other writing situations. So try them. Be playful. Have fun.

Purposes of Discovering

For many writers, discovering is the most fun, most energizing part of the writing process. Discovering a subject you've long wanted to explore or a detail you've forgotten can be as exciting as discovering a new rock band, making a new friend, or finding a hidden waterfall or great Thai restaurant.

You have to start somewhere, but it certainly doesn't have to be at the beginning. The conclusion might come to you first: "Divorce affects teenagers more than other children." Or perhaps you have in your mind a voice that's going to tell the story for you, taking an aunt's view of a divorce rather than a child's. Or maybe to get going you need to find a detail that really moves you or symbolizes the whole issue—the day your father missed your school play because he was pursuing his "other interests." If you're assigned a writing topic or subject, you may need to discover some way that it relates to you, some way to make it your own . . . and have fun with it.

Discovery is logically the first step in a writing process, but in a successful, enjoyable process it may be part of every step—revision can yield many discoveries, as can coming up with a title or laying an article out on a page. Some writers are tempted to skip discovery and just write whatever seems most obvious when first faced with the issue. But without some element of discovery, of freshness, of insight into yourself and your ideas, the subject may get old quickly—for you and for any potential readers.

There are analysis moves in this chapter, lots of reflection and introspection, as well as recommendations to do things that may seem to have nothing to do with writing. For most of us, discovering requires not just the right prompt or activity, but the right frame of mind. We need to be ready to recognize and pounce on discoveries when they arise.

Discovering Moves

Prepare

If there's a universally necessary move in this book, it's the next one. School seems to train us to be harsh, critical, and demanding, even though early in the writing process it's much more productive to be accepting. **Shut up the critic** (MOVE 47). Quiet the "watcher at the gate," the critic on our shoulder always ready to "express adverse or disapproving judgments." Instead of being critical, we need to listen to or see what's really there and what we think about it. To get in touch with your gut reaction, dismiss the critic for the moment and concentrate on initial, unarticulated feelings. What grabs you about the music or art? What one detail stands out for you? How does it relate to your gut feeling?

Early in the writing process, we need to look at the writing situation to see what the uses and limitations will be for a piece of writing. **Ask your teacher or boss** (MOVE 48). I debated where to put this move, since some of the questions and answers are most relevant at the end of a writing process. But because talking to your boss or professor is probably the smartest way to start a writing project, I decided to put it early.

These are questions to ask of whoever assigned you a writing project or whoever will read it. Be wary of someone telling you "just do it the normal way" or "write a *report*," as if there were only one kind of report. Someone who thinks there's only one way to do an assignment may not be self-aware enough to realize his or her own biases and preferences. If that's the case, you may need to do some digging to find out what sorts of work have been accepted—and praised—in the past. Models are great things.

If possible, find answers to the following questions in the material you've been given, like a syllabus or website. If you can't find the answers, ask the assigner:

1. Are models available?
2. Are there guidelines?
3. Do you have format, font, margin, or layout preferences? Do you want a title page, abstract or summary, headers?
4. What is the ideal, minimum, and maximum page or word count?
5. Do you expect certain steps or sections in the paper?
6. How do you feel about headings, subheadings, and bullets?
7. What should I assume about my audience—that they're knowledgeable or new to my subject?
8. Is "I" acceptable? "You"? Contractions?

9. Should I use or avoid certain language, ideas, or terminology?
10. Is there a preferred citation form? MLA, APA, Chicago, something else?
11. May I get feedback about my paper from peers and others?
12. Do you have any writing pet peeves that you're aware of? Words or constructions I should avoid?

Often an idea will arise from getting back to the basics—the sense impressions that spark so much writing. **Explore with your senses** (MOVE 49). Writers are the people who see significance in the everyday, who pick up on the details that others overlook. Writers need to be alert to anything they can see, hear, feel, taste, smell, or touch. Yet the usual advice to "keep your eyes and ears open" is not enough; to go beyond sight, most of us need conscious practice. Sit in one spot—familiar or new—close your eyes, and spend five minutes on each sense, smelling, tasting, hearing, and feeling things that you would normally miss because of the dominance of sight.

> *I stand at the water's edge,*
> *smell the seaweed and mud,*
> *listen to waves lapping my feet and*
> *halyards clanging masts,*
> *crunch snails, pebbles, seaglass,*
> *taste the salt on the wind,*
> *watch the boats swing their noses around*
> *in a puffy northerly.*

Ironically, we sometimes get the best writing ideas when we're doing something that seems unrelated to writing. **Take a hike** (MOVE 50). Walk, run, ski, shower—do whatever you do that's physical, that absorbs one part of your brain and lets other parts be heard. Being physically involved but aware of your thoughts can be useful for developing, gathering, and integrating your ideas—I could bring it up again in each of the next four or five chapters. I put it in this chapter because of my fondness for the concept of woolgathering, "fanciful daydreaming," something that many people do when they're exercising. The term is often used to dismiss, but think about it: a wool gatherer is someone who picks up the bits of wool that sheep leave on bushes as they brush by— someone who can see a little value in every thicket. That's the kind of person you want to be when you're *discovering:* a person on whom nothing is lost, in the words of the American novelist Henry James.

You may discover personal meaning and interest in a subject by looking inward, but to make it meaningful for others, you'll almost certainly have to **Dig into contexts and connections** (MOVE 51). Discovering new ideas for your writing is largely a matter of being prepared and sensitized to the possibilities that observation and reading may reveal. New ideas result from

- Connecting the reading to outside information and seeing how the reading relates to other ideas and facts.
- Digging into everything from word origins to philosophies that you admire to sayings your grandmother used and you never understood.
- Discovering relationships among sound, feeling, and meaning.

Most readers recognize that context—surroundings, situations, frames—is not only legitimate to bring into the discussion about a piece of reading but often holds the key to the most interesting and insightful perspective. The first readers of Charlotte Perkins Gilman's (1996 [1892]) "The Yellow Wallpaper" saw it solely as a horror story about a woman going mad; it took most of a century before feminist readers began to see it in the context of nineteenth-century medicine and its sexist treatment of women. The details of the author's life and of the story's reception complement and deepen the story's meaning.

What about contexts for your subject, the Abu Ghraib pictures? One context might be the history of wartime leaks of classified information and how such leaks have affected the war effort. Another would be about the power of pictures and why written accounts of similar events didn't provoke anywhere near as much attention. How about the still-uneasy role of women in the military? And of course you could see the pictures in the context of the use of torture.

Sometimes students emerge from high school thinking that all English classes are about the search for "hidden inner meaning," an elaborate game played by writers and teachers and in which normal people often don't have a clue. But when you're reading or researching for ideas, you need to find ones that are personally meaningful or useful. **Look for what's valuable** (MOVE 52). For me, the central question about an insight is "Does it help me see more or appreciate more in the subject?" If it does, then I'm interested in it, whether it's the smallest detail or the largest philosophical concept. If it's valuable, interesting, illuminating to you as a reader or observer, it's a worthy discovery, whether or not others care about it.

Before we get very far into digging into a subject, it's useful to understand the keywords in the process and to remember that you can find the crucial element in a topic without taking a judgmental attitude toward it. **Define the critical** (MOVE 53). Almost any trip to the dictionary yields discovery, as the origins and evolution of words tend to live on in whiffs of connotation and overtones of meaning. One such discovery for many students lies in the word "critical" itself. Students tend to associate it with the negative comments of a "critic," "expressing adverse or disapproving comments or judgements" as the first entry in the online Compact Oxford Dictionary puts it. Many people are surprised to realize that the "critical" in "critical thinking" or "critical mass" is very different, critical as in "crucial" or "just enough." What might a reader discover by looking for something crucial rather than something to criticize? If you're asked to do "critical thinking," or even if you're just supposed to write about the major points in a topic, look for the crucial, don't immediately whip out your critic's pen.

What's *critical* in your paper? If a reader takes away just one thing from it, what should that be?

Analyze

How much do you know about how you write? Getting a sense of what's normal for you can help you decide where you need to experiment and change. **Analyze your writing process** (MOVE 54). Make three columns on a piece of paper. In the left column, jot down all the steps you took in writing your most recent paper. (The questions below will lead you through that process.) In the middle column, note whether this step was typical for you or unusual. In the right column, indicate whether, given your history with this step, you'd like to change it or stick with it. Answer the following questions [example answers are in square brackets].

a. Why did you write this paper? [required for my history course]
b. How did you come up with this subject? [came to me while jogging]
c. Did you talk to anyone about your subject? [explained it to my roommate]
d. How did you refine (narrow, make specific) the subject? [decided to focus on economics because that's what the professor keeps talking about]
e. What did you do before the first draft? Was it all in your head? [just got on the computer and started writing when I thought I had an idea that would work]
f. What writing tools did you use? (For instance, pen and pad, computer, particular software) [laptop and Microsoft Word]
g. What steps did you take after the first draft? (Did you let it sit for a while, talk about it with anyone, reread and revise?) [put it away for three days before reading it again]
h. Did anyone else read any of your drafts? [printed it out and showed it to roommate]
i. How did you come up with your lead? (The opening or introduction to your paper.) [wrote down the first thing that came into my head—but by the time I got done, it didn't fit any more]
j. What reactions did you get from your readers? [roommate said it was fine]
k. What parts of the process were particularly difficult or painful? [getting started, finding a better lead]
l. What parts were easy or enjoyable? [turning it in, getting rid of it]

When discussing such issues with other writers, keep in mind that there's no ideal or best approach. Learn what works for others and try new things. Keep a close eye on the activities that come easily for you and/or are particularly productive. They're the ones you'll want to build on with other moves.

Why are you writing? It's a simple question, but writers sometime waste writing time because they haven't answered it for themselves. **Analyze your purposes** (MOVE 55). If you're writing for a class, "to get a good grade" is probably one of your main purposes, but your teacher almost certainly expects your writing to have other purposes. What function can your writing fulfill for your readers? Do your readers need you to persuade them, inform them, present them with all sides of an issue? How will they use your text? Keep in mind that different audiences may have different purposes: your boss might use your report to prove to upper administration that your unit is making progress, while a programmer might see your report as providing general guidelines for writing code. Keeping such different purposes in mind can help you aim different parts of your document for different audiences: your boss might be satisfied with an executive summary, while the programmer might want all the technical details in your appendix.

One of the most basic questions writers need to keep in the back of their minds is, who am I writing for? **Analyze your audiences** (MOVE 56). You can discover a lot about what needs to be in your text by analyzing your audience(s).

- Who is the primary audience—the person who will read or hear your message? And who are the secondary audiences, the people to whom the primary audience is likely to pass your message?
- What do you know about them?
- What is their relationship to you?
- What do you represent to them? (Young upstart? Arrogant expert? Clueless novice?)
- What in their background might affect their response to you?
- What part of your topic is most important to them?
- Are there aspects of your topic that would be irrelevant to your audience?
- On the ladder of authority, is your audience above you, below you, or on the same level?
- What authority are they likely to grant you in relation to your subject?
- How are they likely to feel about your conclusions or approach?

Often looking at your topic through the eyes of your audience can reveal to you what you need to focus on or emphasize.

The next move has a dual purpose: to help you become aware of what writing habits and skills work best for you so that you can build on them, and to convince you that you DO have writing strengths and therefore should be more confident as a writer. **Analyze your strengths as a writer** (MOVE 57). What are you good at that has anything to do with writing? Not just "grammar" but "getting up early in the morning to write." Not just "comfortably write long sentences" but "take feedback well." Photography, calligraphy, geography, linguistics . . . many areas of expertise can make for a stronger writer. And the smart writer builds on strengths.

What have teachers, classmates, and friends praised about your writing? What subjects work for you? What tools (computer, pens, pads)? What moves or processes? Do you have critics who give you good feedback? Are there words, phrases, tones, or constructions you should stay away from because they don't have the desired effect (like sarcasm) or because you use them too often (like parentheses)? (See **Learn the red flags of your prose** ➡ 196.)

What values, opinions, and prejudices do you bring to your writing? Knowing your own stances and biases can help you predict audience response to your work and prepare you to deal with alternative perspectives. **Analyze your "cultural eye"** (MOVE 58). In their book, *Literacy in the Secondary English Classroom*, Lynn Langer Meeks and Carol Jewkes Austin propose a clever way to make sense of the varying perspectives or "lenses" through which each of us sees the world. These lenses develop from our experiences with religion, politics, education, and a host of other cultural influences. Meeks and Austin suggest that every writer or reader who wants to understand his or her unique stance on an issue should analyze the lenses through which they see. They identified nine lenses (see Cultural Eye figure; Meeks and Austin 2003, 29). My classes have suggested that health, family, and interests should also be included as lenses.

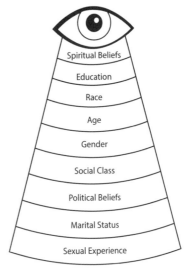

To get some practice in understanding how the lenses affect you, think about how your lenses influence the way you respond to some national issue, the latest war, for instance, or the latest health-care proposals. (For example, my age—well beyond draft age—gives me a different perspective on war than I'd have if I were nineteen, and my education in history has been good enough that I can compare the current war to wars of the past.) Thinking about those lenses whenever you're approaching a new subject can give you insight into your own stance and others'.

I worry that too often writers abandon their own opinions when they write an academic paper, so I like to encourage them to see that tastes and opinions, likes

The Cultural Eye

and dislikes, can be the basis for analysis, meaning, and even a possible thesis. **Analyze your tastes** (MOVE 59). Write down the name of a song that's floating through your head at this moment, or that you'd like to hear on the radio next time you're in the car, or that you might find on your iPod next time you put the buds in. I'm not asking for "all-time favorite song," just something that you like playing in your head. Got it?

Now let me tell you my story about the Neil Young song "Down by the River." I fell in love with the idea that there might be a woman in the world who could, in the words of the song, "Drag me over the rainbow," and it took me ten years to really grasp the fact that the narrator of the song I was identifying with was a murderer: "Down by the river I shot my baby." I learned two things from that realization: I needed to stop thinking like a sicko and expecting women to make life good for me; and it's worth analyzing your tastes and preferences, because they may tell you something about yourself and your world. The first idea could turn into a short story showing the dissolution of a relationship because the boyfriend couldn't hold up his end of a truly equal relationship. The second could lead to an editorial about why it's important for schools to connect with kids' own interests.

So . . . what about the song you wrote down? Why does it speak to or for you? Is it connected with a memory? Is there a particular line that hangs in your head? Do you dance to it? Fastwrite for seven or eight minutes on your connections with the song. You may come up with a paper topic, as I did when I started looking into my affection for "Down by the River."

We can do similar kinds of analysis with everything that comes to us through sight. When you're examining a visual artifact, you need to look closely and to enter into the designer's mindset. **Analyze visuals** (MOVE 60). In order to create interesting visuals, it helps to understand the kinds of choices that graphic designers and visual artists in general make when they start to conceive of an illustration or layout. For instance,

- Where does the designer place the main element? (Usually top left or top center.)
- What font is used? (Usually one with serifs, those little points at the ends of letters; the difference between A and **A**.)
- How many important elements are there? (Usually not more than three or four.)
- What elements are repeated in the design? The repetition can be of color, shape, placement, size, or other features.
- Is there an element that breaks the pattern?
- What are the biggest and/or darkest elements? They attract our attention first.
- What is the relationship of illustration to text—does one explain the other, or are they both working together toward a meaning greater than the individual parts?
- Are there any parallels in the visual elements

that might contribute to an analogy? (If a man and a goose are the two vertical shapes in an image, we wonder how the man is gooselike.)

- If there are people in the illustration, what are they feeling? What did the designer want to make us feel in response to the people?
- What personal, cultural, and aesthetic associations do you have with elements of the visual? Do you think the designer meant to call forth those associations?
- What colors are used? Are they saturated colors, yelling at you, or paler colors, drawing you in? Are colors used to distinguish one section from another, or to set off individual elements?

Inventory

For some of the easiest and most fun moves, you don't have to leave your chair or your computer; they just require introspection and thoughtfulness. **Inventory** (MOVE 61). So far we have been looking at processes without content. In making inventories, *we* are the content: our histories, likes and dislikes, strengths and weaknesses. We examine ourselves in new ways that may produce valuable ideas. Listing is one of the easiest of all processes, and writers seldom spend more than a few minutes doing it before they come up with something long forgotten or recently overlooked. As James Adams says, "List-making is surprisingly powerful, as it utilizes the compulsive side of most of us in a way which makes us into extremely productive conceptualizers" (quoted in Mack and Skjei 1979, 83). After you've come up with a list in one of these categories, try picking the most likely topic on the list and freewriting about it. Some of my favorite kinds of lists are listed here.

Authority (MOVE 62)—what do you know better than the people around you? You don't need to be a world authority, just have enough expertise to give you insights about a subject, whether it be planning a wedding, shopping in second-hand stores, break dancing, or playing World of Warcraft. If you don't have free choice of topics but have to work on a given subject, can you connect it to one of your areas of authority? If you had to write about global warming, for instance, perhaps you could connect it to the experience of living through Hurricane Katrina and the possibility that global warming creates more violent storms.

Authorities
pancakes
college scholarships for figure skaters
growing up an only child
Civil War battles
relative value of different makeup
Alanis Morissette
Lincoln Elementary School
biscuits at fast-food places

Places (MOVE 63)—What places have been meaningful in your life? Your grandparents' apartment? A summer cabin in the mountains? Why? Can you describe a favorite place in such a way that a reader would understand some of what it means to you without having to be told directly?

Places
behind the football bleachers
Cape May mini-golf course
the spot on Cannon Mountain where I broke my leg
swimming hole on the Lamprey River
town of Big Sur
the new Wal-Mart
Moe's backyard
the Radnor train station

Conflict (MOVE 64)—What tensions or unresolved conflicts are there in your life or in the subject you're dealing with? Why don't you get along better with your mother? Why can't physicists agree about the universe? Why does your stomach drop every time you think about your old school? Writing about such subjects, trying to answer such questions, can be therapeutic as well as surprising and enlightening. Sometimes conflicts are too recent, wounds too raw, to write about. But get them down anyway. In a list of twenty-five conflicts, there's sure to be one old enough to give you some distance but important enough to be worth returning to. When you're looking at a subject outside yourself, concentrate on the things that don't make sense or seem to contradict.

Conflicts
me and Mr. Algebra
wrestling versus band
trying to be smart AND cool
selling out to the football team
gun owners' rights on campus
privacy versus school safety
NBA salaries

Strong feelings (MOVE 65)—What in your life, in your school, or in the course you're taking do you feel most strongly about? What makes you happy or mad, ready to rant or cheer or argue? At this point, write down whatever comes into your head, but you probably don't want to choose a subject that you feel you have entirely figured out—getting up on your soapbox and ranting to the world may feel good, but it's an impulse that doesn't often yield good writing. You're more likely to discover something that's interesting for you and your readers if there's a question or doubt about it. If you want to write about something that you know well, pick an aspect of it that you're not as sure about.

Strong Feelings
gun control
pastrami
"the good old days"
Coach Clark has got to go
Jennifer Aniston
tea partiers
slide guitar

Territories (MOVE 66)—Each of us writes about a small number of broad subjects or territories that we return to again and again. Many people would include "family" as a territory, but you might add "first aid" and "civil war," while I might list "skiing" and "rock music." Becoming conscious of our territories can help us focus our discovering efforts: rather than search randomly for subjects throughout the universe, we can concentrate on the eight or ten territories that we know well. We have to get over our fear of returning to the same well—the idea that "I've already written about that"—and realize that all writers focus on a small number of topics, over and over again. Looking for subjects outside of our territories may seem adventuresome, but it's likely to be a shallow and frustrating adventure.

Much more productive is to connect territories, looking for some combination that's unique to us but still meaningful. Most territories are broad enough to be shared by large numbers of people, but when you look at the overlap of several territories, the numbers drop considerably. For instance, millions of people are interested in family, in music, in teaching, and in writing. But there aren't that many who have interest and knowledge in all four. One of my first published articles came about because I realized that my expertise in all four areas allowed me to write something that few others could write but that would intrigue people with a stake in any of the four territories.

If no overlaps spring to mind, try randomly connecting territories by closing your eyes and drawing lines between two of them. Don't reject bizarre connections—ponder the unusual possibilities. "Skiing" and "rock music"? What about people who hurtle down the slopes—or drive down the highway—with Led Zeppelin in their earbuds? Is that just part of the fun, or potential homicide, something that should be outlawed?

Don't ignore your feelings, particularly when you're writing about reading. It's okay to FEEL about your subject and to base your responses on your feelings. It seems silly to have to assert that gut feelings can and perhaps should be the basis of any critical response to reading, but many people come out of high school thinking that their responses to literature are "wrong" and likely to get in the way of a "proper" response. Most of us need to learn that it doesn't work to go straight from the text to its meaning, skipping the gut response. **Write down your gut feelings** (MOVE 67) as you read or shortly after you finish, or in response to anything you encounter. Your gut feeling may be "I like this" while your analytical brain is already comparing it to other things, categorizing it, labeling it. Write down the parts or the reasons you like it first. Try not to move into analysis right away.

As icons replace words and even Olympic athletes' outfits are an advertising medium, our world becomes ever more visual, and visual images ever more meaningful. To discover meaning in an image, we need to bring to it the same seriousness of purpose, the same willingness to examine closely and question, that we have traditionally applied to printed text. A classroom is a perfect place to question visual information and find possible topics in the ordinary. **Do a visual inventory** (MOVE 68) of what's around you.

How about Sam, the classmate who furtively keeps one earbud in but makes the best contributions to class discussion? Could this new generation of iPod kids actually be superior multitaskers because of their childhood training?

Or consider the whiteboard. Whiteboards replaced blackboards as quickly and as thoroughly as cars replaced horses, but why? How did the whiteboard manufacturers get thousands of schools to give up something almost perfect in its simplicity and elegant functionality?

What do you learn by thinking back over all the school desks you've sat in, or all the drinking fountains you've slurped from? The visually inspired topics in just one room are endless.

Brainstorm

A main purpose of many of the moves in this book is to shake up our thinking, get us out of mental ruts, make it possible for fresh, unusual ideas to storm the brain and perhaps take over briefly. **Brainstorm** (MOVE 69). Any fairly random process of putting ideas down on paper qualifies as brainstorming, and you can do it alone or with others. I like to make lists. Other people like to fill the page with little clusters of ideas. Write down everything that pops into your head; save the analysis for later. Don't worry about any of the niceties of writing, spelling, sentences, grammar. Brainstorming should be fun—you're just jotting down whatever your mind freely feeds you. If there are no restrictions on what you're going to write, great! But *Focused* **brainstorming** (MOVE 70)—jotting down everything you know about a topic, say, the origins of AIDS—can be just as useful.

> **Brainstorming**
> swimming camp
> taking Latin
> growing giant pumpkins
> Girl Scout cookies
> best way to choose a college
> chess club

Mrs. Martin's weird clothes
pajama Fridays

Focused brainstorming
pajama Fridays
fun
value of seeing teachers looking silly
kids enjoy coming to school
no outfit competitions
attendance rates would rise on Friday
admin treats Friday as football game anyway

Models are useful throughout the writing process, and some are valuable to get us thinking at the beginning. **Use a song template to tell your story** (MOVE 71). Templates or model sentence structures can be borrowed from anywhere, even songs. You just fill in the blanks and see where the sentence leads you. One of my favorite blues songs is "I Got a Mind to Give Up Living," as performed by the Butterfield Blues Band. It starts out,

"I've got a mind to give up living / and go shopping instead.
Pick me a tombstone / and be pronounced dead."

I love the way the song goes from serious in the first phrase to comical in the second and back again. And it provides a valuable template for digging into your own thinking. Try this fill in the blanks:

I got a mind to _____ and go _____.
Pick me a _____ and _____.

Try three or four different ideas. "I've got a mind to put on a helmet and go biking away. Pick me a bagel and leave work for the day." That could lead to an essay on why so many people daydream about quitting their jobs and what truly satisfying work could be. By leading you into new thoughts and comparisons, such a template can help you break out of rutted thinking.

If there's a single move that's useful throughout the writing process and across all kinds of writing, situations, and writers, it's **Freewriting** (MOVE 72). Also now called fastwriting, garbage drills, vomit-alls, nonstops, free-intuitive writing, and a host of other names, freewriting is brainstorming in lines, following a thought wherever it leads and taking any tangents that present themselves. Quantity of words, not quality, is key. Surprising, interesting, fruitful thoughts appear when you write too fast for your internal censor to keep up. Though primarily a tool for the beginning of a writing process, freewriting can be useful any time a writer is stuck or looking for more to say.

People who can't at first free their minds and hands enough to freewrite have, I think, the most to gain by it. So if you just feel stuck and awkward the first time you try it, try again later.

I tend to brainstorm in a list running straight down the page, but using more of the surface area can provoke other kinds of thinking and particularly reveal connections. **Map** (MOVE 73). Mapping may be most useful for visual thinkers. Start with a key concept in the middle of a piece of paper, then branch related ideas off from it and branch from the branches. (Your central thought might be "High school trauma" and the branches could include "sports," "parties," "French class," "lunchtime" etc.) Sometimes an idea in a subsidiary branch (perhaps "sports") will grow so many branches itself that it becomes the new center of attention. Why? What does that tell you about your subject? Often, even five minutes of mapping will show the writer how broad and complex the topic is and compel the writer to narrow and focus. Sometimes, because of the physical limitations of the page, two ideas will butt up against one another, challenging the writer to explore their relationship. For instance, you might expect both "choir" and "unsuccessful athlete" to show up on a map of your high school years, but you might never have thought about their relationship. Would it be interesting to analyze the choices you made in high school?

Perhaps we've been too logical in our thinking so far. To break out of that straitjacket, it may help to turn to the comics. **Think like Zippy the Pinhead** (MOVE 74). Zippy the Pinhead, a comic strip character, makes no sense to some disgruntled readers and hilarious nonsense to fans. He's known for non sequiturs—words that have no connection to the previous ones—and associative (not rational, logical, or linear) thinking. Most of us have trouble writing associatively, not making sense in a way that others can quickly grasp. But try it. Start the next sentence with a rhyme, or an animal, or the opposite of what you just said. If you're writing about your grandmother and a funny scene with your cousin pops into your head, go with it for a while. Maybe you'll discover a connection later. As James Adams, author of *Conceptual Blockbusting*, writes, "Many techniques of conceptualization . . . depend for their effectiveness on maintaining 'way-out' ideas long enough to let them mature and spawn other more realistic ideas" (quoted in Mack and Skjei 1979, 37).

> *Fructose is the main ingredient*
> *in most alphabet soup,*
> *along with pigs' knees,*
> *strontium from the Moon.*

In general I encourage writers to be honest in their writing and avoid the "tangled web" of deceit, but I also believe that we can and should create different versions of ourselves for different circumstances. **Create a persona** (MOVE 75). A persona is a mask or front that people put on to hide their real

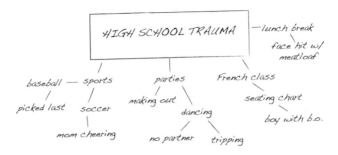

selves and function better in a certain situation. (You may have a "dealing with partner's mother" persona that you put on, or a work persona that's different from your weekend persona.) The "you" that comes across in a gripe letter to the town council is different than the "you" praising the values of a university you want to get into. Decisions about persona depend on decisions about purpose and audience. Is there room for humor or casual language in this persona? Or is this a black-tie affair, everything stiff and proper? Experiment. Try writing a paragraph from the perspective of the most formal, uptight person you know. Or choose a persona from among the people you're writing about—a high school senior debating going to college for instance—and write about your subject for ten minutes from that person's point-of-view.

My friend from Oxford could easily slip into The Robe, his name for an alter-ego of a very upper-crust sort, Eaton or Harrow for school and either Oxford or Cambridge for university, old money of course, and more importantly, old land, the kind of person you can turn your back to without worrying, not the sort of rabble you see living in million-dollar, sinfully ugly American-style homes in a treeless plot of what used to be cow pasture.

Writing is a process of making thousands of small decisions, for many of which there's no right or wrong choice. **Choose** (MOVE 76). You define yourself—and your ideas and papers—by the choices you make. This book poses endless choices, and I wish I could give you a simple-but-sure way to make them. Writers seem to agree that the best choices come from the right brain—the "felt sense" or "subconscious" or "preverbal." Go with your gut, in other words. Or make a provisional permanent choice today and then see if the choice keeps you up tonight second-guessing. Don't worry too much if you can't articulate the exact reason for your choice. Your left brain will get its turn when you edit.

You may think of graphs and charts as purely for the benefit of the audience, but they can also help a writer think through a subject and learn from it. **Graph to discover** (MOVE 77). You can learn a lot about your material, including potentially how to focus and organize it, by graphing your data. Chapter 7 includes a chart to help you decide which type of graph to use.

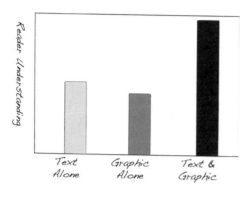

For now, play with your data. Sketch out as many different ways to present the material as you can. You're mining the material for insights, not yet thinking about how best to present it to an audience. Each of the "moves" chapters (22 through 30) includes a window into writing in a particular area of study and communication—a discourse community.

Discovering in Science

In the sciences, discovery can occur at any point, from the first decision to conduct an experiment or observation to the final write-up. One way in which the sciences differ most radically from the humanities is in the use of figures or graphics to illustrate results and thus spark discoveries. Berkeley geologist Luna Leopold advocated thinking about the figures early in the writing process. What kind of graphic presentation will best illustrate the data and/or best captivate or inform readers? Trying to decide early about figures can help the scientist determine what's most interesting, unique, or noteworthy about the project and thus help to focus and organize the material as well. Is there anything in your project that you could represent visually?

Share

You probably already use friends as sounding boards and discovery agents. Become more conscious of the process. **Tell your story** (MOVE 78). Ironically, we often overlook discoveries we've already made and therefore miss some of our best subjects. What stories do we tell friends? What incidents in your life would you bring up if someone wanted to know how you ended up where you are today? What do you tell friends about the class or project you're working on? What "story" can you relate about the historical figures, the theories, the financial data, that you need to write about? The insights, events, and people that come to mind as the result of other discovering activities can all be transformed into stories.

Anyone with a willing ear can be an audience for your stories, but if you prepare them right, an audience can be much more active and helpful. **Tell me what I'm saying** (MOVE 79). If you're willing to tell your stories to others, choose one that you haven't completely figured out yet and tell it to a willing audience, asking the audience to listen for the core of the story, the meaning, the answer to "So what?" It's often easier for someone other than the teller to hear what's central to a story. The listener may focus on elements of the story that the teller has taken for granted, having told the story so many times.

To demonstrate the process, I often tell my classes the story of the big decision I had to make at the end of my junior year in high school—to keep my word and spend the summer as a volunteer at a Quaker day camp, or to follow my heart (and my brother) and work on a trail crew. To me, the story is about how we make decisions, but my students see in it possible essays about high school "outsiders," the allure of the macho, how relationships with parents affect who we become, what creates the political beings we turn into as adults.

You may have had a whole class focusing on your work in the last move. In the next one, you get quick, anonymous feedback from a lot of people and you get to see what others are working on, which might spark some ideas of your own. **Pass the ideas, please** (MOVE 80). Hearing what others think about our ideas almost always sparks new insights. One way to involve others in the dis-covery process is to have everyone in the group write on a piece of paper what their topic is, some of the things they know about the topic, questions they hope to answer, and sources they plan to consult. Then everyone passes their paper to the right and reads the new paper they got from the left. Each person around the circle adds at least one question to the list, jotting down sources and information if they happen to know any about the topic, then passes on again. The writer gets back a whole roomful of thoughts about what aspects of the topic others found interesting.

What's Next?

A key difference between fluent writers and those who get stuck, blocked, or frustrated is that the fluent writers generally know what they're going to do next. They tell themselves a story of the steps they're going to use to produce that content, a narrative that might include a section like "Brainstorm titles. Pick the best title and brainstorm ten leads for it. Then start with the best lead and write three pages." Writers who have identified the next step have some place to turn when they run out of gas on the current step. So I end each "moves" chapter with suggestions about where to go next.

After discovering something—an idea, an image, an angle, an insight—you may want to write as much as possible about it, creating a freewrite or discov-ery draft perhaps many times longer than it needs to be. Some writers work well on the **Accordion Principle** ➡152, expanding a draft as much as possible, then whittling it down as much as necessary, then perhaps repeating the pro-cess. Getting everything possible said in the fewest words is, after all, a goal of much writing.

Another good approach after an initial discovery is the simplest—talk it out. Explaining to an interested, uncritical party what you're thinking and where you plan on going with it can lead the speaker to new connections and tangents worth pursuing. Sometimes in meetings with my students, I feel that my most important function is just to be someone to talk to. When asked to elaborate, most speakers find ideas they didn't know they were contemplating.

Most importantly, if you can forget "no pain, no gain" thinking, you'd probably do well to take the path of least resistance and make the next step the most fun one you can dream up. If you take an easy and enjoyable step that gets something accomplished, you may find another painless step and another. Pretty soon you have a substantial portion of the whole written without any tears.

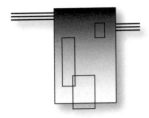

24

Develop

Most wonderful ideas die, unseen, from lack of development. Development is the difference between an outline and a draft, an idea and a proposal, a thought and a plan. Many teachers try to ensure good development by giving page minimums for assignments, but usually what they really want is not a certain number of pages but a certain level of development.

If you find yourself thinking, "I don't have anything to say," or "I don't know what to say," you should practice the moves in this chapter. A writer who has summed up the germ of an idea in a sentence or two may well feel that she has "said it all." "We should just respect the earth. What more is there to say?" The activities in this chapter are designed to stir up connections, relationships, examples, generalizations, all the materials that answer "What comes next?"

Using developing strategies can be appropriate, even necessary, at almost any stage in the writing process. Obviously the ideas generated by discovery activities need to be developed, if only to give the writer a clear sense of whether the initial idea will pan out. The great idea that peters out after a page holds less promise than the conflict that keeps getting more complex as each page leads on to another. We may also need to develop later in the writing process—sometimes good proofreading will reveal to the writer a hole or gap in the logic of a presentation, an aside or tangent that doesn't fully make sense, a term that needs to be defined or a generalization that needs an example.

Purposes of Developing

Occasionally, the only communication required of us is a simple yes or no. Much more often, developing our initial response by expanding—adding details, explanations, definitions, connections—will make our communication

- more concrete
- more interesting for the reader
- more persuasive
- more lively and compelling
- more memorable

Even if you're limited by having a small amount of space or a word maximum, develop your ideas as much as possible and then condense them, rather than shoot for the required length from the beginning. Writing about something complex in a limited number of words may be the writer's hardest task.

In the developing stage, many writers do the work that will make their writing stand out: they come up with hundreds of telling details and select the best one; they create a scene with enough sensory information to make it come alive; they show that the summarized idea isn't so simple when it's expanded. Developing often requires the writer to change perspectives, at least temporarily, in order to see more completely everything involved. Some of my choices for the chapter may surprise you; you may think of "thesis," for instance, as a limiting or organizing factor rather than a developing one. But a good thesis opens up possibilities for the writer, showing the writer within what narrow boundaries the paper can grow. And even though most of the moves in this chapter position the writer alone, developing can be a very social stage. Catch good ideas wherever you find them!

Developing Moves

Any form of writing develops the writer's idea, whether it's fleshing out a scene, listing reasons for a decision, adding details to a memory, or giving examples of someone's job performance. If you're putting down meaningful words, you're developing. (And if your words aren't meaningful, our slang has a specific and biting term for what you're doing—BS.) It's worth playing with some of these moves even if you can't make them directly relevant to your own writing project; many writers need to convince themselves that they CAN develop material. And as you're making these moves, keep track of information that you need to look up or gather. That will make the transition to the next set of moves easier.

Experiment

The following moves involve mental changes that might result in changes in your paper. **Change perspective** (MOVE 81). Prodding yourself to look at your subject in new ways and from new angles can reveal to you how much more there is to say about it and help you develop it in surprising directions. In their book, *Rhetoric: Discovery and Change*, Young, Becker, and Pike (1970) suggest a series of metaphors from physics. First, they say, look at your subject as a *particle* or object: what do your senses tell you about it? What parts make it up? What are its boundaries? How would you define and describe it? If your subject is, for instance, cheddar cheese, you would talk about color, smell, taste, texture.

Next, think of your subject as part of a *wave*. What comes before it and after it? What causes it or is caused by it? As for cheese, think of processes. How is cheese made? What does it come from and what does it turn into? What led to Wisconsin's reputation for cheese? Where does cheese fit in the history of humanity's relationship with bacteria?

Finally, consider your subject as part of a *field* or network. What is it similar to or related to? Think of a spider web—when you touch one part, everything else moves.

You could consider cheese in the intricate set of interrelationships that is our economy; or its place in the diet of Americans, particularly vegetarians; or how it fits into the complex web of human-animal relationships.

This next move will seem familiar to anyone who has ever tried to walk in another's shoes. It's a simple move, yet it can have major effects, especially on a persuasion paper. **Take the other side** (MOVE 82). A radical version of changing perspective is to take the side opposite your own. If you're a global warming skeptic, outline a paper or write a couple of pages from the perspective of Al Gore or another global warming worrier. If you usually tell a story one way—as a tragedy, for instance—try creating a comic counter-story. If you can seriously take on an opposite position, you'll see new avenues for research and development in your own stance.

Don't be content to note and analyze the present and obvious. **Freewrite on what's missing** (MOVE 83). What's outside the frame of the picture or the perspective of the reporter? What might you have looked for or noted if you had been on the scene? Sometimes we can learn as much from figuring out what has been left out as we can from what's there.

Often we can choose the details of the story we tell and the contexts into which we put that story. To make those choices, it helps to **Play with time** (MOVE 84). It's valuable practice to take control of time and prove to yourself that you are indeed the master. Choose a period in your life and summarize it in a short sentence: "I played hockey goalie my senior year." Then take one small event from that period and stretch a few seconds as far as you can: "I watched the puck come toward me in slow motion. I felt as if everyone in the arena had stopped moving to watch me as the puck slid across the ice, clearing itself a path through the skate shavings of 45 minutes of hockey. As soon as it came off his stick, I knew I had to move to my left but my stick seemed stuck to the ice and it took much too much effort for me to stab it over to my left to where the puck was heading . . ."

Just as writers can manipulate time to their advantage, they can play with the distance between themselves and their subjects. **Adjust distance** (MOVE 85). What did writers do before they had lens metaphors? Growing up in the era of powerful zoom lenses, we've seen the earth from space and we've seen pictures of DNA. We should have no trouble adjusting that zoom.

In general, close-ups create interest and wide-angle shots promote understanding. The article on changes in the welfare system will spark sympathy by introducing Jane Doe and her five kids, then pull back and put the system in the larger context of the American economy so we can understand why our senators vote as they do.

Question

It may be easier to spot disagreement than agreement, but this move is crucial if you want to get results, not just win an argument. **Find the overlap** (MOVE 86). If you've spent some time making sense of both sides of an issue, you're ready to take a crucial step in the creation of a persuasive paper: you're ready to define where the two outlooks overlap, what they have in common. If you're interested in finding a solution and not just in making an argument, you need to take this step. Any two positions agree on something. The basketball players and skateboard riders might not be friendly in the vacant lot, but they can unite in their opposition to the place being sold for a high-rise.

We start looking outside ourselves with one of the most familiar moves, **Answer the journalist's questions** (MOVE 87). Who, what, when, where, how, why? And which of them are important to the story you want to tell?

Move your lens up close to your subject. Maybe jot down details for half an hour, then read back through and **Find the one detail that best speaks for your subject** (MOVE 88). Save that detail. It might become part of a lead or end, or possibly you could organize your whole paper around it. Now **Brainstorm a list of contexts** (MOVE 89) in which your subject is meaningful. What does it mean in economic, social, political, or historical terms? How will it affect other people? Come up with as many contexts as you can before you choose one to elaborate. If you pick one and run dry, it's good to know that you have a list of others to return to.

Maybe my detail is the recent death by alcohol poisoning of a student undergoing a hazing ritual. Do I want to put that detail into an economic context, perhaps investigating how alcohol makers promote college drinking in order to get young people hooked for life? Should I put it into a social context and look at the victim's social network and whether he felt so alone that he HAD to take the opportunity to join a group, even if it involved hazing? I could put it into a political context and discuss how the incident might affect calls to raise the drinking age. Or I could research alcohol-related deaths over the years and try to reach a conclusion about whether our era is different from or similar to past years. We tend to think of "imagination" as creating something out of nothingness, but in a move like this, you need imagination to see the webs of meaning in which a detail already exists.

To a large degree, developing is a matter of responding to questions, so if you're ever short on development, **Probe with analysis questions** (MOVE 90). We expand and develop our ideas by asking analytical questions that make us aware of what we're looking at but not seeing. *Why* does the hero choose the fair heroine over the dark heroine? *Who* benefits from the banking crisis? Good questions force us to articulate our hunches and detail our generalizations. They make us see how much more the reading offers than we got from a first time through. The journalist's basic questions are a great place to start, but asking some of the more subtle and specific questions in the following list can get you much further. "Critical thinking" may sound like an arduous, time-consuming task, but anyone can go down a checklist and answer each question with a sentence or two.

The categories below move from relatively objective questions of examination and observation to more subjective questions that require more thought and personal input. Keep in mind that two readers may disagree about even such seemingly objective issues as "What rhymes?" and that even the most subjective issues of interpretation and evaluation need anchoring in close observation and examination. Many of these questions could legitimately be put under other headings. Most concern particular kinds of written texts but many could also be used to analyze other things.

Examine

1. Who, what, when, where, why, how?
2. What does it look like?
3. What does it sound like?
4. Does it have a feel, taste, smell?
5. What rhymes?
6. What are its denotations and connotations?
7. What is its rhythm?
8. Who is the teller?
9. Who is the audience?
10. What is the tone or mood or voice?
11. What images are used?
12. What motifs do you notice?
13. What details stand out?
14. What kind of documentation is used?

15. How does the author establish authority?
16. What is its structure, skeleton, or outline?
17. What are its parts?
18. What larger whole is it part of?
19. What is its form, genre, pattern, or shape?
20. How can you describe it?
21. What can you name or label it?
22. How can you define it?
23. What identifies it or makes it unique?
24. What questions does it raise?

Connect
25. How can you group the observations or details?
26. How does it connect with you and your experiences?
27. How do the whole and parts relate?
28. What is it related to?
29. With what similar things could you group or associate it?
30. What analogies could you use to describe it?
31. What have you read that is similar to it?
32. What context can you put it into?
33. What character do you connect with?
34. What connections can you make between specific and general?
35. What reflections or parallels do you see?
36. What is it different from or opposite of?
37. What research sheds light on it?
38. What does it allude to?

Interpret
39. What expectations does it raise? Are they fulfilled?
40. What does it mean? Are there layers of meaning?
41. What is its focus or point or message or theme?
42. What is its thesis or argument?
43. What are the most important details or pieces of evidence?
44. What is fact and what opinion or speculation?
45. What is your reading or understanding of it?
46. What does it symbolize, represent, or stand for?
47. What are its effects and causes?
48. meaningful (e.g. , historical, geographical, social, political, artistic)?
49. Does it reflect the values of a particular class, race, sex, religion?
50. What were its creator's intentions or motivations?
51. What is its creator's angle or point of view?
52. What in its creator's life seems relevant to it?
53. What can you conclude about it?

54. How can you summarize it?

55. How can you justify or explain your reaction or judgment?

56. What assertions can you make about it?

57. What is the basis for your reactions and preferences?

58. What judgments does it make?

59. What politics or assumptions or beliefs underlie its judgments?

59. How can you understand its ambiguity or your ambivalence?

61. How can you answer the questions it raises?

62. How does it exemplify or differ from others in its category?

63. How is it relevant?

64. How can you evaluate it?

65. How can you apply its lessons or insights?

If you've exhausted your ideas about a subject you've been examining or an image you want to use—a photograph or drawing or graph or picture—**Ask yourself, "What's not there?"** (MOVE 91). "What does this perspective emphasize, and what other emphases might there be?" "What was outside the frame or behind the photographer?" "What additions might make for a 'complete picture'?"

Expand

Occasionally I'll suggest a move that won't directly help you finish an assignment but can be fun and teach you about your own abilities. The following move, particularly the "compulsive housecleaner" sentence, has provoked more laughter in my classes than almost anything else I've done. **Expand** (MOVE 92). Writers need to learn that they can turn the spigot of words, of description, of detail, on and off, up or down. If you can write five pages about what you see from your desk chair, you can certainly write that much on your anthropology paper. If I can find twenty words to describe a pebble, I can write forever about Eminem.

To prove to yourself that you have control over that spigot of words, try the following. Imagine that each of the numbered sentences below is the first sentence of a long paragraph. Choose one of those sentences to expand on. Write as much as you can in ten minutes. Humor is a bonus. Feel free to change the pronouns.

1. She was a compulsive housecleaner.

2. He was a soap opera addict.

3. More than anything, he hated little dogs.

4. It was disgusting to watch him eat.

5. It was the hottest day of the year.

If the sentence you expanded on is a meaningful one related to your project, don't stop with a page full of details. Find the detail or word or image that is liveliest, most interesting, most accurate. If you have room for a single extra sentence, it should include that detail. Or you can put your detail at the top of the page and expand again. My favorite expansion on the "housecleaner" sentence began, "She hated anything that looked, smelled, felt, or flew like dirt. But most of all, she hated hair. In her worst cleaning moments, she would stick her sponge blindly behind the toilet . . ."

The following is a type of expansion targeted to where it's needed most. **Explain your code words** (MOVE 93). What you did with the "expand" exercise was to treat a word within the sentence—"compulsive" or "disgusting" perhaps—as a code word, a word that means much more to the writer than to the reader. All writing is a code of sorts, and the communication is bound to be imperfect, but we can improve it by trying to explain for our audience what some of our code words mean. Consider the common sentence "It's been a good week." One word carries the entire meaning of the sentence: good. "Good" doesn't say anything *concrete* and specific about the week, it only establishes the speaker's feelings about it, ignoring the listener/reader, leaving the listener/reader hungry for details. How many parents or spouses have asked in frustration, "What do you mean, 'good'? Good weather, good relationships, good digestive functioning? Success on the job, at the gym, or in the car, beating your commute record?"

Code words can pop up anywhere, but you're almost sure to see some in the first paragraph and especially in the thesis statement, if there is one. If some of your discovering activities have left you with a simple statement of your subject, look in that statement for code words and explain them all.

Many theses and critical arguments rely on definitions; defining one's terms is important in just about any discipline. Sometimes a writer can take the definition of a keyword and expand it into an entire paper: "What Patriotism Means to Me." **Define** (MOVE 94). Besides a trip to the dictionary, defining terms requires one step that people often overlook: determining the class or group of the term. "A mallard has a green head" is a weak definition; it needs a class—"duck" or even "bird." Within that class, the differentiating characteristics—"green head"—can specify the particular bird: "A mallard is a duck that has a green head." A good template for definitions is "A _____ is a _____ that _____."

Formal definitions need not be dull. Consider Ambrose Bierce's *Devil's Dictionary* (1958 [1911]) definition of "aim"—"the task we set our wishes to"; "bore"—"A person who talks when you wish him to listen"; or "cabbage"—"A familiar kitchen-garden vegetable about as large and wise as a man's head."

You may have a bad history with formal outlines, but give other kinds of outline a chance. **Outline** (MOVE 95). Like many writing teachers, I have mixed feelings about outlines. Often I find myself arguing against the use of outlines when, for instance, a colleague wants to require of students an outline and thesis statement weeks before the first draft. Creating a formal outline too early can lock the writer into old modes of thinking and prevent the productive clashes of ideas or temporary confusion that can lead to creative thinking.

On the other hand, various kinds of outlines have scores of useful purposes, some of which you'll encounter elsewhere in this book. In listing "outline" as a developing move, I'm thinking of the kind of outline that records and generates ideas without limiting them. What is your biggest point or question? What three to ten key ideas contribute to that major point or answer that question? They are the big headings of your outline. Jot down what might be sections under each heading. If you come up with five headings and several ideas under each heading, you'll have plenty to work with.

Structure

If your eyes glanced ahead, you may have seen that we're moving into thesis territory. Don't panic. I aim to take some of the mystery and stress out of thesis development. **Find a thesis in four easy steps** (MOVE 96). First step: gut reaction. Write down your initial feeling about your subject, which might be something like "ugh" or "wow" or "surprising" or "sappy!"

Next choose a detail—it might be a fact, a scene, a quotation, a number.

With gut reaction and detail in mind, freewrite about the connection between the two—how does the gut reaction relate to the detail? Why do the harmonies surprise?

Finally, boil down your freewrite into a single sentence, which, if possible, should make an assertion. And there you have it, a thesis: "Imogen Heap's song is so refreshing because the harmonies in "Hide and Seek" [detail] sound surprisingly soothing [gut feeling] even though the genre of electronica is known to shock more than soothe and for distance more than beauty." You could do the same thing writing about a book or about the economic situation in Sudan. And you can build on that initial sentence by thinking up three or four examples that illustrate the thesis.

The following move is a more detailed, formal, and serious way to **Develop a thesis** (MOVE 97).

1. *Start with a brief statement of your idea for a paper.* "The drinking age is too high."
2. *Look for code words in your statement.* "Drinking age" itself is a code, but that's easily dealt with: "The age at which young people are allowed to consume alcohol." But "too high" is less quickly explained; it raises the question, Why?
3. *Come up with three reasons for your statement,* three answers to whatever key question your statement has raised: "because it's unfair that you can get drafted before you can drink, because young people grow up much faster than they did when the law was made, and because the current high age turns experimenting adolescents into criminals."

4. *Consider adding some context.* Is the argument you're making true only for a particular time, place, or set of circumstances? Can you work those circumstances into your evolving thesis? Maybe you feel that the drinking age is an attempt to legislate morality: "The age at which young people are allowed to consume alcohol, a holdover from a time when the government tried to legislate morality, is too high because . . ."

5. *Watch out for promising more than you can deliver.* Your thesis statement should *not* cover a lot of territory, though it can suggest how your limited topic fits into larger issues. It's better to stick to a single topic rather than try to show that you know everything there is to know about the subject—and all in the first paragraph! If your paper is good enough, your reader will assume you know it all. Don't make generalizations you can't back up.

6. *But don't box yourself into a corner with your thesis.* Although you may limit and define your statement of purpose quite well, you could lose all complexity and all possibilities for exploring new ideas. Be careful not to prove a point that needs little proof. It's obvious that teens today are different from those of a century ago, but you don't want to get hung up on arguing exactly how they're different. Is that really crucial to your point? Step back and ask yourself a few more questions to give your assertion more complexity. What really is the connection between drinking age, voting rights, and the draft? What's the history of the drinking age? Has there always been one, and was it once higher or lower? What have been the traditional justifications for fixing the age at twenty-one? Try to anticipate a reader's questions. Get in the habit of asking yourself as many questions as you can: How do I know this? Why is this important?

7. *Make sure you define key terms and any code words in your evolving statement.* If you assert that current laws aren't "fair" to young people, what do you mean by "fair"? Don't rely solely on dictionary definitions; you may need to explain how *you* read the definition. The dictionary may provide interesting information about the word "fair," but it won't say what *you* mean by "fair."

8. *Don't alienate your reader with a too formal or too defensive statement of your purpose.* It's unnecessary to say, "In this paper my purpose is to examine the reasons for and against lowering the drinking age." Explain your purpose without the extra words and the formal tone; your thesis doesn't have to be labeled. Don't apologize for areas you won't be covering; that's the same thing as apologizing for narrowing your topic, related to the let-me-show-you-I-know-everything syndrome. A related problem is the "fear of assertion" statement: "It may be possible for some readers to agree that the drinking age is too high." Simply begin: "The age at which young people are allowed to consume alcohol, a relic of the time when government tried to legislate morality, needs to change because it is fundamentally unfair."

Then prove it. You can't fool anybody by being wishy-washy. If you assert your point directly and concretely, you'll find you have more to say.

9. Even if you can limit your topic to avoid both vastness and narrowness, you must still *express your thesis as clearly and as fully as possible*. A thesis statement is poorly expressed if you choose inexact words, garble the syntax, or attempt to impress your reader with an elaborate display of language that buries the chief idea. Although an introduction to an essay should attract the reader's attention, it is more important to inform the reader precisely of the purpose than to attempt to dazzle the reader with ornate words and phrases that circle the thesis.

10. In summary: A good statement of your thesis will be clear, positive, assertive, and inclusive, though not necessarily all-inclusive. It will present the purpose effectively, without formality or apology. It will accurately reflect a sensible idea, and it will present definitions of key terms. It will also, if possible, foreshadow the organization of the body of the essay, thus helping the reader see how the parts will work together to support the whole. In the process it should help the writer with transitions.

A good thesis will help solve your organizational problems. It becomes the backbone of the essay. Be careful not to mistake an organizational approach—comparison and contrast, for instance, or chronology—for a thesis. A comparison is a tool to get you to an end, not an end in itself. You must still discover something in the works to assert. Everything in the essay should be related to the thesis; the essay can be seen as an orderly examination of parts stated or implied in the thesis. If it is carefully constructed, it will provide the basic structure for the essay.

A good specific title focuses the reader's attention before he or she even gets to the opening paragraph. Whenever readers know what to look for, they see connections and implications they might otherwise miss.

After you've worked so hard to develop a thesis, you may not want to hear that not all papers, not even all essays, have a thesis, and that some develop their theses in very different ways. **Try an alternative thesis approach** (MOVE 98). Songwriter Greg Brown, an "itinerant Iowa Zen beatnik folkie," according to the *New York Times*, sings something very like a thesis in "If I Had Known": "It's just as well we don't know when things will never be that good again." He suggests that some things, like catching giant bass in a little creek and kissing for the first time, are so good, maybe you shouldn't do them again, because you'll never match the initial wonderful feeling. After Brown presents two convincing examples, you're probably nodding in agreement. But then his third example—having sex for the first time—turns the others on their head: "Oh if I had known / I'd do it all over again / some things just get better and better / and better than they've already been."

If I Had Known

GREG BROWN, 1990

A little creek you could spit across
Jimmy & me each took one more toss
our spinners bright in the evening air
People always said, There ain't no fish in there
Well grown-ups they ain't always right
Jimmy and me walked home slow that night
Right down main street in our P.F. Flyers
With two five pound bass making grown men liars

Jimmy if I had known—
I might have stopped fishin right then
It's just as well we don't know
when things will never be that good again.

A hayride on an Autumn night
well we was 15 if I remember right
we were far apart at the start of the ride
yeah but somehow we ended up side by side
oh we hit a bump and she grabbed my arm
and the night was as cold as her lips were warm
and I shivered as her hand held mine
then I kissed her one more time.

And Jane if I had known
I might have stopped kissing right then
It's just as well we don't know
when things will never be that good again.

She was older than me I guess
summer was invented for her to wear that dress
oh I knew about risk and she knew about proof
and that night she took me up on the roof
we could see the lights of the little town
we could watch the August stars come down
oh the shooting stars and the meteorites
yeah we went on a ride through the sky that night

Oh if I had known
I'd do it all over again
some things just get better and better
and better than they've already been.

Try it yourself. Think of an issue that you've been mulling lately—maybe look at a list you came up with in a Discover move. (We'll take offshore oil drilling.) Figure out where you stand on the issue. (We're against it.) Now come up with two examples that seem to prove a point opposite of your own. (We need the oil, and we should be pumping our own as much as possible.) Write them out in enough detail so you'll remember your own logic. Now find an example that proves your point and somehow trumps the previous two. (But the BP oil spill in the Gulf of Mexico proves that companies can't be trusted to safeguard our environment.) Good luck!

Developing in Business

Even writers who have nothing to do with business can learn from business and technical writers, who have taught us to use things like whitespace and headings. **Use a tree diagram** (MOVE 99). I believe that businesspeople first developed the tree diagram, a move that can be particularly useful for someone planning research. A tree diagram (or "decision tree") can quickly give you a fairly comprehensive idea of the material you need to gather. While it looks like an outline, it's really an ideal activity for when you have a lot of gathering to do. You can find many "tree" variations; I use questions at every level.

You start with the big, final question on the left side of a sheet of paper: "Should student fees subsidize athletic programs?" In the next column to the right, list all the second-level questions that would have to be answered before the big question could be answered. Perhaps that would include "What are the arguments for?" and "What are the arguments against?" These questions could be broken down into questions about students, athletes, and dollars, the process continuing until you have nothing but questions that can be fully answered with a number, like "How many students would this affect?" and "What is the proposed fee per student?"

Share

You'd think you could explain your subject to your pet gerbil or a local brick wall, but somehow it's much more effective to talk to a person, even if the person says nothing. **Talk** ➨3. One of the most common and natural ways to develop ideas about a project is also one of the best—simply talking about it with friends, people who will ask intelligent questions and make surprising connections. Talking about the specific subject with the professor or boss may be the best conversation you can have, but even trying to explain it to your sixth-grade nephew can help you see new answers to the "So what?" question. Try to become conscious of when in your writing process it's most useful to

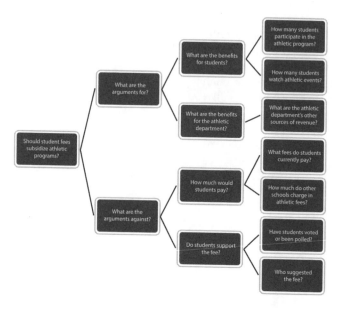

talk to others—When you're first trying out the idea? Not until you've got it pretty clear in your own head? Try to talk with someone who's smart and inquisitive. You may need to choose your sharing partners carefully, but the right person can unearth your assumptions, illuminate your contradictions, challenge your easy generalizations, and in general complicate your topic enough so that you'll have to whittle it down.

What's Next?

I put developing before gathering because I like to expound on my own ideas before I start gathering—and potentially becoming overwhelmed with—other people's ideas. Many writers take the opposite approach and gather as much as they can before developing their own ideas. If you don't need any information from beyond your own head, you can go straight from developing to focusing or organizing. More commonly, after you've written down your ideas and developed them as far as they will logically go, you'll probably want to gather all the material you don't have at hand. In any case, as you gather, keep your mind open for titles, details, connections, quotations that might provide a focal image or useful comparison in your paper.

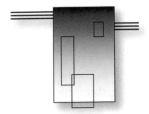

25

Gather

The discovering and developing activities you've done so far should have given you a general sense of where your writing project is heading and of what you know and need to know about your subject. It may be time to start gathering more material. As you gather, try to stay flexible about the focus and emphasis of your project so that you can make full use of the best information you find.

Purposes of Gathering

We write not just with words but with information. Whether we get that information from our dreams or our library research, it will seldom come to us at the moment we need it, especially if we're desperately trying to get a first draft done. Rather than interrupt the writing every few minutes to try to find the right information, it's better to take a conscious step to gather material. The moves in this chapter complement whatever developing steps you've taken; in fact, gathering could be seen as one kind of development. Most of the moves will seem familiar; you just need to make the move.

We gather for inspiration, to help us convince, to show us the core of the subject, to prompt us to develop ideas further or in new directions, to give us the momentum to draft. Writers want to have way more material than they can fit in their papers; if you have to leave out some pretty good details, you know you're doing well.

Most of the information writers gather, no matter what the discourse community or purpose, comes from a small number of activities. If you're proficient at researching online and in libraries, if you know how to ask good questions and listen well, if you can create at least a rudimentary questionnaire, then you're ready to learn the truly specialized gathering techniques of your chosen discipline—the chemist's experiment, the psychiatrist's diagnosis, the social scientist's statistical surveys. In the era of Google Scholar, full-text databases, and email interviews, gathering is easier than it has ever been. But the novice writer's instinct is often to just write down whatever is in his or her head and ignore gathering because it doesn't seem to contribute directly to writing. Try to fight that urge; it's a rare paper that doesn't require some gathering outside your own head.

I've put gathering fairly early in the writing process, but don't let that fool you. An alert writer needs to be open to gathering all through the process. Some people like to gather everything they can think of before they even start discovering moves. If you like to start with an abundance of information, maybe you should gather first. On the other hand, discovering and developing moves may help clarify the topic in your mind and therefore narrow the field from which you gather. One word of caution: unintentional plagiarism is often a *gathering* error rather than a *writing* error. If you forget to put the quotation marks around a great line, in a week you may assume that line was your own. If you don't write down everything about the website, it may disappear and you'll be left with no citation information. Don't let your readers suspect cheating when really the problem is just laziness or an imperfect system of gathering and notetaking. In the academic world, people love to have their words and ideas recognized, but they're very particular about giving credit where it's due.

Gathering Moves

Virtually any form of writing involves gathering, as we "collect our thoughts" and "marshal our evidence." Even quickly listing your ideas about a subject is a form of gathering—you're likely to call up thoughts from the far reaches of the brain, and by gathering them on a single sheet of paper, you will start seeing possible interactions among your ideas. Possible focuses and organizational structures may start to emerge. As you engage in any of the following activities, make sure you keep your pen and paper—or laptop—handy and record both the information you're finding and your thoughts about it. Keep a list of things you need to know or find out.

Reading is a key element in most gathering moves, but the act of reading alone does not gather anything. Especially if you have spent a lot of time reading material you weren't interested in or for which you weren't being held responsible, you have probably perfected the art of passive reading—your eyes move, your fingers turn the pages, but you retain little or nothing of what you've read. To read in a way that will help you with a writing project, you need to become *active*, and generally that means using some form of writing during or right after reading. To gather information from what you've read, you may need to practice entirely new reading habits. Don't just read and take notes. Collate, combine, expand on those notes. Write and talk about what you're reading with anyone who'll listen. Ask questions of it and work to find an answer that satisfies you. Readers improve by approaching the subject from more perspectives, bringing more context to bear on the subject, and developing greater creativity in analyzing texts.

Use the latest gathering tools if they appeal to you—you can record, comment on, organize, and edit material on virtually any electronic device, from Smartpen to laptop. If you've always hated notecards or organizing your citations, try a program like Firefox's Zotero, which can capture bibliographic information, organize it according to any style sheet, and save your notes with the entry. This last point is the most important one—no matter what note-taking technique you use, no matter which of the moves you try, write your thinking down at every stage, from "this might help me support my point about androids" when you first find the source, to a lengthy diatribe about its misguided definition, a diatribe that, edited, might become a paragraph of your paper.

Think

Much gathering can be accomplished without moving from your desk chair. **Memory joggers** (MOVE 100). Your memory and the associations you bring to your topic are your most important tools, even when you're working on a technical subject that requires considerable research. Most of the moves in chapter 23 can help jog your memory and get you thinking about important connections. If you don't yet have even a general idea of your topic, try some of the moves from that chapter. The "joggers" below assume that you've focused on at least a vague idea.

- Why did this topic spring to mind?
- What personal connections do you have with the topic?
- Do you know anyone with expertise in the area you're studying?
- What were your first encounters with this topic?
- Have you ever taken a class related to your topic?
- What questions do you have about the topic?
- Do you have any strong feelings or "answers" about your topic?
- Have you written anything related to your topic? (You can't just turn in the same paper again, but most writers return to the same general subject time after time, building on the writing, thinking, and research they've done in the past.)

Many think in the language of song lines, and it's a habit to be exploited, not ignored. Earlier generations used classical poetry in their epigraphs, those little quotes at the beginnings of poems; nowadays, people use lines from Jim Morrison or NOFX. Perhaps you want to write about representations of gender in popular culture—what better source than lines from hip-hop songs? How do Mickey Avalon's songs portray women? With your subject in mind, **Brainstorm songs and song lines** (MOVE 101) for four or five minutes—that's likely to bring a dozen or more songs about any given subject to a music lover's head. As we saw in chapter 23, all such musical connections can be meaningful.

You may think of this next move as belonging at the end of a writing process, but it's good to do often, to learn from your trials and experiments. **Reflect** (MOVE 102). Mining the past for today's material is not only smart but sometimes necessary. Reflection activities are so popular in writing classes because becoming actively involved in figuring out what an activity or a week or a semester means to you is a great way to ensure that the activity DOES have meaning.

- What stands out about the experience? What do you remember best?
- What feelings do you now have about the experience? What sparked them?
- Was there any tension or conflict in the experience? Do you understand it?
- Tell an interested friend about the experience. What do you find yourself emphasizing?

Read

The gathering that you can't do in your own head you'll likely do in a library, with a book, or on the Internet, so most of the moves in this section are about reading strategies. **Skim** (MOVE 103). You need to be *active* to read well, but that doesn't mean you have to devote a lot of time to it. Skimming is one of a reader's most powerful approaches. You have to get over your guilt about not reading every word. Ideally, skimming takes you to the words you need to read carefully; it gives you context in which to make sense of the text's new ideas. It's no coincidence that most of us would label as "skimming" the techniques taught in speed reading and comprehension classes. Try to gather an impression of the text as quickly as you can: read the title and the table of contents, the back jacket, quotations about the book, headings and subheadings and summaries and introductions. Highlight words and passages so you can return to key ideas later. If you need to go into more detail, you can read the first and/or last pages and then start reading the first and last sentences of each paragraph.

Many of these moves are useful for any student, not just someone trying to write. Any good student needs to learn, for instance, how to **Annotate** (MOVE 104). The simplest and most common form of active reading is annotating as you read—underlining, circling, highlighting, writing questions or comments in the margins or, if you don't own the book, keeping a running account of the connections, responses, questions, and new ideas that the reading provokes. Some readers don't like to "mess up" their clean new book, or feel that taking notes as they read will slow them down too much. You need to overcome such resistance. Any form of active reading will seem to take longer than the largely passive reading you may have been used to, but if you add up the time it takes you to reread passages to find the information you know is there but didn't note, you'll find that active reading actually saves you time in the long run.

You may have been doing this next move without being conscious of it. **Keep a log** (MOVE 105). You can create endless variations on a reading log. The simplest is just a list of the notes you take as you read a book you can't mark up. But the more elaborate the log, the more work it will do for you, and the simpler the succeeding steps will be. I like keeping a log on the computer because I can type the quotations faster and then search the whole log when I want to find a particular source or quotation. No matter what kind of log you keep, push yourself to do two things with each entry:

1. Write down all the bibliographic information. There's nothing more frustrating than sending a book back to Interlibrary Loan and then discovering that you didn't write down the page numbers for the source you used.
2. THINK as well as copy: make notes to yourself about how you react to the reading and how you imagine it might fit into your writing project. It's a depressing but almost universal habit of the human brain that the idea that seems so important and obvious to us at the moment may slip away forever unless we get it in writing.

A more elaborate way to keep a log, and one which gets some of your writing done for you, is to **Use a double-entry journal** (MOVE 106). Simply put quotes or paraphrases of the reading on one page or one side of a page, then write your comments, connections, questions, and thoughts for further work on the facing page or other side of the page. Again, the time you invest in this process will almost certainly be time saved from a later step. Here is a brief double-entry for a reading of "Everybody's Gotta Jump," one of the personal essays from Chapter 12.

"When I met poverty I wasn't prepared" "Meeting poverty is like jumping off a winter cliff into a frigid lake" "once you leave the cliff you can't get back onto the dry ground" "His bare feet were flat and cracked from walking for years without shoes. He laughed at everything."	Reminds me of going to Guatemala and seeing true poverty I'm not sure I see the exhilaration I think we're good at shutting our eyes again Great juxtaposition. How can both things be true?

I like this move because you don't have to interrupt your reading to do it. **Transcribe and explain** (MOVE 107). Some readers who can't bring themselves to keep a journal as they read still mark up the text and occasionally write marginal comments. As anyone who has purchased a marked-up text knows, those comments soon become meaningless. But a terrific way to rethink a text is to transcribe to the computer all the marginal comments and all the passages underlined and then explain why you marked what you did.

For instance, let's say the last entry in the double-entry journal was a comment you'd written in the margin of the personal essay. When you copy that entry into a computer file, you might expand on your thinking so you'll remember better what you had in mind: "We're so used to linking laughter and happiness to consumption and excess, we find it hard to imagine that someone living in abject poverty could laugh all the time."

Actively reading on the Internet requires a set of new procedures in addition to the ones that apply to any kind of reading. **Read from the Internet** (MOVE 108). Whole books have been written about how to use the Internet wisely, and chances are, if you've been surfing the Web for a few years, you have developed your own strategies to avoid getting lost or distracted. Here are just a few basic tips:

- **Maintain your focus** (MOVE 109). Don't take the side trip to test your rock music IQ or see which old friends are looking for you. As with any kind of reading, you need to keep your questions in mind and not waver.
- **Keep track of where you are** (MOVE 110). It may be helpful to open up a document in your word processor and paste in URLs and other information from every worthwhile webpage. There's nothing more frustrating than realizing you can't find your way back to that page that looked so promising twenty minutes ago.
- **Take notes** (MOVE 111). The other moves in this section are doubly important when you're surfing the web instead of reading a piece of paper. Many people move so quickly through websites that they may wind up knowing the answer to their question but having no idea how they found it. Keep a log.
- **Consider your source** (MOVE 112). Google and Wikipedia are wonderful, but they can lead you astray. There's a lot of misinformation on the web, and you don't want to be accused of falling for an urban legend or believing the information of a radically biased source.
    1. Try to find as much source information as you can: author, date, organization, contact information. People and organizations with legitimate authority are usually willing to identify themselves.
    2. With the information you gathered in step 1 and the last three letters of the Web address, guess what kind of organization created the website and how trustworthy it is: **.edu** is an educational institution, **.gov** something from the

government, **.org** an organization, **.com** a business, and I'd trust them in that order.

3. Read some of their material. Is it well-written? Is the tone reasonable? Does it make any mistakes or say anything you know to be untrue, even small things?

4. What is the purpose of the page, and who is its audience? Is it strictly informative or persuasive? You need to be more careful with websites that obviously have an agenda.

5. What gives authority to the page? Does it cite other authorities, or provide links to other organizations? Do the links work?

Interview

Despite the infinite amount of information available on the Internet—or maybe because of it—people may still be your best source of information. **Interview** (MOVE 113). A good interview requires many things: preparation, a functioning recorder, efficient note-taking skills, the "people skill" of putting someone at ease . . . but fundamentally, it's about good questions. Quality of questions is definitely more important than quantity. If you have a lot of little specific questions, you should do your homework and find answers BEFORE you talk to your subject. Try to come up with four or five questions that are

- *open-ended.* You want the subject to be talking, so you want to ask questions that will get them going and not allow a simple yes or no. Not "Have you enjoyed your years at Default High?" but "What have been some of your most memorable experiences at the school?"
- *respectful.* Not "Can you tell me about your job?" but "From what I've read, you do really interesting work. What part of it would you say is most rewarding?"
- *focused* on the interviewee's expertise. People talk best about what they know best. Give them that chance. "You're well-known for turning failing schools around. Could you explain what that means, to turn a school around? How do you measure that?"
- *relevant.* The disadvantage of open-ended questions is that they allow the interviewee to go off on tangents that may not be relevant to your project. Make sure that at least a couple of your questions get to the heart of the material that matters to you. "Do you have anything to say to the Default High students calling for your removal?"

Gathering in Folklore

Folklorists do a lot of interviewing, and though their goals may be different from those of people from other discourse communities that use interviews, people outside folklore can profit from their methods. First, according to folklorist Lynne McNeill, folklore interviews are "conversational and emergent"; that is, interviewers aim for the feel of a true, two-way conversation, rather than keeping the roles of interviewer and informant distinct and static. And they allow key ideas to emerge from the flow of the conversation, rather than going into the interview with a preconceived notion of what they want to hear.

Folklorists also strive to get three things from an interview or observation: text, context, and texture. The "text" is the story, joke, song, or riddle that the informant knows and that the interviewer is interested in. The context includes all the elements of the situation in which the text might be produced or repeated: when, where, why, and by whom would the song be sung? "Texture" refers to the feel of the text—the tone, pitch, timbre, humor, body language, and expressions with which the text is delivered. So it's possible for a single text (a joke, for instance) to take on different meanings depending on the context (a locker room or a wedding) and the tone (jovial or biting) with which it's told.

You may never find yourself interviewing teenagers about urban legends, but try to **Interview like a folklorist** (MOVE 114), bearing in mind the possibility of "emergent" ideas and keeping your eyes and ears open for the context and texture as well as the text.

Survey

Readers are interested in what others think, so a quick survey, even of just your classmates, can be a fine addition to the other material you've gathered. **Survey** (MOVE 115). Generally an on-campus survey requires the approval of your Institutional Review Board, but surveys done just for a class project are exempt. Surveys are not difficult to create or conduct, but you need to write the questions carefully, so you're asking what you really want to learn. If you ask, "Do you ever get irritated at the parking problem at Default U?," almost everyone will say yes; administrators will respond, "Well, duh," and no one will pay it much mind. But if you ask, "Has the parking situation at Default U. made you consider transferring?," your results just might wake up an administrator.

Gather Visuals

The acts of gathering feed the acts of developing and discovering. Finding good visual materials that complement your writing will almost certainly spark new ideas for your writing. Visuals should not, of course, be just sprigs of parsley dropped in for color. Ideally, they should be interesting, arresting, captivating in their own right as images and illuminate an important point in the writing. Don't leave the selection and placement of images for the last minute; doing so deprives you of the chance to learn from the images and strengthen your text.

I think it's fair to say that you can find an image of anything, real or imagined, on the Internet. **Copy images** (MOVE 116). Your use of images almost certainly falls under the fair use doctrine and therefore you don't have to worry about copyright, the most troublesome issue in getting images from the Internet. You can get many images simply by right-clicking on the image, selecting "copy," moving to the target document, and clicking "paste." Get all the source information before you leave the site. More serious image-hunters might consider websites like ARTstor.org.

But don't rule out creating your own images, making something unique. **Take pictures** (MOVE 117). Digital cameras and image manipulation software have made integrating pictures into papers commonplace. When taking a picture of an object to insert into a document, take a close-up with as few visual distractions as possible. You may want to put a sheet behind the object to provide the plainest possible background. Get as much lighting as possible onto the object. If photographing a place, try to have people actively doing something in the shot, both for scale and to give a quick sense of what the place is used for.

Share

Writing groups are often smart enough to use some kind of rubric or protocol to guide their meetings, but they should also work to **Use group members' strengths** (MOVE 118) to make gathering activities as efficient and varied as possible. Think of "strengths" broadly: besides "being a whiz on the Internet" or "having friends at the reference desk at the library," gathering strengths could include a keen sense of the visual, for picking out images; an ability to draw or design; an easiness with people, on the phone or in person, perfect for interviews; a fabulous collection of *National Geographic* and *Discover* magazines; being related to a local school principal who could get 1000 surveys passed out in an hour.

What's Next?

Do you collect all the information you can imagine needing before you move on to the next step? Or do you start focusing or organizing the material? Or do you jump directly to writing a draft, confident that the focus and organization will reveal themselves as you write? You can't take a wrong step from here as long as you remember that writing is recursive, moving forward and then circling back—after you come up with an organization, you may decide that more focusing and gathering are in order.

If you're lucky and observant, a focus—a point, a thesis, an angle, an opening—will have suggested itself as you gathered material. If so, you may want to do some developing activities on the new focus. If you're feeling overwhelmed with material and wanting to get it down on paper, try one of the organizing moves.

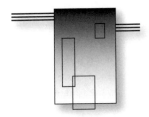

Integrate

As you're gathering material, you need to start thinking about how you're going to integrate it so that facts, opinions, quotations, graphs, images, definitions will flow seamlessly together and contribute to the overall desired effect. Successfully integrating material is not just a matter of learning the conventional ways to punctuate quotations. More than perhaps any other single stylistic feature, the smooth integration of outside material tips the reader off about the experience and professionalism of the writer. Awkwardly managed quotations undermine the writer's authority and may make the reader more suspicious about the quotations themselves and the writer's argument. Sometimes the way the writer handles the outside material is just as important as the material itself.

Purposes of Integrating

Writing projects would be much easier if everything we wanted to include came straight from our heads, no quotations, no paraphrases, no data, no flashbacks. But even people who write memoirs often have to gather material from outside their heads and find a way to work it into the text. Did it really snow on your tenth birthday in May? Was your great-grandfather really a pirate? Readers aren't going to be happy if you say "maybe."

We integrate outside material for a number of reasons: facts, details, images, and opinions from respected sources add interest, variety, and intellectual weight to the writing. They can complement the writer's own ideas and make points clearer by wording them in different ways. Most importantly, they add authority and credibility to the writing. Generalizations often carry only the authority of the writer: a statement like "Roger Federer is the greatest tennis player in history" is likely to be met with the response, "Who says?" But add some information, and the statement is much more compelling: "His record 17 Grand Slam wins prove that Federer is the greatest tennis player."

It's possible to imagine a writing style or tradition that didn't practice integration, didn't care about flow, didn't emphasize coherence or connection; the writer would be expected just to produce individual units of material, and it would be up to the reader to make connections between the units. We would probably call such a work a collage, and indeed it has been successfully used over the years. But in most situations, the reader wants to know what links the writer sees between unit A and unit B—the transition is the most interesting part.

Some of the moves in this chapter, such as summarizing and synthesizing, are core techniques of critical thinking. To think critically, we bring different elements together and put them in conversation with each other; we compare and define and analyze. And to make the final product readable, we integrate.

Integrating Moves

Some writers build a draft around quotations and paraphrases. This strategy is likely to make the integrated material feel integral to the text rather than like an after-the-fact addition. But if done carelessly, it can give the text a sense of being a quote quilt, other people's ideas stitched together with a few words from the author. Because I find the actual drafting to be the hardest part of the writing process, I'm inclined to hurry through it with as few interruptions as possible, noting where I want a particular fact or quotation but not bothering actually to stick them in until after I've drafted a section. Like the other moves, integrating moves can be useful at any stage of the writing process; you should keep yourself open to relevant facts or quotations from the minute you decide on a topic until you submit the finished paper. Finding a good line from a respected source can lead to discoveries, development, new gathering efforts . . . to any other stage in the writing process.

Prepare

As I've encouraged you to do throughout the book, learn as much as you can about your audience before you start writing. **Probe attitudes about**

integrating sources (MOVE 119). Even if you have a model for the kind of piece you're trying to write, you need to determine

- Does your audience want you to include material from other sources and voices? If so, what?
- How are such materials introduced? Are they just listed or given long block quotes?
- What citation system does the audience expect? Footnotes? Endnotes? In-text citations? APA, MLA, some other system?
- Is there a specific section, like the literature review, where most of the outside material appears?
- Is there room for the author's voice, opinions, and stories?

You know that we add other voices to our papers to engage those voices in a conversation about the subject, but how can you best do that? One approach is to **Talk with your sources** (MOVE 120). Pose a provocative question and write out what several of your important sources would say in response. Add yourself as a voice if you want. When you're not tethered to reality, sometimes you can see things in a new light. Maybe if you speak for them, some of your confusing sources will start to make sense.

Perhaps your subject is fluoridation of public water supply, and you decide that rather than ask directly about the science, you'll approach the subject by asking, "Are people who oppose public water fluoridation just cranks?" If you wrote in their voices, the "cranks" would answer with their best scientific evidence, the pro-fluoridation scientist might have to concede that the worries have some scientific basis, and the politician might cite polls about how many "cranks" there are. All three bits of evidence would help you build an argument.

Whenever you're working with sources, you need to remember to **Leave a research trail** (MOVE 121). When you're researching, often all you need for a good start is to find one relevant article. Then you can look at the articles it refers to and continue expanding your search by reading through the footnotes or works cited pages of every new source. Just as you have probably followed research trails, other people may follow yours. You want to leave breadcrumbs of your own, so that someone reading your article can find your sources.

The documentation that allows readers to find their way back to your source generally includes author, title of piece, title of whole book or magazine or website, publisher, place of publication, year of publication, volume or edition number, date, and page. If you're documenting something other than traditional books and articles, the best rule is simply to collect and include as much information as you can, whether it's from a strange website or an anonymous pamphlet. See "How to Cite a Cereal Box in MLA 2009" on YouTube http://www.youtube.com/watch?v=dPyB3bl7GY0. If you keep in mind the question "What would help a reader get back to this source?" you'll gather the important information.

There are now several Internet services—including http://citationmachine .net/ and http://www.easybib.com/—that will turn your information into citations properly formatted according to the style you choose—MLA, APA etc. I'd double-check any citations made by one of those machines. The first time I tried one, with the book *Outcasts United*, the program gave the wrong citation, confused by Warren St. John's last name.

Probably the most popular and useful website for documentation assistance is the Purdue University Online Writing Lab, or OWL (http://owl.english.purdue .edu/). It answers almost any citation question you could come up with. Another excellent citation resource is http://bcs.bedfordstmartins.com/resdoc5e.

Before we look at how to integrate text, we need to discuss what for many writers feels like a minefield: how to **Avoid plagiarism** (MOVE 122). "Plagiarism" is sometimes applied to a whole spectrum of actions, from forgetting a set of quotation marks to buying a paper online. But you don't need to get paranoid about it. You're not likely to mistakenly fall into the kind of plagiarism that drives teachers crazy and can result in a failed class or even expulsion. You know about the actions that are serious plagiarism crimes—copying a paper from the Internet or from a friend or copy-and-pasting large expanses of text from other documents. To avoid the smaller, but still potentially disastrous forms of plagiarism:

1. Take meticulous notes. Use quotation marks whenever you're quoting something directly. Write down all source information, even if you don't think you're going to quote the source.
2. Be wary of Internet sources, especially if you're copying and pasting. Stealing Wikipedia's words is just as bad as stealing those of a print author.
3. Proofread carefully. Try to keep a copy of your sources so that you can compare the original to what you're quoting. Make sure every source mentioned or borrowed from is indicated in the text and fully cited in the works cited or references list.

How to Integrate

The most direct and perhaps most common way to include others' ideas is to **Quote** (MOVE 123) their words directly. Quotations can add weight to your argument, sometimes in language better than you could come up with. A bit of the quoted authority's credibility rubs off on you. Using them smoothly takes practice, so it's good to get in the habit of strengthening your paper with quotations. Paring the quotation down to just the right kernel is an art; the entire Gettysburg Address is worth quoting, but you just don't have room— and your readers don't have patience—for it. Play around with different combinations of paraphrase and direct quote.

Pure quotation: "The world will little note, nor long remember what we say here, but it can never forget what they did here."

Paraphrase leading into quotation: Lincoln belittled his own role in history, but said of the fallen soldiers that history "can never forget what they did here."

Quotations mixed into paraphrase: Lincoln said that people would "little note, nor long remember" his own role in the drama but could "never forget" the deeds of the fallen soldiers.

If the writer you're referring to has not put the ideas in as simple or succinct a way as you need, you can **Paraphrase** (MOVE 124). With a paraphrase you retell a portion of text in your own words. A paraphrase may be as long as, or even longer than, the text itself. The non-quoted parts of the previous two example sentences are paraphrases. A paraphrase of Lincoln's quote might be "We'll be forgotten" or "Lincoln predicted that he and his audience would be forgotten while the soldiers who died would be remembered."

If you want to include a lot of ideas quickly, **Summarize** (MOVE 125). Summaries, close cousins of paraphrases, tend to cover more ground in short space: a summary might be a tenth or a hundredth as long as the text itself. A summary of the entire Gettysburg Address might read, "Lincoln asks his audience to dedicate themselves to the struggle for a democratic union as the dead they were burying had dedicated themselves."

Once you've gotten good at finding your own words for what others have said, you're ready to put ideas together, to **Synthesize** (MOVE 126). Synthesis is the most difficult and sophisticated of the ways to work other people's ideas into your writing. You need to make sense of all the relevant ideas and blend them together, connecting practical and theoretical or seemingly different ideas, perhaps using a phrase like "The latest research has shown . . ." or "X, Y, and Z agree that . . ." Read the sample literature reviews in chapters 9 and 14 and see if you think the authors successfully synthesize their sources.

Writers trying to integrate song lyrics or lines from poetry often confuse their readers because they assume the meaning of the lines is obvious, and therefore they don't bother to explain how they see the lines connecting to the larger point in the paragraph. For instance, in a paper about my growth in understanding feminism, I might write, "I fell in love with the idea repeated throughout the song: 'She could drag me over the rainbow.'" Now to me, it's clear that the line from the Neil Young song means the "she" could, despite some resistance from the "me," help the "me" to get "over the rainbow" to some pot of gold—a great relationship—at its end. But I imagine there are many different ways to read that line, and I don't want the whole meaning of my paper to be undermined by someone not getting my point about the lyrics. So I would expand my sentence: "I fell in love with the idea repeated throughout the song: 'She could drag me over the rainbow,' which to me meant that she could lead me, kicking and screaming, to an ideal relationship."

Go through your draft and look for lines from songs or poems—or even from prose—that might be clearer to you than to a reader. **Explain to integrate**

(MOVE 127)—add a "which" or "that" clause, as I did, or a parenthesis or an explanatory sentence. Step back for a minute to look at how the quotation is supposed to fit in the flow of your ideas, then see if you can briefly explicate your quotation, emphasizing how it fits in and adds to that flow. Try not to end a paragraph with a quotation.

This might seem to be getting too picky, but sometimes if you force yourself to find an alternative to "said," your sentence will bloom. **Vary your verbs** (MOVE 128). Some writing authorities will advise you to just leave "said" alone; it's an almost invisible word, something we don't even see in a sentence, especially when we're reading dialogue. Writing with "said" forces the reader to pick up the tone of the utterance from the words themselves: did the source "assert," "argue," or just "add"? Other writers get tired of writing "said" and want the verb to convey more. Certainly finding other verbs can make your writing more lively and interesting, though you need to be sure you grasp the full meaning of the verbs you use and don't wind up with a word that has a connotation that doesn't fit the context. (Using the verb "ejaculated" comes to mind.)

As in many other situations, models can be very helpful, even at the sentence level. **Use sentence templates** (MOVE 129). Unless you've done a lot of writing where you refer to other people and sources, you may not be familiar with the many different ways you can introduce such material. You may want to use some of the phrases below as models or templates for some of your own writing.

> "In her book *Silent Spring*, Rachel Carson argues . . ." [You can cut "her book" if your readers are likely to know that *Silent Spring* is a book, or if you've already referred to it. Note the use of the present tense—"argues." It's customary to use the present tense when referring to something in print—*Silent Spring* still presents the same arguments, even though Rachel Carson is long dead. Note also how this construction sounds better than, "In Rachel Carson's book, *Silent Spring*, she argues . . ."]
>
> "According to Rachel Carson, 'XXX' . . ." (page #) [Since the text refers to the author's name, and assuming there's just one source from Rachel Carson in your works cited, in MLA format you just need to put the page number of the quotation in parenthesis after the quotation. In APA format, you'd put the date after Carson's name and just the page number in parentheses.]
>
> "As Rachel Carson noted many years ago, '. . .'"
>
> "Rachel Carson wrote in *Silent Spring* about the effects man-made chemicals were having on the environment." [Here we use the past tense ("wrote") because we're referring to the historical act of her writing the book, rather than quoting directly from it.]

I borrowed this next move from a technical communication textbook because I liked the way it linked "story" and graphic. **Choose the appropriate graphic** (MOVE 130). Generally you want to use a graph to help readers understand complex ideas or to call attention to a particularly important point. The graph should be simple enough so it can be understood quickly, and even if you think the graph is easy to understand, it can't take the place of text; you need both. The graph needs to be placed close to the text that discusses it and labeled so that its function is clear. Both word-processing programs and spreadsheet software can quickly turn data into a variety of different kinds of charts and graphs. The table below will give you some help in deciding which graphic to use. Examples of different kinds of graphs are easy to find on the Internet (from Richard Johnson-Sheehan, *Technical Communication Today*, 3rd ed. [New York: Longman, 2010], 280).

The Story to Be Told	Best Graphic	How Data Are Displayed
"I want to show a trend."	Line graph	Shows how a quantity rises and falls, usually over time
"I want to compare two or more quantities."	Bar chart	Shows comparisons among different items or the same items over time
"I need to present data or facts for analysis and comparison."	Table	Displays data in an organized, easy-access way
"I need to show how a whole is divided into parts."	Pie chart	Shows data as a pie carved into slices
"I need to show how things, people, or steps are linked together."	Flowchart	Illustrates the connections among people, parts, or steps
"I need to show how a project will meet its goals over time."	Gantt chart	Displays a project schedule, highlighting the phases of the work

What to Integrate

Before you start working with what others have to say, make sure that your ideas get a hearing. **Integrate your own ideas** (MOVE 131). This chapter focuses mostly on weaving others' ideas into your own, but for many writers the greatest challenges lie in weaving together their own ideas and fragments of writing. The secret to stitching together two ideas lies in the concepts that connect the ideas, not in finding the perfect transitional phrase.

For instance, say one paragraph of your paper on bees ends with the assertion "These threats to bees are real and should be taken seriously," and in the next paragraph, you want to start talking about possible solutions. You could start the next sentence with a "therefore," but it will usually make a better connection if you take one word or idea from the previous sentence and echo it in the next: "Each of these threats requires a different response."

Here are some other approaches. Get yourself a printout or summary of the paragraphs or ideas you're trying to bring together and then:

1. Reread your opening paragraph. Jot down ways it connects to one of the ideas you're wrestling with. Do the same with the other idea. Now see if there are connections in what you've jotted down. There should be—every part has some relationship to the whole and therefore to every other part.
2. **Cut and paste** ➥205.
3. Forget what you've written down, and **Talk Out** ➥3 the connection between your two ideas.
4. Consider the non-integration option: use a heading instead of a transition.

Often it's the voice of the writer, rather than the writer's ideas, that you want to include in your paper. **Integrate voices** (MOVE 132). My wife, who is also an English professor, got her first teaching job in part because she was good at integrating voices. She published an article on Flannery O'Connor that everyone found hilarious—not so much because of my wife's writing but because of quotations from O'Connor. One key to integrating voices is to read actively and mark phrases and sentences that capture your imagination. The best quotations, like the O'Connor quotes that my wife used, let the voice of the source shine through, adding not just the quoted text but the *ethos* of the quoted author to the authority of the paper.

Are you getting ideas or information from a writer with a strong voice that could make a nice complement to your own writing voice? If you run across a good quotation from such an author, consider quoting two or three sentences rather than just a phrase. If the quotation runs to longer than three lines, make it a block quote: indent it from both the right and left margins and put the page number in parenthesis and after the final period.

Another way to augment the voice of your writing is to interview someone. The transcription of their actual voice can make them a more believable and authoritative presence in your text.

Good persuasive writing offers the reader not just more than one source but more than one kind of source, moving the reader with facts, data, opinions, impressions from surveys, interviews, books, scholarly journals, and popular articles. **Integrate sources** (MOVE 133). Skim your draft to see what kinds of sources you've relied on so far. Is there a variety? Can you balance data with authoritative opinions, interviews with graphs? If the voice of the source is not important to you, you can just present the material in your own sentence, announcing the source only in a footnote.

This chapter is concerned with many kinds of verbal balancing. Among the most important is to **Integrate showing and telling** (MOVE 134). As we saw in chapter 24, to develop our ideas often we need to expand a "telling" line by "showing." If you have trouble grasping the difference between the two, imagine the two in a movie—the telling would be done by a narrator, while the showing might be done without any words at all, just the actions on the screen. While the edict "show, don't tell" is good advice for poetry and sometimes for fiction, show AND tell is more appropriate for the writing most of us do. Think of one of the lines we expanded in Chapter 24: "She was a compulsive house-cleaner." Telling. But then we *showed* by picturing something that housecleaner did: "She scrubbed the bathroom grout so hard, she broke a knuckle on her index finger." Much good writing integrates showing and telling, often within the same sentence: "She was a compulsive housecleaner: she scrubbed the bath-room grout so hard, she broke a knuckle on her index finger" or "She was such a compulsive housecleaner that she broke a knuckle on her index finger scrub-bing the bathroom grout" or "She scrubbed the bathroom grout so hard she broke a knuckle on her index finger. What a compulsive housecleaner!"

Search your own writing for spots that could be developed or enlivened by showing as well as telling. Get a picture in your mind and describe it. Or maybe you've been using lots of description and you need to add a line of telling or summarizing so that readers know what they're supposed to be seeing in the description. We're not just talking about personal or creative writing here. Most kinds of writing move between showing and telling, describing and sum-marizing. Think of a corporate report: "This has been a very good year for our company," it summarizes. And then it uses pages to describe exactly how and why it has been good.

Most writers also try to find a balance in the kinds of persuasion strategies they use. **Integrate *pathos*, *logos*, and *ethos*** (MOVE 135). These three Greek terms refer to three kinds of rhetorical appeals, three ways to move and per-suade the audience, roughly translated as "emotion," "logic," and "character." These are fundamental characteristics of almost any writing; readers develop a sense of the character of the writer, and react to logical and emotional appeals in the writing, whether or not the writer has planned to create a persona or particular appeals. Paying attention to these appeals may help you spot weak-nesses in your presentation and work to reinforce your credibility, tighten your logic, or come up with new details to appeal to specific audiences.

Most of us probably think first in terms of *logos*, the logic of our argument, appealing to our readers' sense of reason. We may worry about being caught in a *logical fallacy* with a Latin name that we don't understand, or we may have a favorite kind of outline that always seems to produce a tight argument. Writers try to create a strong, clear structure, with each element related clearly to the whole, to improve their *logos*. Any of the focusing and organizing moves should help make the logical appeal of your writing clearer.

Ethos refers to the writer's authority and credibility. For some audiences, a writer's title—the Pope, the President, the Prophet—carries tremendous weight and immediately establishes *ethos*. Most writers, though, need to build authority through writing carefully and without exaggeration, through establishing credentials and through augmenting their own *ethos* with quotes and ideas from other authorities. If you're writing honestly and directly, your audience will get at least some sense of who you really are. So you don't need to worry about somehow creating a demonic *ethos*; if people generally think you're a kind, reasonable person, your readers will probably get that impression too.

Pathos, the appeal to the audience's emotions, can be the most controversial of the three. A writer who leans heavily on emotional appeal can be called "sensationalizing" or even "pathetic." Writers generally want the weight of their facts to convince audiences, but those facts can be presented in many different ways. You can move your readers by including pictures, either verbal or visual; by presenting details, especially those that readers can relate to; by establishing common ground with readers; and by exploiting the human element in the text.

Look at the next appeal for money you get in the mail. It tries to establish common ground with you ("Don't you hate to find chewing gum stuck under the table?"), personalizes the appeal ("Brock, I forced myself to examine every table in the Lower High cafeteria"), presents possibly exaggerated details ("If squished one micron thin, the amount of gum I found in the cafeteria would stretch three times around the equator"), and wrings your heart with stunning photographs.

Like most other elements in writing, these three appeals depend on the rhetorical situation, on the specific audience and purpose for the writing. What kind of writer will appeal to the audience—knowledgeable academic? Commonsense regular guy? Calm or angry, confident or self-deprecating? Will the audience react best to stories, statistics, expert testimony? Will they care if the argument is tightly reasoned or notice if there are logical gaps? Check through your paper to see if you have used the three appeals as effectively as possible.

Song lyrics may seem an easy and obvious source for quotations, but getting meaning from a song is not as easy as it may appear. **Integrate music** (MOVE 136). Music can be a powerful bridge between different concepts and between different points of view. But integrating music involves more than simply quoting song lyrics in a paper or playing a song at the beginning of a presentation. If you quote lyrics, don't let them stand on their own; explain what you see in them. Similarly, if you play music for a presentation, show the audience key lyrics and explain clearly what the music adds to the rest of your presentation. It's too easy, and usually wrong, to assume that your reader or audience is going to get the same meaning that you get from a song.

You may have been integrating text and visuals since the fourth grade, when you dropped some clip art into your report to make it come out to five pages. But now you need to do it more thoughtfully, with a clear purpose in mind. **Integrate text and visuals** (MOVE 137). How will an image help to make your point? Where should you put it for proper effect—on a page by itself, in an appendix, or right along with text? Be sure to refer to the image directly in the text, give it a number (for example, Figure 1), and consider adding a caption to the image to help clarify. Others won't necessarily see what you see in an image.

Integrating in Publishing

Western American Literature is an academic journal that uses visual images in bold and innovative ways on every cover and throughout each issue. Editor Melody Graulich credits research. "I've been going to museums and taking notes for 15 years," says Graulich, who chooses most of the images. But, she adds, "We couldn't do what we do without Internet research."

Sometimes the images illustrate the text: an article about animals mentioned in James Fenimore Cooper's *The Prairie* was "postmodernly peppered" with pictures of mammoths, sloths, and other animals. More often, the images serve as "counterpoints to the text"; image and text can have a conversation that invites the reader to join in. For instance, when the journal ran an article on modernist writer Willa Cather's use of space, Graulich looked for women painters also interested in modernist renderings of space. Because many *Western American Literature* readers are teachers, one of Graulich's considerations is whether an image in question would work on a class projector screen.

If you're using images in a paper, **Study how a favorite magazine or journal relates its images and text** (MOVE 138). Do you want to create a similar relationship? Do you want your images to represent the text or, as Graulich suggests, provide counterpoint to it?

Share

Having integrated quotations, other voices, and information into their work, writers justifiably worry about flow—will the integrated sections fit in smoothly, or do they create a bumpy road full of potholes for the reader? **Check the flow** (MOVE 139). One way to find out is to read your work aloud to a listener whose only job is to give you a sign—holding up a finger would work—whenever the flow of your ideas stops or stutters.

What's Next?

You can integrate outside material into your own writing at any point in the process, but you need to be careful to connect, prepare for, and contextualize any material you bring in. Additions of good quotations or ideas tend to create ripples forward and backward in the draft, and you need to deal with the effects of those ripples. Making those kinds of minor adjustments can lead you painlessly into a next logical step—focusing or revising.

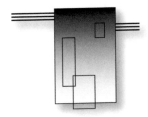

27

Focus

Success at a sampling of the preceding moves makes some writers anxious to write the actual draft. And there's nothing wrong with that. If you're eager to flesh out a discovery, fit an expanded idea into context, or put all the information you've gathered to work, it may make sense to jump right into a draft. Never waste enthusiasm and momentum. Just remember that the writing process is recursive—you can, and probably should, return to any steps you've skipped. You can focus—and organize, and gather—after you've written a draft, after you've seen where your words take you. But it probably won't be the most efficient way to work. If you can wait until you've done some preliminary focusing and organizing—quick, low-stress work—then your draft will be more on target and will likely need less revision.

Focusing may be the step most often neglected by inexperienced writers. Some writers are used to, and may have gotten away with, an information dump, simply cramming all the material they've gathered into their draft, leaving it up to the reader to decide what's most important. Others have a fairly clear sense in their own heads about what's key, but it doesn't occur to them that they haven't provided the reader with clues about their thinking.

Occasionally a writing assignment will come to you with a ready-made focus. The boss will say, "Write a report on company B, explaining why we shouldn't partner with them," or a professor will say, "Write five pages on the differences between Western and Islamic economics." But even when you're pointed in a particular direction, you probably have more focusing to do. Which reason are you going to emphasize? What effects will you concentrate on?

Purposes of Focusing

Consciously focusing helps the writer as well as the reader. Writers may have a vague sense of the reason they're writing and what they're trying to get across, but unless they ask themselves some focusing questions, their work is likely to remain vaguely centered on a subject, rather than aimed at accomplishing a specific goal. Focusing is a crucial part of a writer's thinking.

If a writer hasn't sufficiently narrowed and aimed material so that it's focused in his or her own head, imagine the difficulties the reader will have. Unfocused material may be interesting and may provide the reader with useful informa-tion, but it will seldom be persuasive or move the reader to action, which is the point of much that we write. Writers who haven't been thinking about audience, purpose, and especially genre earlier in the writing process should be considering those issues at this stage. For your purposes, what should your focus be? What does your audience see as your focus? Does your genre give you encouragement for one kind of focus but not others? A report to the company CEO about a project, for instance, would not be the place to critique or reward a particular employee's contribution to that project. But that contribution might be topic number one in a personnel evaluation.

Besides focusing the writing product itself, the writer also needs to focus his or her activity. The individual moves in this chapter should help you choose where to put your time and effort. There's nothing more disheartening than facing what seems like an impossibly large task with no idea where to begin. The first step is to break the huge into manageable chunks and focus on a chunk at a time. Always know what the next step is going to be.

One purpose of this book, and especially the order of the moves section, is to help you write as efficiently as possible, spending little time on activities that don't pay off. The earlier in the process you focus, the more targeted your efforts can be, and your whole process can be efficient. BUT (and it's a big but) if you focus too early and ignore the tangents that spring up in discovering and devel-oping moves, you may end up with a focus, but not the most interesting or rel-evant one. Many writers go through quick cycles of the first five sets of moves, with focusing leading to new discoveries, which require more developing, gath-ering, and integrating, and then the expanded material needs focusing again.

Some of the moves in this chapter, including brainstorming titles and leads, are among my favorites because they can do so much work for the writer so quickly. A good focusing move draws on what's been done before and highlights what is key, gives a direction to new thinking and effort, and can even provide an organizational structure, as a good lead often lays out a skeleton for a whole paper. When I intervene in someone's writing process, I most often recommend one of this chapter's moves.

Focusing Moves

Whereas almost any kind of writing helps the writer gather and develop material and open the way for discovery, writing alone will not create a focus. The writer must make a conscious effort to separate what for him or her is wheat and chaff, though that effort may be as minimal as recognizing that one detail, one perspective, one line of thought has stood out in the previous steps.

Brainstorm

As always, my advice is get something down on paper as quickly as possible. **Focus with freewriting** (MOVE 140). "Focused" freewriting may seem like a contradiction in terms. It's true that writers who limit the scope and the direction of their writing aren't writing totally "freely." Give it a different name, if you will, but practice the process of starting with one idea in mind and then writing without limitation or restriction wherever your fingers take you. It may start in a different place than truly free freewriting, but it has the same benefits. Try **Mapping** (➡ 73) to focus as well.

Imagine, for instance, that you start with a freewrite about your general topic—why you think amusement park rides are dangerous—and you find yourself writing about this one gruesome story you'd read about a suicide ride in Serbia. You spend the whole five minutes remembering details. Later, you Google "amusement park safety rates lightning" (thinking that fatality rates are always compared to the "hit by lightning" rate) and discover that you're more likely to get hurt riding a bike than going on an amusement park ride. But those images in your mind affected you so strongly that you wonder why? And what are the consequences of being moved by such images? You head for the library to talk to a librarian about researching how opinions get swayed by rare real-world events. At least that's where you'll start. Maybe there are some studies on how dangerous people think amusement park rides are . . .

This next move is an easy one. All you have to do is **Fill in the blanks** (MOVE 141). Don't try to fill in all of these blanks—it would get irritating and repetitive. But when your eye lights on one that seems interesting, fill in that blank and see if it helps you focus the whole piece. (These sentences can also be useful for prompting responses to someone else's essay.)

1. When I tell friends about this subject, I emphasize _____.
2. _____ is my best detail so far.
3. My thesis will have something to do with _____.
4. When I think about _____, I get excited about writing the paper.

5. If I were to choose just one image to represent my subject, it would be _____.

6. The central conflict in my subject is between _____ and _____.

7. The biggest surprise for me so far was _____.

8. The aspect of the subject I've written most about so far is _____.

9. _____ is the thing I've been thinking about that's most relevant to the class or major project.

10. I have most experience dealing with _____ aspect of the subject.

11. _____ upset me most about my subject.

12. _____ sticks in my mind and seems to stand for the whole subject.

13. The face or name I associate with my subject is _____.

14. The one thing my readers need to know about my subject is _____.

15. As I worked on my subject, I began to see this pattern or order _____.

16. The story or anecdote that I remember best is _____.

17. The statistic that seems most relevant is _____.

18. I think that _____ results from _____.

19. After they read my paper, readers should be thinking about _____.

20. The main problem with this subject is _____.

The next move is one of my favorites, useful and fun at many points in the writing process. You're just playing with words, imagining papers that could be. **Brainstorm titles** (MOVE 142). Most people leave the title for last and then agonize about it because nothing seems both catchy and fitting. Take the pressure off and try to come up with a title earlier in the process. But don't come up with just one—write down at least twenty or twenty-five, so you have a lot to choose from and can take pieces from one and add them to another. Each different title, as catchy or accurate as it may be, points in a slightly different direction, to a different focus. Adopting one as a working title will funnel your thoughts and probably spark new ones, and it serves this same role for readers, narrowing their focus to exactly what you're writing about—thus making you work less hard in the opening paragraph to orient your readers.

Let's play with a few titles for a paper about a proposal to eliminate fraternities from a particular college. "Fat Cat Frats Fight Back" is catchy and promises a critical look at fraternity finances. Is that a focus we're prepared to support? "Frats Part of Campus Life for Seventy-five Years" indicates the paper will be about history and tradition, and it hints of support for the frats. "Frats Offer Students Unique Growth" will look more into the current fraternities and the positive effects they have on members. "Greek No More" seems to look forward to a time when fraternities will be gone and might sketch out the benefits of a frat-free campus. If we came up with twenty such titles, each a signpost pointing us to a new destination, we should be able to choose one that points in a direction we feel excited about.

A natural sequel to brainstorming titles is to **Brainstorm leads** (MOVE 143). "Lead" is a journalist's term, meaning the opening or introduction, except it doesn't have the "yawn and skip" connotations of "intro." Leads can be a few sentences or a few paragraphs—enough so that the text seems to have a direction or momentum. That's why they're particularly useful for focusing—if you can come up with a lead that you like, particularly if it's linked to a title that seems to work, you've got a focus, and you can work on modifying and refining rather than finding that crucial element.

Many people who understand the focusing effects of a good lead get stuck trying to come up with the perfect lead, the perfect opener, one that will grab the reader, forecast some of what's to come, explain the significance of the subject or perspective, explore the consequences of ignoring the point, develop an interesting voice, present a thesis . . . We ask our leads to do a lot! But trying to craft a perfect lead before writing the rest of the piece is a losing proposition, an almost certain recipe for writer's block. Instead, do as you did with titles: write as many as you can as fast as you can. Work on each one only long enough so that you know where that lead is headed, then start another one. Write at least ten. Then go back and read over them. Each lead is a trailhead; look down each path and ask yourself if that's the direction you want to go. Consider whether you could weave pieces of various leads together to make a new, improved one.

Let's try a few leads on the fraternity issue.

1. Among Podunk's students, it's unanimous: the nicest houses, the best housing at Podunk U. is to be found along fraternity row. If there's a heart of Podunk, this is it. [Sounds as though it could be in the Sunday magazine section. This will be a genteel look.]
2. "Should Podunk do away with fraternities?" Ask Jennifer Dure, Head Facilitator of the Other Project. "Do you realize," she asks rhetorically, "that every alcohol death at Podunk in the past fifty years has occurred as a result of fraternity drinking? Those places are poison." [This one comes out swinging. Will there be an equally forceful speaker for the other side?]
3. I'm not sure I've ever been to an official fraternity party. They don't have a great reputation. But over the years, fraternities have brought some great bands to Podunk. So maybe you have to pay a little for the good you get. [This one sounds student-centered and balanced. It might lead to an essay that students could believe.]
4. The issue is simple: fraternities' existence at Podunk depends on the Greek Charter, signed by founder Ephraim Podunk and by the only fraternities

ever allowed on campus. The one-hundred-year charter runs out next year. What should the school do? [This objective, almost legalistic lead promises just the facts, with little on the scandal.]

5. People who oppose fraternities generally know nothing about them. I've spent four years in a fraternity, and I've never once vomited on the floor or forced myself on a young woman. The fraternity has been a major force in getting me through college in four years, and I'll start my career off with a job at a company owned by one of my frat brothers. [We know where this speaker stands, and he sounds confident that he can persuade you to see things his way.]

If you've ever written an entire draft only to conclude, "That isn't what I wanted to say," you can appreciate the value of writing multiple leads. Brainstorming leads allows you to say, "Nah, try again" after a paragraph rather than after an entire draft. See ➡20 for ideas about more specific kinds of leads.

One more in this series, and maybe the hardest: **Brainstorm ends** (MOVE 144). A good ending is crucial to some kinds of writing, yet it can be as difficult to come up with as a good lead. All the types of leads listed in ➡20 can also work as ends. Comb your draft during one reading, looking for a detail or turn of phrase or clever point that might make an ending. Look for questions you raised or claims you made with your lead. Can you circle back to something from the beginning? Don't be afraid to just end. Sometimes the instinct to explain yourself one more time produces redundancy, and you're better off cutting the last paragraph or two. A few rough ends for our fraternity paper:

1. The neighbors down the street say the parties bother them only about once a year. Eventually they quiet down, and by dawn you would have trouble picking out the fraternity from the other old, elegant houses that surround it.

2. It may be difficult to reconcile the two sides of the fraternity issue, and each side accuses the other of being blind to reality. It has been debated for almost all of the school's ninety-eight years, and even after the university makes a decision, the debate is sure to continue.

3. The irony is, fraternities have the university over a barrel. If a fraternity is barred, its members may transfer out, and the university can't afford to lose hundreds of students in these difficult economic times. The fraternities will stay. And they won't even have to bring their big guns to town.

4. "I'm just as glad all those alcoholics are concentrated on one street," says sophomore Noah Reinslot. "That way, they cause less trouble for the rest of us."

5. The University doesn't want to be seen as breaking the old man's will, but keeping to the original fraternity list angers both the anti-fraternity activists and the other wannabe fraternities.

This one cuts to the heart of a piece of writing: **Find the problem/tension/conflict** (MOVE 145). Many of us shy away from conflict because we don't like face-to-face confrontation, but in writing it's different: we can control, clarify, perhaps even resolve the tension or conflict. Almost all published writing answers a question, eases a tension, or fills a gap. Look for a central problem in your subject. You may not be able to solve the problem or resolve the conflict, but you won't know until you dig into it. And sometimes just clearly laying out the problem is a triumph by itself.

Is the major conflict in the fraternity paper between old and new conceptions of education? Or about gender roles? Or really about alcohol, and fraternities are just incidental?

All good writers use details, and sometimes a good detail can unify a whole project. **Find a focusing detail** (MOVE 146). Sometimes there's a single detail, perhaps a quotation or statistic, that seems to encapsulate much of what you want to say. If you bring that detail up early in your paper, you can refer back to it several times, and it can become a focal point for the entire paper. A paper arguing for the ouster of the university provost for instance might focus on the number of faculty members who have walked out of meetings with the provost, slamming the door in disgust. For the parking paper, the exact time it takes the bus to get to school might be a focusing detail.

Experiment

Doing this next one can complicate your understanding of audience. **Play with perspective** (MOVE 147). We usually start our thinking about a subject with one perspective in mind—we write about the campus parking problem from the commuter student's point of view, the one we're most familiar with. There's nothing wrong with that, but considering your subject from other points of view can help you see what you need to develop and gather and sometimes can lead to a discovery. In chapter 24 ("Develop"), I encouraged you to consider different perspectives by playing with distance and by seeing your subject through metaphors from physics. Here I'm suggesting that you ponder all the different people, positions, or institutions that have a stake or an interest in your subject.

Put your subject in the center of a piece of paper and then circle it with all the interested parties. With the campus parking subject, among the various perspectives might be that of on-campus students, faculty, staff, campus police, visitors, citizens of the surrounding area, alumni, people who would be affected by the building of a proposed parking garage, the contractors involved in that building, people who bus students from the remote parking lots to the heart of campus. The list is just about endless. Coming up with all those perspectives can give you a sense of just how large and complex the whole issue is, which should impress upon you the need to focus. And you might find the focus in one particular perspective or in the tension between two competing perspectives. Maybe your issue isn't really with campus parking but with the routes of the buses that get you to your classes so slowly.

If thinking about other perspectives on your issue was useful, you might want to **Focus for different audiences** (MOVE 148). You may feel that you don't have time for this tangent, but it could save you lots of time in the long run by helping you figure out your audience and focus. Spend five minutes summarizing your project for your target audience. Now choose a very different group that has some interest in the project and write a quick summary for this second group. Finally, address a third group, as different from the other two as possible. What do you end up emphasizing differently? Can you possibly take into account the desires of all three groups, or at least address the issues of all three?

Let's say we're writing a paper about changes in the way the public gets music. For your target audience, your peers who know nothing but iTunes, your summary might be "iTunes takes us back, in some ways, to the era of the 78 rpm record, when you'd buy music one or two songs at a time. Such listening habits can have a major effect on what music people listen to—and what they miss out on."

For a record industry publication, you might write, "The iTunes phenomenon has opened up for the music industry a scary new prospect: people buying only the music that they really want. No more need for filler. No more waiting until the band can produce six or seven more good tunes. Very few albums are sold now because someone liked the single."

For a Free Music! blog, you could write, "Back when there was some connection between the amount that a song made and the amount the musicians made, record companies could make a moral argument—if you ripped off the company, you were ripping off the artist. But as a result of changes in the industry, that seems no longer to be the case."

If you're soon to be on the job market, consider the different possible focuses for an application letter. Some job-seekers run off dozens of copies of the same letter without considering that different audiences are going to want to see different qualities in applicants, even if they're hiring for what's essentially the same position. A generic, one-size-fits-all letter is likely to be just enough off-target for purpose and audience that it will get ignored.

So try it: take a recent application letter or one you write just for this purpose, and target it for two different jobs. This will require a close analysis of the job posting. What qualities are key for the particular job? Can you highlight those qualities in your letter? What's the tone and level of formality of the posting? Can you match these in your letter? What particular duties will the job holder be asked to do? Can you manipulate your background so that it shows your ability to perform such duties?

This one uses creative writing to help you understand your subject better. **Try a different genre** (MOVE 149). We seldom have the luxury of switching from writing a corporate report to writing a sonnet, but sometimes experimenting with a different genre helps us see what the real core of the subject is and therefore points us to ways to focus. So try writing a poem about your essay assignment, or an executive summary, or a short story. Spending just fifteen or twenty minutes on this alternate genre may help you see your real task in a new light.

Often we're asked to take this step, to generalize from or **Abstract** (MOVE 150) a much longer work. Writers may grumble at such a task, but it inevitably makes the longer work clearer in the writer's mind. Stand back and ask yourself what the key issues are, how you can generalize from the specific. Sum up your thinking in a sentence or two. Polish them. The clearer you can make your abstract, the clearer your focus will be.

The most basic advice may be the most useful: **Frame it** (MOVE 151). The one writing tip I picked up from high school was to frame your subject first, then fill in the picture. Framing indicates to the reader what's important, what to look for in the picture. "This report will consider the causes of the recent recession" is not yet a thesis statement, but it does frame the upcoming discussion, letting the reader know that *causes* will be the focus. Conceiving of a frame can be a useful move early in the writing process, and by the time the writer is to the focusing stage, a frame—a sense of context—is almost required. So if your subject is the picture, what's your frame?

If your goal is conveying the most meaning in the fewest words, you might find this move useful. **Expand then choose: The Accordion Principle** (MOVE 152). If you've ever watched someone play the accordion or some other kind of "squeeze box," you know that the instrument plays both when it's expanding, taking in air, and when it's contracting, pushing the air out. I encourage writers to use the accordion as a metaphor for their writing. Freewriting or doing any of the development activities is like the expansion phase of the accordion. You get as much down on paper as you can, defining, following tangents, spinning out descriptions, shutting up the censor, and telling yourself "Keep going." But eventually, after your burst of expansion, you must compress.

Read through your freewriting to see if one detail, word combination, perspective, or line of thought sticks out for you. Where is there the most tension, the most energy? Is there a line that you want to build on? Taking successive steps of expansion and selection will almost certainly make your ideas clearer to you and in turn help your readers.

To focus your responses to a visual image, **Divide your comments into "aesthetic" and "argumentative"** (MOVE 153). Which aspects of the image strike you as having a persuasive purpose? Which add beauty or mood to the image? How do the aesthetic and argumentative elements interact? Do they seem to be working in concert?

Question

As you develop a focus in your writing, your reading can become more directed and efficient. **Force yourself to read intelligently** (MOVE 154). If you're like me, you have a little inner voice that says that if you don't read the whole text from beginning to end, you're somehow "cheating," you haven't really "read" it. But the secret to good reading is knowing how and when to vary your reading style. If you're reading a poem or novel, yes, read each word, savor the rhythm and music of the language. But if you're writing a paper about comparative child-rearing practices and you've found a thousand-page anthropology book about a tribe in the Amazon, you'll never get finished if you read the whole book. You need to know WHY you're reading a particular text, what questions you're trying to answer, and use the index, the table of contents, the introduction, the afterword, and headings to guide you to the important material quickly. Yes, this kind of reading takes more thought—it's more active—than reading start to finish, but it's much more efficient.

An honest, in-depth answer to any of the following questions can lead to a focus for your project. **Ask focusing questions** (MOVE 155) to find a focus by making connections between parts of your project and between your project and other things. Most of the analysis questions in MOVE 90 will help you focus. Here are a few more:

1. Why are you interested in it?
2. Who else is interested in it?
3. What caused it?
4. What effects will it have?
5. How can you group the observations or details?
6. How does it connect with you and your experiences?
7. With what similar things could you group or associate it?
8. What are its functions?
9. How did it start, and how will it end?
10. How is it relevant to our lives?
11. What context can you put it into?

Focusing in Family Therapy

Sheila McNamee writes books and articles at the intersection of communication, psychology, philosophy, and therapy, but she strives to make her work accessible, so that someone picking it up off the street could understand it. "My first job is to answer the 'So what?' question," she says about her focusing techniques. "Here's what other people say and why it's inadequate and why you should care about what I have to say." She also finds that she focuses while editing, making her points sharper for herself and for her readers. She compares her writing process to the improvisation of a jazz musician—"you really need to know the music or material."

Ask yourself the "So what?" question (MOVE 156). Why does your subject matter to anyone but yourself? What's the point, the moral, the conclusion, the reason your piece is worth reading? How will your piece fill gaps in what others have written or set right what you consider to be a wrong? What do you want your readers to be thinking about when they finish your piece?

Those questions may sound daunting, but with some creative thinking you can find an answer in virtually every paper. Jonnie's essay about becoming paranoid as a result of a life-guarding experience might convince the town to hire older lifeguards. That's a significant "So what?" Deidre's paper about her father the alcoholic would help anyone understand better the dynamics in a family of an alcoholic. Spencer's paper about building a Tinkertoy-and-duct-tape facemask to amuse his laid-up father speaks volumes about the way love can be expressed. If you chose your subject because it mattered to you, there's almost certainly a way to get it to matter to others. But you may need help to find the right angle.

Share

This is a great way to learn about yourself and those around you. **Talk . . . and listen** (MOVE 157). In chapter 23, I encouraged you to talk about your subject to anyone who would listen, because simply formulating your ideas and summarizing them in a way that will make sense to others is a powerful technique for discovering what you want to say and where you need to expand. But if you have an audience that's willing to do more than nod and approve, having a discussion about your story can be a powerful focusing device. First, tell your story, with all its tangents and holes. Then ask your audience if they think there's an essay ready to emerge from your story, and if so, what is it and what parts of your story need to be trimmed or expanded to form that essay. Be ready for possibilities you never imagined in your story. Your listening audience may be particularly useful at answering the "So what?" question. Ask them.

What's Next?

Often, when a writer has found/imposed/developed a focus for a writing project, the best next step is developing that focus, or the focused project, using some of the moves in chapter 24. Such a step is particularly appropriate if the chosen focus is very different from the working focus that was in the writer's head while the writer was engaged in other steps in the writing process. But if you're eager to move forward and feel that you've done enough discovering and developing for the moment, try some of the organizing activities in chapter 28. I urge you not to write a full draft yet, although you may be tempted. You now have a sense of where you're headed, but you probably still don't have a clear idea of how you're going to get there. Spending a few minutes with the moves in the next chapter can help you develop an outline or other kind of plan, which can be tremendously valuable in preventing you from getting stuck, not knowing where to go next. It may seem as though I'm trying to slow you down, but really, I'm trying to make this easy for you: the more preparation you do before the draft, the easier the draft itself will be.

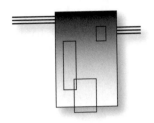

Organize

*A frequent cause of blocking is the confusion that ensues when you
try to hold the entire pattern in your head at one time.*
—Mack and Skjei

You have insights into your material, you've developed some of your ideas, and
you have at least a working focus around which all of your ideas cohere. Why
not just jump into a draft?

Without a sense of the organization of the whole, you're likely to start with
the most obvious point you want to make, write a page or two, and then . . . get
stuck, because you didn't provide yourself with a next step. One of the principal aims of this book is to help you avoid getting into that position—stuck,
frustrated, and spinning your wheels. So if you can hold off on drafting for just
a little longer, your overall writing time will, I think, be shorter, and the drafting process will go more smoothly.

Learning HOW to organize material should serve you well no matter what
you write. But individual discourse communities have specific preferences
on such issues as the order of materials, where the thesis or key point goes
and if the piece even needs a thesis. One of the mistakes writing courses have

traditionally made is to implicitly teach students that the "right" organization is that of the personal essay, which is in fact a genre unusual outside the humanities. A student writing about business or biology using personal essays as a model is not likely to do well. So some transfer can be negative, harmful to your writing in a new situation. The possibility of negative transfer is yet another reason to learn as much as you can about audience, purpose, and genre when you're in a new writing situation.

Purposes of Organizing

I doubt I have to convince you that the organization of a piece of writing is important. Yet many writers never think consciously about organizing; they just assume that the order in which ideas come out of their heads will be a good order for readers. Unfortunately, that isn't generally the case. (See **Write reader-based prose** ➡️158.)

To organize an entire project, the writer steps back from it and tries to see the whole and its parts. Because this valuable step can be difficult if the writer is caught up in the details or the flow of the story, many of the moves in this chapter help ease the writer into this distanced position. If you think with a pencil, now's the time to sharpen it: a doodle could turn into an outline or sketch. And as you play around with rearranging the big chunks of your paper, always be alert for surprises and discoveries. If you move paragraph ten right after paragraph two, what kind of transition will that require? What new thoughts spring from connecting those two once-distant ideas? If you use software to keep track of your notes, does the way it organizes your material tell you anything?

Many writers shy away from organizing because of bad experiences with outlining, the simplest and most commonly used organizing technique. Teachers and professors often require outlines too early in the writing process, or they require too formal an outline, or students feel that they must follow the outline too rigidly. In almost all cases, an outline should be an aid to the writer, not an impediment or an end product. It's up to you to figure out what kind of detail you need in an outline or if a non-conventional outline would work for you. Be guided by one central goal: any kind of outline or organizational aid should lay out future steps for you, so that you're never stuck, wondering "Where do I go next?"

Organizing moves can help you figure out an organizing principle for your writing. Will you present all the benefits, then all the costs, then your conclusion? Will you list events in chronological order? Will you reveal your evidence most important to least important, or the reverse? **Group, label, and order** ➡️162 and **Try standard organizing patterns** ➡️166 should help you make a decision about your organizing principle.

Organizing Moves

Unlike some of the other processes we've looked at, organizing doesn't happen automatically as you write. In most cases it takes a conscious effort, a stepping back from the details to see the big picture, and a good enough sense of the whole so the writer can imagine how all the parts could best fit in.

Outline

You may have your own unique way of organizing your material. If it works, don't mess with it. But most people need some kind of **Outline** (➡95). In chapter 23, we talked about outlining as a technique for development. But for most people, outlining is an organizational tool. Bestselling author Judy Krantz says, "Blocking is the panic of not knowing where to go next, and outlining is the way to avoid it" (Mack and Skjei 1979, 104). The simplest outline may be the most useful—you jot down the five or five hundred things you want to cover, group them if you have a lot, then number them. For some writers, that's plenty—all they need for a memo or a novel. If you want to make another list under each of your major headings, great. Just don't convince yourself that you have to follow the outline exactly as it came to you. And you don't need to use Roman numerals.

Most writers should go beyond simply being conscious of their audiences and strive to **Write reader-based prose** (MOVE 158). Linda Flower gave the writing world the terminology to make a useful distinction between "reader-based" and "writer-based" prose. Understanding the distinction can be very helpful as you work to organize your material.

The easiest way to make sense of the distinction is to spend ten minutes doing this little exercise. Think of something that you've learned to do relatively recently—a sport, a game, perhaps something academic. Jot down the steps as they happened or as they occur to you. This is writer-based prose, organized by the writer according to some preexisting order in the writer's mind, with no thought of an audience. Now imagine that you're trying to interest someone in the process you just wrote about. What would hook them? What questions would readers ask, and how could you answer them? What is the key point you want them to grasp?

When I do this exercise, I write about learning to windsurf. My writer-based list is long and dull, full of frustration, equipment problems, and, at about step twenty, finally getting the ecstatic feeling of skimming over the water. When writing about windsurfing for someone else, though, I start with step twenty, that magical feeling of flying, because I need to create interest, show readers the goal, before I get into cautions about how long it takes to learn and how frustrating it can be. Doing this little exercise is, of course, simpler than creating a successful organization for a thirty-page thesis. But if you can remember the principle—and the fact that your initial draft was so reader-unfriendly—that may convince you to think through your subject with a reader's questions and interests in mind.

A simple form of organization builds on the insights from the last activity. It takes imagination but not much work. **Answer readers' questions** (MOVE 159). First, jot down your subject, or your title if you have one: windsurfing. Now imagine that you're a reader who knows nothing about the subject. What would your first question be upon reading the subject or the title? "What is it?" Then you have to shift back to your own shoes and answer that question: "It's a cross between sailing and surfing that one person does with a fairly simple rig." What new question does this statement raise in the reader's mind? Perhaps, "Where can you do it?" Answer: "You can windsurf in any body of water at least a couple feet deep: ponds, lakes, the ocean, even rivers." Reader: "Is it fun?" Answer: "It's more personal and immediate than other kinds of sailing, and doesn't require the surf—and the endurance—necessary for surfing. It's the most fun the average person can have on the water." And so on. Notice that if I put my answers together, with slight modifications, I'd have a pretty good opening paragraph. I've started a draft without being aware of it—and without the trauma that usually accompanies drafting.

If you're going to do only one thing to organize your paper, this next move should be it. **Outline your draft** (MOVE 160). This move requires that you have at least a very rough draft. It yields a **descriptive outline**, the most useful analysis you can create for reorganizing and revising. In about half an hour, you get a clear sense of what you've written so far, where your emphasis is, where there might be flow or transition problems, and how well the whole thing hangs together.

1. *Number each paragraph.* This is the only thing you do on the paper itself. Part of the point of this activity is to take attention away from the individual pages of the paper and focus it on the skeleton you're about to construct. It's much easier to get a sense of the whole when it's all on one page.
2. *On a clean sheet of paper, jot down a number for each paragraph, spacing evenly.* (In other words, if you have twenty paragraphs, number one through twenty.)
3. *Summarize each paragraph in as few words as possible.* Write each summary next to the appropriate number.
4. *Reflect on what you just did.* Why were certain paragraphs difficult to summarize? Are they unfocused or incoherent or compound? Should you break a paragraph into two? Did you find you could use ditto marks because a number of paragraphs in a row were about the same subject? Does the subject deserve that much attention? Could someone glancing at the summaries of your opening and closing paragraphs get a sense of how they connect?

5. *Group the summaries into blocks.* Use brackets or different colors or whatever works. First get every summary into a group, then bracket some of those groups into larger blocks until you get to the one block that they all fit under. Label each group.

6. *Reflect again.* Are some summaries out of place, requiring you to draw an arrow to the correct group? Does the number of paragraphs in each block roughly correspond to the relative importance of that block? You have now created a kind of an outline sometimes called a tree diagram. Do its major blocks correspond to what you see as the major sections in your paper? Are you missing parts? Do the blocks appear in the best order?

7. *Mark junctions between blocks and summarize what the transition at each spot needs to do.* Between every pair of blocks, big and small, there should be some indication of a change of subjects: a paragraph break or a bullet if not some kind of verbal transition. Resist the temptation to see what transition you *did* use. First figure out what *should* be there and write it down at the crucial spot in your outline. Then see if you can find it in the paper.

8. *Write down all the changes you want to make.* This process in effect X-rays the draft, and this new form of seeing can open your eyes to many kinds of re-vision, not just organizational problems.

A fine way to prepare for outlining your own paper—or to analyze a reading—is to **Use the descriptive outline on a piece of professional writing** (MOVE 161). The outline can demonstrate that even a seemingly complex piece of writing has a simple skeleton. And it can help make connections between the writing that we read and the writing that we produce. So try it. Go through the eight steps of the previous move using a relatively short essay or article, perhaps dividing it up among classmates. What do you learn about the article? About how to organize your own writing? Does the article in fact have a simple structure?

I outlined Sam Abbott's "Everybody's Gotta Jump" (chapter 12). When I summarized the paragraphs, I saw new things in the article. For instance, I noticed that in each paragraph about the family members, Abbott details both a hardship and an example of transcending the hardship, so his point about the family as a whole is reflected in each individual's story. The key transitions occur in paragraph 1, where Abbott moves from a focus on himself to a focus on the Dolas, and paragraph 8, where he reverses that focus. Perhaps wisely, Abbott doesn't slow down his story by explaining under what circumstances he met the Dolas; he gets right to the things they taught him. And his transition back to himself is simple—he contrasts the way poverty affects the Dolas to the way it affected him. The analysis reveals what might be a weakness in Abbott's essay: he spends just two quick paragraphs on what he hopes to accomplish with the essay, and he never explains what the metaphorical "jump" translates into in everyday actions.

1. Not prepared for poverty
2. Dola family—working overtime but "very happy"
3. Tiny cement shack but Ramakrishna "laughed at everything"
4. Dwarka the youngest and their games
5. Ganesh—goes hungry for his family
6. Ganesh's callused hands—the jump off the cliff
7. Prasad—quiet, providing father
8. Family not governed by poverty but changed him
9. Some of his luxuries
10. Got to get others to jump in
11. Inviting others to join him

I connected paragraphs 1, 6, and 8 under the heading "speaker's story"; I put 2–5 into the block "family portraits" but wondered if 7 should also be part of that block. I labeled paragraph 6 "insight" and realized the whole essay could be seen as "before insight," "insight," and "after insight," with this last category including "consequences."

A key organizing move—grouping—can help the writer understand more about the writing project and therefore figure out how best to present it. Sometimes when we brainstorm, we're just looking for one thing, like the best title, and once we've found it, we can discard everything else. More often, all the elements of the brainstorm are relevant and worth keeping. And if you're going to keep more than one of them, **Group them, find labels for the groups, and order them** (MOVE 162). Such grouping can show you that you have just three big things to say, not twenty-one, and can help you focus. Best of all, it can provide you a plan for the whole writing project—you just need to preview and explain the three or four groups you've come up with, present those groups in the order listed, and then tie them together again at the end.

For example, let's say you're writing about the need to save the bees, something you're interested in because you have an uncle who's a beekeeper. You brainstorm details about it and find that they sort out into three groups:

- Why bees are important to humans
- Current threats and challenges to bees
- Solutions—what we can do

Seeing the paper in such simple terms may make a focus or thesis obvious to you. In the case of bees, it might make clear that there are three major parts to the paper, all of which should probably be included in a thesis statement: "Bees are so important to human existence that we must try every possible solution to the threats and challenges bees now face."

Experiment

More than perhaps any other element in a writing project, the ordering of materials is specific to, and dictated by, the traditions of the genre and the discourse community. So the smartest, most efficient way to figure out the organization of a new genre you're working in is to **Find a model** (MOVE 163). Discovering that you're supposed to present "problem—solutions—debate—decision" or "lit review—methods—discussion—conclusion" can answer all your organizational questions and speed you on your way. Part I of this book presents models for a number of genres, but the best approach always is to see if your audience can provide you with recent, approved models.

Many student papers follow an understandable but ineffective pattern: they tell a story for three or four pages, then in the last paragraph, the writer extracts a meaning or moral from the story. This is a natural way to write, because in real life we don't know what the moral to a story is until we've lived through it. But it's ineffective—readers can't make the same connections between details and conclusion that the writer can see. A reader who gets to the meaning at the end will probably have to reread to see the connections between the meaning and the story.

To get a sense of how else you might present your moral or point, listen to Beethoven's Symphony No. 9. In the final movement, see if you can identify the first time the "Joyful, Joyful We Adore Thee" theme is introduced. Then see how many times it is repeated throughout the movement in different registers and instruments. The theme or thesis is *woven throughout the piece* and not just repeated but repeated with variation. Can you do the same thing with your paper? **Weave your theme** (MOVE 164) throughout, giving at least a hint of it in the first paragraph and using it to create transitions and highlight important points.

The secret to conquering any large piece of writing is to break it into manageable sections. If you're organizing a substantial report, that means you need to **Use headings and subheadings** (MOVE 165). Some writers in the humanities are reluctant to use headings because they look like business writing. But they can do a quick and effective job of organizing and highlighting a paper for both writer and reader. Imagine this book with no headings! Does your paper logically break into sections? (Look for places where you have transition problems—that's likely to be a break.) If you use an outline, would the parts of the outline work as headings? Break a big piece into smaller chunks any way you can. For my windsurfing paper, my major headings might be Why Do It?, Where Can You Do It?, and What's Required?, which would have subheadings like Equipment, Training, and perhaps Staying Warm.

The structure of many pieces of writing grows organically from the combination of audience, purpose, subject, and genre. But if your writing doesn't have an organic structure of its own, **Try standard organizing patterns** (MOVE 166). Some organizational strategies are so common in our culture that we give them names like "cause and effect" and even organize writing courses around them. Critics make the valid point that good essays and articles seldom stick to one organizational pattern, but the patterns can still be useful for any writer trying to find a logical way to organize material. Readers are used to these patterns and may assume that your paper is logically organized if you use one of them. Here are a few of the most common patterns:

Chronological, start to finish: "The Civil War started on April 12, 1861 . . ."
Cause and effect (or effect and cause): "These factors caused the Civil War" OR "These were the results of the Civil War."
Specific to general (or general to specific): "These data lead me to conclude . . ." OR "All Xs believe Y, as we shall see in the following examples."
Most important to least important (or the reverse): "Of the many causes of the Civil War, the most important was . . ."
Definition: "The Civil War was actually a blood feud."
Classification: "The Civil War was caused by economic, social, and political factors."
Partition: "We can divide the Civil War into three phases."
Compare: "The war did not visit the two sides with an even hand."
Process: "How did the generals arrive at their decision?"
Analogy: "The Civil War was a train wreck with a multitude of causes and effects, but the fuel that drove the train was slavery."

All the traditional text-organizing patterns apply to visual organization as well. Two faces on a billboard invite comparisons and contrasts. The "effect" is boy-gets-girl, and the "cause" is the advertiser's miracle product. Visual marketers try to redefine "home" for you.

Visual organization can play a role in many stages of writing. Some brainstormers use the whole surface of the page to put each new idea into loose categories. Many people prepare to draft by creating something visual, whether it's an outline or a script or an image—the boxcars of thought pulled by the lead and cabooseed by a red lantern. You might see a paper as a river with tributaries, waterfalls, and eddies, or as a triple-length truck. You might see your job as doorman to the reader's imagination, or wilderness guide to the reader's adventure. You might think in symbols and forms that you couldn't explain to anyone else but that guide you through your work. For some writers, seeing the text printed out on the page sparks ideas for layout, highlighting, and emphasis. **Sketch the organization of your paper** (MOVE 167). It may not make sense to anyone but you, but that's fine; the point is to help you get organized. Cultivate the ability to think visually.

Organizing in Marine Biology

Megan Dethier, a marine biologist, advises students to "spend a chunk of time graphing up and studying your results. See what's there that's nifty." To write her own papers, she graphs the data in as many ways as seem logical and then sees "what kind of story the graphs tell." Lining up her graphs so that they tell their story most effectively gives her an outline, an organization for her data. Then she just has to explain and connect the various graphs through writing.

This graph of the survival and sizes of clams in Puget Sound confirmed one of Dethier's hunches and surprised her by revealing unexpected information on another front. The clams were grown in tubes, some of them covered by nets to protect against predators. Dethier used three different sites around the sound—Budd, Brown, and Carkeek. She expected more clams to survive in the protected "Net" tubes at each site than in the "No net" tubes at that site, and the results confirm that expectation—the "Net" column of each pair is taller than the "No net" column. What she didn't expect was that so many more clams would survive at Carkeek

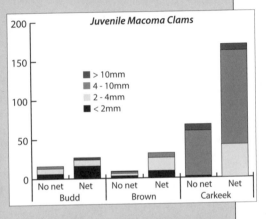

than at the other sites, and that the Carkeek clams would be bigger. The Carkeek results confirmed the "Net" hypothesis but also opened up possibilities for other experiments and possibly new insights into marine growth in the sound. Graphing helped the researchers both to communicate results and to open up new areas of inquiry.

Writers with a strong visual imagination might want to use a similar method, arranging material in terms of the visual images it suggests. Try to **Graph your data** (MOVE 168), put it in a table, or come up with an image that represents it. If you can create a logical series of visual images, you'll be halfway there.

Share

This quick exchange gets to the heart of your paper. **Analyze your thesis** (MOVE 169). Do you worry that your point is either vague or not as powerful and reverberating as you hoped it'd be?

1. Write as brief and complete a summary of your thesis as you can. Don't just choose a sentence from the paper. *The government should license people allowed to gather mushrooms on public land.*
2. Identify two or three major subpoints, the major building blocks upon which your thesis rests. *In the current unlicensed situation, the health of the public, the mushroom pickers, and the fungi themselves are at risk.*
3. List the most important details or minor points that contribute to or exemplify the subpoints. *Recent mushroom-eating deaths, some from mushrooms picked and sold by professionals; the wars among pickers; evidence of the mushrooms' decline.*
4. Exchange papers with a friend or someone in your revision group, and go through the same process with your classmate's paper. Then compare results. If there are serious discrepancies, discuss with your partner ways to make the hierarchy of your ideas clearer.

What's Next?

Creating some kind of outline of the points you're going to make should prepare you for the actual drafting of those points. But if the organizing process has raised new issues, don't feel bad about doing a little more developing, gathering, or focusing at this stage. Looking at your outline will probably reveal to you areas you've sufficiently developed, focused, and researched and ones you've neglected up until now.

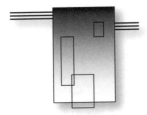

29 Draft

A sense of organization, of where you're headed, may be the single most important thing to have before you start actually writing a draft. But the more you do before the draft, the less painful the draft will be. A major goal of this book is to make drafting—the most difficult part of the writing process for most people—easier, less scary, less overwhelming. I try to take the pressure off the draft by making moves before and after drafting, but eventually you have to sit down and write in full sentences, and it's work. The first part of this chapter offers eight different ways of writing out those full sentences. The second lists tips for the sweaty work of getting developed ideas down on the page.

Drafting Approaches

Approaches three and six start with something written on paper. The others begin with just a blank page or screen but differ in the writer's attitude, the stories in the writer's head about just what this draft is for.

1. "I just want to get some ideas down and see if they're worth anything."
   Draft to explore (MOVE 170). Sometimes the smartest thing is to promise

yourself that you're not even trying to write a draft; you just want to explore the subject with words. Call it a "discovery draft" or a "sketch" if you want. If you're lucky, your exploration will result in a revisable draft. If that doesn't work out, at least your stress should be under control.

2. "I want to get my ideas down as fast as possible without worrying about purpose, audience, all that stuff." **Draft by freewriting** (MOVE 171). Just sit down at the computer with a headful of ideas and go . . . and hope you don't get stuck, when you may wish you had SOMETHING written down beforehand.

3. "I've got a good outline; I just need to flesh it out." **Draft by outline** (MOVE 172). The opposite of approach #1. Move meticulously from branch to branch of the outline, each numbered or named entity on the outline getting its own paragraph.

4. "I tend to get distracted and go off on tangents when I write." **Draft with blinders** (MOVE 173). Develop your own code—like "LLL" for "later"—for dealing later with the subjects and perspectives you ignore the first time through, as you work to put down the most direct word path possible toward your goal.

5. "It's all too hard." **Pick the draft of least resistance** (MOVE 174). Working from some kind of outline, pick the first discrete unit of work that strikes you as "easy" or "fun" to accomplish. Do it. Then look around for another easy thing.

6. "I've got a thesis. What next?" **Draft with thesis** (MOVE 175). Many readers expect a thesis-based structure, so thesis-driven drafting makes a lot of sense. You can regularly look back at your thesis as you draft, making sure you're not getting too far off target. See **Develop a thesis** ➡97.

7. "I like to perfect as I draft." **Draft recursively** (MOVE 176). You can use recursive drafting with any of the preceding approaches. Recursive means circling back around to—taking two steps forward and one step back. Try to figure out how large your recursive circles are. Do you want a complete draft before you come back to the beginning, or should you work on a couple of pages of yesterday's writing before you start fresh today?

8. "I usually don't figure out what I want to say until I'm polishing." **Three times round** (MOVE 177). Write a complete draft, as fast as you can. Put the draft away. Write another complete draft, as fast as you can. Again, put it away. Write a third first draft without looking at the other two. It will be far superior. Cut and paste pieces from the first two drafts into the third one if it seems appropriate

Drafting Tips

1. Everyone should do this. If you've got a "magic pen," whip it out! **Use your favorite tools and habits** (MOVE 178). Writers are famous for having strange habits—writing standing up or in the bathtub, or with

a particular kind of pen and pad. Sure, writing on a computer will save
the step of typing it up later, but do you actually work better writing
longhand? Keep track of when, where, and how you do your best, most
relaxed writing. Figure out what you're doing when the ball goes in the
hoop and replicate the situation.

2. No, this isn't a copout. You just need a way into the draft, to get the
words flowing. **Start with what's easiest** (MOVE 179). You don't have to
start at the beginning. Choose a part that will seem to write itself. It's
good to have some writing momentum before you tackle the difficult
parts.

3. This tip may seem counter-intuitive, but it works. **Use your best stuff**
(MOVE 180). Don't worry about "using it up." Writing itself generates
memories, ideas, connections. Build your project around the strongest
details and information.

4. You may already have done some valuable writing without knowing it.
Mine what you've already done (MOVE 181). If you wrote multiple leads,
could some of the rejected leads turn into paragraph two or three? Could
any of your discovering or developing moves help you ease into the
draft?

5. Another universal necessity. **Shut up your internal critic** ➡47. "It's good
enough for now." That's my motto when I'm drafting, and I encourage you
to develop something similar. Yes, you can be a perfectionist; just wait your
turn. It's amazing how often the line that seemed like trash when you were
writing it turns out to be okay when you reread it later.

6. Trying to be too perfect too fast can destroy your momentum. **Ignore
all rules** (MOVE 182). Drafting is a time when anything goes. Don't worry
about spelling, transitions, wordiness . . . just get it down.

7. Keep track, at least mentally, of what moves work for you, so you can
Return to earlier moves, if necessary (MOVE 183). Try not to strain, beat
up on yourself, or force yourself to write. It shouldn't be torture. If you
get stuck or frustrated, try one of the easy moves from one of the earlier
chapters to get yourself going again.

8. Maybe just the act of sitting in front of a screen stresses you. **Try a different recording mode** (MOVE 184). Talk into a recorder or even dictate
a few pages if you know someone who will type them out for you. Many
writers find it easier to compose without the blank page or blank screen
staring at them.

9. Play any kind of mind game that gets the words flowing. **Address a
specific audience** (MOVE 185). The sense of trying to write to a vague,
universal audience makes many writers freeze. Instead, write for a friend
or teacher. You might even start your draft, "Dear _____." Imagine that
instead of writing the paper, you're writing an email to a friend about the
paper or about your subject.

10. To get started easily tomorrow, **Stop in the middle** (MOVE 186). That is, stop when you know what the next sentence, paragraph, or idea is going to be. Stopping at the end of a section, when you need to make a big transition, will make it more difficult to get your momentum going again.

11. But if you do have trouble, **Back up to restart** (MOVE 187). When returning to a partly finished draft, build momentum by backing up a page or so, reading and perhaps slightly revising what you've done, and then using that impetus to charge into new work.

12. For the long haul, **Make drafting a habit** (MOVE 188). Many professional writers keep a daily appointment with their writing chair, sitting there even if the ideas aren't coming. Try it for a couple of weeks—go to your writing spot each day at the same time and spend an hour there. Even if you manage to produce only a few words per day, eventually those words add up.

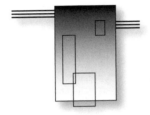

30 Revise

I can't understand how anyone can write without rewriting everything over and over again.
—Leo Tolstoy

If you're like me, you can keep your nit-picky, perfectionist critic from interfering in the early stages of your writing only by promising that eventually you'll let the critic out of its cage, give it a magnifying glass and a red pen, and let it rule the day. That time is now. Whether you're writing an important email, an essay exam, or a report, you're shooting yourself in the foot if you don't leave yourself time at least to proofread what you've done. The little blunders you catch on a ninety-second proofing of your email may seem irrelevant compared to the big content issues, but if you don't catch the spelling error or the decimal out of place, your reader may see nothing but the mistake. We have to remember that our readers have their own picky internal critics, probably uncaged, and those critics' whisperings may drown out any other response to your work. The time you spend perfecting may pay off in reader response better than anything else you do. Your creative products are who you are—they're worth perfecting.

Purposes of Revising

I almost didn't include a "purposes" section in this chapter because I thought that the purposes of revising were so obvious. You want to make your work look good and read well so that your message will be taken seriously by its audience, not dismissed for being sloppy or inaccurate. Some writers argue that polishing is for copyeditors, and they're just interested in explaining BIG IDEAS. But their ideas will never to get to the copyediting stage if they're not polished.

Much more happens during this stage than meets the eye. Changing a single verb from passive to active may highlight a relationship you'd never thought about and lead to a whole new line of thought. Making sure your beginning and end connect can lead to changes not just in those two parts but through-out the piece, as the thread becomes clearer in your own mind. Looking up the spelling of someone's name can remind you that you were going to check one more source about that person. You may be surprised to find that revising includes analysis as well as editing. We need to see what we have before we can decide if it needs to be changed.

Revising should give the writer a satisfying sense of completion that may elude the writer who scrambles to meet a deadline or sends the piece off knowing it's half-baked. It's no surprise that our cliché for meticulously get-ting things right is "dotting every 'i' and crossing every 't.'" The final stage in writing allows compulsives to shine. And it pretty much forces writers to leave lonely learning. Almost no one revises without some input from a friend, writ-ing partner, or editor.

Revising Writing

Unless you've skipped all the previous chapters and have come to this section to find a quick fix to your writing problems, you know that I advocate put-ting off the revising stage until you have your writing focused, organized, and chock-full of meaning. It doesn't hurt to correct spelling and punctuation mis-takes as you go, but most people need as much momentum as they can accu-mulate to make it through the drafting stage.

Revision is, literally, re-seeing. When you re-see your writing, you might decide to approach it from a different point of view, cut 90 percent, or expand one paragraph into a dozen. Often, revision is the difference between a "C" paper and an "A" paper, between a report that does an adequate job and one that moves the audience to action. Most professional writers see revision as central to the work they do, but many beginning writers have a difficult time believing that more advanced writers revise again and again, sometimes throwing out most of a draft, sometimes turning what was a tangent into the main focus.

Rather than make distinctions among the slippery terms "rewriting," "edit-ing," and "proofreading," I have included all my suggestions about revision in this one chapter, the moves starting with re-seeing both process and product and evolving toward more specific suggestions for later in the revising process.

Many writers find revision particularly satisfying because you can do it in short bursts of time, and often just two or three minutes of work will result in a noticeably improved sentence.

There's no substitute for a good **Model** ➡ 163, since when we revise we generally try to do it the way the audience wants it done. Try to capture the tone, the voice, the attitude of the genre. In the model, what is the writer's stance toward the material and the audience? Brainstorm words that you associate with the writer's tone and style. Are there traces of humor or irony? How is opinion expressed?

Revision Moves

Revise Your Process

Process revisions are most important, since they may affect all the writing you do and could potentially last a lifetime. If you've been keeping track of which writing process approaches work for you and which don't, you may have some concrete ideas about how to revise your own process. These are just a few suggestions for changes and additions late in your writing process.

1. **Read aloud** (MOVE 189). Note where you stumble and where everything seems to flow. It's amazing how much this simple step reveals. Listening to someone else read your piece can be equally instructive.

2. **Print it out** (MOVE 190). You'll see things in a hard copy that you didn't see on the screen.

3. **Revise for voice** (MOVE 191). It's what editors look (or listen) for, what persuades teachers to give the paper an A even if it has errors, what makes the casual reader keep reading. Voice is one of the mysteries of writing. Most readers recognize voice as the sum of the elements of writing that give the impression that an individual consciousness is communicating with you. But how do you build or create or find or encourage that voice? I think the secret is getting rid of deadwood, passives, clichés, tired phrases, anything that doesn't sparkle. And making sure the prose breathes with your own rhythm. You'd think if everyone did the same kind of tightening and pruning work on their prose, everyone would come out sounding the same. But in fact, the more we revise down to our core, the more your core differs from mine. So do everything you can to improve your writing, and whenever possible say things in your own way, making your own connections. The result will be a strong, individual writing voice.

4. **Listen to the draft** (MOVE 192). Most professional writers agree with Donald Murray that "the piece of writing will, if I listen carefully, tell

me how it needs to be written" (Murray 2009, 68). You may think that your draft is terrible, and you may be right, but it's still worth reading carefully. Does it seem to want to head in a direction different from the one you had planned? Do some ideas get more space and time than others? Imagine this were a friend's draft and that friend asked you, "Where do you think it's headed?" What would you say? It takes a lot of experience to trust your draft, but it's worth the effort.

5. **Let it sit** (MOVE 193). Fresh eyes are a reviser's best friend. Figure out for yourself how you can best freshen your eyes—a shower, a nap, nothing less than twenty-four hours away from the desk? Even an hour away from a text can help you return to the text able to see new things. A few days or weeks can give you more perspective, if you have the luxury of time.

6. **Start as close to the heart or climax as you can** (MOVE 194). This fiction writer's adage is just as true for business writing, where you have to assume a very busy reader. Some writers habitually throw out their first few pages, knowing that they use them for warming up. Is there any warming up in your paper?

7. **Keep a revision checklist** (MOVE 195). Inevitably, a change in one sentence or section will require further changes, but it's easy to forget those secondary changes as you're focusing on getting the sentence of the moment right. So keep a list of revision ideas that you need to pursue but are putting off for the moment.

Analyze Your Text

The first move in this section is something that many writers do intuitively and anyone could benefit from. Five minutes of analysis could save you hours of rewriting time. The other moves are ways of re-seeing what you have written, highlighting the most important ideas.

8. **Learn the red flags of your prose** (MOVE 196). Seeing the glitches in your writing as useful "red flags" requires a major attitude shift: we're so used to thinking in terms of shameful "errors" and "mistakes" that we have trouble seeing anything positive in such "failings." But if you know that you overuse passive verbs (your red flag), you can fixate on every passive verb as you revise and very quickly make your prose more lively and interesting.

You may need help from a reader or teacher to see your own red flags. Common ones are any kinds of repeated phrases, "There is / this is" constructions, "seems," unnecessarily negative phrasings ("we didn't lack anything"). One of mine is using "but" too often: "This . . . but that . . . but this . . ." What things have English teachers always bugged you about?

Your writing process may also have red flags for you. Are there certain things you tend to do in the process of writing that you should look out for? Do you get stuck at odd times? One of my process red flags is what I call the Threshold of Nausea—a sick feeling I get when I've read over a text one too many times. I know at that point, I'm not going to do any useful revising or proofreading, so it's time to print it off, send it on.

Keep a list of your red flags. It may be your best revising tool.

9. **Make ends meet** (MOVE 197).

    a. Look at your title and opening paragraph. What issues do they raise? What promises do they make? Do they point to what's truly important?

    b. Does the body of the text deal with those issues and fulfill those promises?

    c. Does the final paragraph complete some of the thoughts begun in the opening?

        These crucial elements—title, lead, and closing—should fit together logically, and if you've strayed, in the body, from your original intent, the difference between the opening and the conclusion can give you a sense of what went astray and what you should do about it.

        Consider, for instance, a paper titled "Fascists are Skinny" that begins, "Why is fatism the one kind of prejudice considered perfectly respectable in America?" and ends, "We should no longer tolerate these kinds of blatant attacks upon our civil rights." The end is certainly connected to the beginning and title, but it seems to be answering a different question, "What should we do about these fatist attacks?" Somewhere, the focus changed.

10. **Examine the links** (MOVE 198). Without reading the rest of the paper, look at the last sentence of each paragraph and the first sentence of the next. Have you linked the ideas in some way? Could you make the links clearer, perhaps by having your new topic sentence refer back to a word or idea in the previous sentence? Try not to use "this" or "that" alone to make this link; follow the "this" with a noun that repeats or summarizes previous ideas: "This recent research (or "This data" or "These results") demonstrate[s] the vapidity of the professor's ideas." And don't overdo it. If you've made the order and connections in a paper clear from the beginning, you may not need to add overt transitions between paragraphs.

11. **Analyze readability** (MOVE 199). Believe it or not, government and corporate documents are easier to understand than they used to be, thanks in part to the Plain English movement that advocates making all public documents *readable* so that they make sense to nonspecialists. Plain English fans puncture the myth that big words are better and generally prefer short, punchy words—"use"—rather than longer, multisyllabic words of Latin origin—"utilize." They argue that if you can write about your subject so that almost everyone can understand you, you should do so.

There are several reasonably simple ways to calculate readability, and getting a sense of a document's readability can let you know whether you should aim for more simplicity or complexity as you revise. Most readability formulas measure two things: average sentence length and unfamiliarity of words, the latter determined by counting the syllables in a sample or the words not on a list of familiar words.

To calculate one readability measure, SMOG (Simple Measure Of Gobbledygook), count thirty sentences from a document. (Taking some from the beginning, some from the middle, and some from the end improves your accuracy.) In those thirty sentences, count the number of words of three or more syllables. Round that number to the nearest perfect square. Take the square root. Then add three. That's the grade level of the writing. In the first thirty sentences of this chapter, there are fifty-six words of three or more syllables. The closest perfect square is forty-nine; the square root is seven; plus three is tenth grade. So by that calculation this chapter is written at a tenth- (or if you round fifty-six up to sixty-four, eleventh-) grade level. If you're interested, you can find many other readability formulas on the Internet.

12. Another way to measure the readability of a text is to **Use a "cloze test"** (MOVE 200). You delete every fifth word of a text, then give the passage with blanks to a member of the target audience. If the audience can fill in 80 percent of the blanks correctly, the text is within the audience's comfortable reading level. If the audience can fill in fewer than 60 percent correctly, the text may be too difficult for them.

Revise Your Text

Yes, we're finally looking closely at the text, what most people think of as revision. But as these first three moves make clear, we still need to guard against having too narrow a focus, assuming that the problem is "the wrong word."

13. To make it look good, **Polish out your weaknesses.** To make it matter, **Build on your strengths** (MOVE 201). Spelling and grammar mistakes may be what strike the reader first, giving the reader an initial negative impression that may be difficult to erase. To avoid that negative

impression and give the reader instead a sense of professionalism, make the surface perfect.

At a deeper level, spelling doesn't matter as much as an intelligent flow of ideas, deep currents of thought that aren't totally obscured by surface interference. To improve those deep currents, you'll probably have to expand on what you already have done well—your analysis or description or insights. More of that good stuff.

14. **Expand the scope of your revision** (MOVE 202). If you're getting frustrated finding the "right word," try revising the whole sentence. If a sentence is giving you trouble, look at the paragraph or back to the idea or outline. If a paragraph seems wrong, maybe it's because the previous page has been leading you off on a tangent. I wouldn't spend more than a few minutes on the perfect word hunt. If you get stuck, back up.

15. **Revise first for meaning, then for coherence, then for language** (MOVE 203). (See "Eddie's Full-Service Rewrite" later in this chapter.) I can't honestly say that I pass up the chance to change a spelling error as I'm revising for meaning, but it's a matter of emphasis or focus. If on the first rereading you start trying to rehabilitate tangled sentences, you may spend a lot of time reworking something that will eventually be discarded because it's part of a section that did not contribute to the meaning. And if you don't consciously set out to work on meaning or organization on a particular read-through, you're likely just to focus on the easy stuff—proofreading.

16. In general, **Follow the most basic English sentence pattern** (MOVE 204):

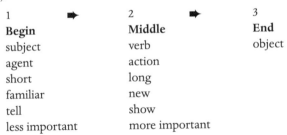

1		2		3
Begin		**Middle**		**End**
subject		verb		object
agent		action		
short		long		
familiar		new		
tell		show		
less important		more important		

Of course millions of wonderful sentences violate this generalization, but if you find yourself puzzling over how to make a sentence clearer, see if it follows or reverses one of these sentence patterns. For instance, consider the sentence "Chewing gum and talking on the cell phone to dignitaries around the world to try to avert the next world war, the President jogged by." We have to hold our breaths as we wait for who is doing all these important things. The long part comes before the short. Try putting the short first: "The President jogged by, chewing gum and talking on the cell phone to dignitaries around the world to try to avert the next world war." Notice that we've also created a sentence that puts the most important detail at the end and moves from familiar to new and from agent to action and subject to verb. Once the President gets by us, we could keep that sentence going for pages, just adding detail to the things the President was talking about.

17. **Outline your draft** ➥160.

18. **Cut and paste** (MOVE 205). Yes, this was fun in kindergarten, and it's fun now. Print out your text, literally cut it into paragraphs, then play around with the pieces. Try sorting the paragraphs into piles—perhaps one for "keepers" and one for "not so sure." Can you spread them out in a way that suggests a new order, a new focus? Could any of them be alternative openings or closings for the text? The process is fun because you're playing with your own mind.

19. **Show AND tell** ➥134.

20. **Break the sentence into parts** (MOVE 206), expressing each idea in a short, simple sentence. Then, if you want to, recombine the ideas in a new way. But don't rule out the option of simply leaving the sentences short and simple. Clarity is usually more important than "flow."

21. **Try rephrasing the idea in four or five different ways** (MOVE 207), as quickly as you can. Once you've wrestled with a sentence for a while, you're likely to get yourself into a mental rut, able to approach the idea with only one kind of sentence pattern in mind. Try starting with different parts of the sentence, writing down quickly any alternative that comes to mind. You may not produce the perfect sentence, but you may come up with a new phrase or a good way to start. Then you may be able to build a new sentence around one part that you like.

Revise Your Verbs

Maybe it's unfair to pick on verbs, but they're among the most important words in any sentence, so working with them pays off in clarity and meaning, and revising them usually requires improving the rest of the sentence too. Strong verbs carry much of the meaning in a sentence; if you make verbs work for you, the rest of the sentence won't have to carry so much weight. Try these suggestions and see if you like the results. Don't change just for the sake of change; look for improvement.

22. **Change, make consistent, and simplify verb tenses** (MOVE 208). Experiment with present tense and use the simplest past that makes sense.

23. **Replace adverb-verb combinations** (MOVE 209) with more expressive verbs—instead of "slowly walked" say "plodded" or "shuffled" or "dragged."

24. **Substitute a more visual verb** (MOVE 210). Instead of "hurt," try "bit" or "stabbed" or "stubbed."

25. **Convert participles to main verbs** (MOVE 211)—"bite," not "biting."

26. **Replace "be" verbs** (MOVE 212) and other bland verbs—"seems," "exists," "has"—with more energetic verbs. Circle with a pencil every "be" verb in your paper: is, was, were, am, are, being, been. Now look at your "be" verb sentences one by one and see if you can get rid of the "be" verb by doing one of the following things:

27. **Combine sentences or ideas** (MOVE 213). Could an idea that now takes up a whole sentence become a phrase or clause in another sentence? Instead of "Bozo was a big time clown. He frightened any kid who didn't laugh," try "Bozo the big time clown frightened . . ." Could you move information into the preceding or following sentence? Could you make a compound subject or verb and eliminate a repeated word? Instead of "Clowns terrified her. Goats frightened her as well," say "Both clowns and goats frightened her."

28. **Make passives active** (MOVE 214). Is the "be" verb you're looking at part of a passive construction? Is there a past participle (-ed form) of another verb after the "be," and is the subject of the sentence passive rather than active? If so, try to figure out the real active agent in the sentence, get that agent to the beginning of the sentence, and follow it by the real action, generally contained in the passive sentence's past participle. Is your new sentence shorter, more direct, and more informative than the passive original? Usually it will be. Compare "The sheriff was shot by me," passive, to "I shot the sheriff," active.

29. Even if the sentence isn't passive, there's probably a hidden verb lurking somewhere within it. **Look for a noun, especially one ending in "ion," that you could turn into a verb** (MOVE 215). "He is full of admiration for . . ." becomes "He admires . . ."; "She is knowledgeable about . . ." becomes "She knows . . ."

30. If you still can't get rid of your "be" verb, you may not be able to repair your sentence as it now stands. You'll probably need to come up with a new way to express your idea or just leave it the way it is. But before you go on, ask yourself if your sentence really says what you

want it to say. Remember that a "be" verb is, in effect, an "equals" sign, so **Examine your "equals signs"** (MOVE 216). Is your sentence equating apples and oranges? Consider. "A king is when a prince grows up." We know the meaning, but it's sloppy thinking—a king isn't a "when."

Proofread

Proofreading is for most people the least taxing stage of revising writing. You print it out and read it one last time, carefully, making final corrections with a pen if you don't have time to reprint it, catching all the little mistakes that fool grammar-check and spell-check software. Because such a final reading can seem easy, even mechanical, many people leap to proofreading when they need to do some serious re-seeing of their work. This poem of mine tries to convey that message in a convincing if quirky way.

Eddie's Full-Service Rewrite

Revision is body work, overhaul
Ratcheting straight the frame
Replacing whole systems and panels
Rummaging heaps of the maimed.
With blowtorch and old rubber hammer
Pound and pull, bend, use your 'bar
Salvage takes sweat but it pays well
(Though never rule out a new car).

Through editing, tuning, adjusting
You get all the volts to the spark
Knock all the gunk from the filters
Set timing right on the mark.
Trade in your hammer for feeler gauge
Test drive and listen, hush!
A smooth-running engine's a miracle
Though mange mars the bucket seats' plush.

The proofreader's focus is narrow
The weary say "Why should I care
About snotballs of tar on the door here,
Creases of rust over there?"
But oh! If the paint job's neglected
The outside just looks like a mess
Stray commas pock bodies like acne
And threaten to rot out the rest.

Why strain your elbows on hood chrome
If the pistons stick, mired in glue?
No profit in setting the carb right

If the drive shaft is broken in two.
So when you're at Ed's contemplating
How to triage repairs on your wreck
Start with the frame and the engine
Don't waste your polish on dreck.

—Published in *English in Texas*, Spring 1994

31. **Read from the end** (MOVE 217). Start with the very last word and read toward the front. Because you won't get much sense of the meaning, you may see more clearly the little mistakes that we tend to gloss over when the meaning is clear to us.

32. **Read aloud** ➥ 189. You'd think reading silently to yourself would have the same effect, but it doesn't. When you pause or trip reading aloud, you know there's a potential problem. If you read aloud, you'll keep the world from ever hearing your most painful sentences.

33. **Cross-read with someone** (MOVE 218). Have someone else read your piece aloud while you follow along. Many journals use this method to catch any lingering errors—you've got two pairs of eyes and two brains focused on catching imperfections.

Revising Graphic Design

Go to http://nataliescheme.com/ and watch the center of the screen from the beginning. This clever introduction to graphic designer Natalie Young's website goes by so quickly, you might think it was the product of one burst of inspiration. In fact, Young began working on it in an undergraduate design course, where it was reviewed by peers and professor, graded, and revised. When Young first put it up on the website, it was "too long, too slow." So even after it was first effectively published, she has continued to improve it.

Share

Everybody—EVERYBODY—needs a reader/editor/responder, someone the writer can trust to give honest responses and to participate in the creation of a piece of writing. **Share** (MOVE 219). A friend may spot immediately a strength or flaw you hadn't seen in something you've spent weeks perfecting. Find the right person to exchange with. A writing ally is a gift.

Even if you don't have a writing buddy, **Get some feedback** (MOVE 220). The best feedback comes from readers whose opinions and tastes you trust, but any feedback can be valuable. If a couple of readers say, "I don't get it" about a particular point or paragraph, you'd better do something about it, even if your feeling is "They must not have read very carefully."

Listening to or reading what someone else says about your work doesn't by itself produce change. Making something of what others say, and not being defensive or hurt by it, is a skill in itself. **Learn from feedback** (MOVE 221). The trick is to keep control over your writing without being deaf to legitimate concerns. I try to get readers to respond rather than advise, but some readers will seem bent on changing your work to their tastes. Before you get feedback, jot down for yourself the major questions that you'd like answered by readers. Your readers may not address your questions head-on, but you can often glean a sense of where they'd stand on them; you can get your questions answered and thus keep control of the movement of the writing but not feel compelled to make the specific changes that your readers may push for.

What's Next?

Unfortunately, many wonderful pieces of writing sit unread in filing cabinets because the authors followed a writing process that ended here, with perfecting the text. But now you've got to DO something with it. You have to present it—to that special someone, to your major professor, to the world. Hence, the next short chapter on wrapping it up and showing it off.

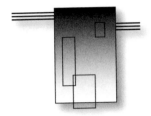

31

Present

This is what you've been working toward during the whole process, your chance to share your work with the world—or at least one small part of it. It's crazy to put in endless hours on your product and then be lazy when you're giving it to the world. Presenting should be a time for celebration, not fear. If you've pursued a successful process up to this point, you're ready, and you shouldn't have much to worry about. School presentations may seem artificial, but you need the practice for your career. No matter what field you end up in, the better you get at what you do, the more likely you are to do presentations about it.

Purposes of Presenting

Throughout this book, I have encouraged you to think in terms of entering a conversation about your subject. With your presentation, you make your entrance. Presenting forces you to think concretely about your audience, which may lead to some cuts and changes in the version you present. This is also your last chance to modify the way you want to come across. Some people take out that bit of sarcasm or that dig at a colleague before they present. The prospect of sharing can put the whole project in a new light, and we shouldn't shy away from the insights that new light can bring.

Presenting Moves

Prepare

The first step in the process of presenting is, of course, to **Analyze your audience and purpose** (MOVE 222). Besides the usual questions (➡1), analyze the specific situation:

- Where and when will you be presenting?
- What kinds of technology are available?
- Are others involved?
- What are they doing?
- How much time do you have? (Going over your time limit is rude, but people often do it. So if you're the last one to speak, you need to be prepared to sum up very quickly.)
- Who are you in relation to your audience—subordinate, peer, or authority?
- What preferences does your audience have for presentation medium?

Think about strong and weak presentations you've seen. What do *you* prefer in a presentation? Do you know anyone who speaks well in public? Can you talk to them about how they prepare?

Most of the moves in this book are thinking activities, useful no matter what product your thinking results in. But at some point you need to decide which medium, or combination of media, to use to present your material to the intended audience. **Choose your medium** (MOVE 223). If you have a choice, don't just settle for the medium you're most familiar with. Seek out and study a poster presentation. Watch a PowerPoint slideshow. Pay attention to the layout and binding you see on good reports. But also consider your strengths and talents. Are you a good off-the-cuff speaker, comfortable and funny with a crowd? Or would you rather write or arrange things graphically?

Write

Writing is still the most permanent and portable form that complex, nuanced thought can take. Whatever other presentation medium you might use, you probably want to write out your thoughts first so that you can manipulate them and have a record of them and possibly turn the writing to other use in the future.

The presentation of writing involves everything from final proofreading to handing it over to the intended audience. Generally the presentation should be professional, clear, easy to follow, not cluttered. No silly fonts or extensive corrections on your final copy.

Things to do the last time through:

- Slow down as you read. Try to look at individual words rather than read for the sense of the whole passage.

- If you've used headings and subheadings, make sure parallel headings use the same grammatical structure and the same typography—font, size, bold or italic, etc.
- Compare what you've done to any models you've found.
- Check your paragraph indentations, your line spacing, whether or not you skip lines between paragraphs.

Should you bind it? Anything not comfortably joined by a jumbo paper clip is a candidate for binding, though you may need to reformat so nothing gets lost in the binding process. Some schools require bound theses. It certainly can't hurt to add a final touch of professionalism. Check with your audience.

Talk

At conferences, in classes, and in business meetings of all kinds, people give oral presentations of all lengths and complexities. All good presentations are similar in that the speaker:

- begins by thanking the introducer, then often tells an anecdote that leads into the topic
- provides an overview, outline, or roadmap of where the talk will go
- helps the audience understand the relationship between parts and whole, examples and generalizations, big picture and detail
- is aware of and responsive to the audience
- sticks to the time limit
- augments the spoken word with visual or audio accompaniment
- makes use of humor and a light tone when appropriate
- leaves time for and prepares for a question-and-answer period

Sometimes you can choose whether to talk or just hand out your document, and you have to decide whether you can give an effective speech that adds to what you've written. More often, you'll know as soon as you're given the assignment that you'll need to do an oral presentation as the culmination of your work. But then you may still need to decide whether to **Read your paper** (MOVE 224). If the paper isn't too long—count on 1½–2 minutes for each double-spaced page of approximately 250–350 words—you can simply read it aloud. Try to:

- Add signposts along the way to help listeners connect key ideas; let listeners know where your argument is headed and how it connects to previous ideas.
- Consider opening with an example or anecdote, preferably a relevant and funny one you can return to at the end.
- Practice enough so you can read smoothly.
- Underline words that you want to stress as you read aloud; practice reading with the natural rhythm and emphasis of the sentence.
- Don't use long quotations.
- Look up and make eye contact occasionally.

- Modulate the tone and volume of your voice; read with pauses and drama.
- Cut from the middle, not from the end, if you fear going overtime.
- Plan for less time than you are supposed to have. Others may go over their limits.
- Consider reordering your material to make it easier to follow. Would it make sense to start with your conclusion or with an example that would catch audience interest?
- Consider trimming some of the more difficult sections and making your language more casual—it's hard to follow an argument you're only listening to, not seeing.
- Practice saying names and words that you haven't said out loud before.
- Determine your tone beforehand. Do you want to be funny, strictly informational, provocative, worried?
- Consider adding to your paper humorous asides, extra examples that the audience can relate to, or stories that can provide an entry into or a context for your paper.

Some conferences or session chairs discourage reading a whole paper, or you may not have time. In those cases, or if you're just good at unscripted lecture, you might **Talk from notes** (MOVE 225). Some speakers bring a print-out of their paper but use it only for quotations. Others jot down eight to ten ideas and improvise. Some memorize. Experiment whenever you can, so you'll know which approach works best for you, which makes you feel most comfortable when you're "on stage." But always rehearse! An underprepared presentation wastes audience time and embarrasses everyone.

Should you read or talk? Reading may make you feel more confident, but it leads to a tendency to hide behind your notes. If you talk you can pay more attention to the audience and respond to them, but you're more likely to wander from the point.

It has become almost standard these days to **Present slides** (MOVE 226). PowerPoint is only one of many brands of slide presentation software available, some of them free. Many people teach themselves the software as they create their first slide presentation; others need a tutorial or human help. A slide presentation can accompany any of the other presentation methods. As you create it, keep in mind:

- Start with an **Analysis of your purpose and audience** ➡222. Cool PowerPoint fade-ins might be appropriate for a family picture show but not for a stockholders' meeting.
- **Try a tree diagram** ➡99.
- Think in terms of slides: break your material down into ten to twenty chunks, depending on the length of your presentation. Count on taking about one minute for each slide.

- Use visuals that advance your point, not clip art.
- Any effects you use should have a purpose beyond impressing the audience.
- Don't just read what's on the slide; use it to highlight your ideas. Talk around it.
- Look at the audience, rather than the slide, as much as possible.
- Practice!
- Be ready for questions. What will shock people? What will they have a hard time believing?
- Try to imagine everything that could go wrong with the technology and make at least a plan B. And plan for plenty of setup time.
- Consider having a handout containing documentation and perhaps your contact information or an outline of your talk. Or you can hand out a condensed version of the whole talk.

Try Alternatives

Alternatives to talks, with or without slides, fit better in certain kinds of situations. **Make a poster** (MOVE 227). Poster presentations have become increasingly popular, especially in the sciences. They allow presenters to communicate with hundreds of people over periods lasting up to a few days. And they can be made to impress both the casual passerby and the interested expert. Posters are as varied as the individuals who make them, but most follow these rules:

- Use the latest technology. Homemade, hand-lettered posters may remind viewers of elementary school science projects. Commercial printers can print the entire poster.
- Get your name, your institution, and a (preferably short, possibly humorous) title top center, big font.
- Even if you're not going to give a slide presentation, you might want to write up your ideas in PowerPoint slides, which you can then print out in pieces or as a whole.
- While the whole should be professional and high quality, give it a personal, low-tech touch. A hand-colored geological map draws the eye, as does precise lettering or a flashy signature.
- The poster should make sense by itself; you won't always be around to explain.
- Organize material in columns rather than rows.
- Use visuals to convey your message as much as possible.
- Don't cram too much in. You need to keep your font big enough to be read from afar, and you don't want the poster to feel cluttered.
- Every presentation is some part show (or showing off), and most these days are some part technology. So experiments in technology or in performance may be welcome. **Try something completely different** (MOVE 228). Could you create a website or even a video game to convey

your ideas? Could you dramatize a paper reading by having someone else read certain parts of it or by planting a friend in the audience to say or do something outrageous? Could you make a diorama or other kind of museum exhibit? Don't forget good old hands-on show-and-tell.

Present with Others

A group presentation needs to steer between extremes—you don't want to be competing for the spotlight, but you also don't want to make it look as though a series of strangers is taking the stage. Try to allow each member of the group a similar amount of face-to-face time with the audience.

What's Next

You're done! For now. If you have the energy for one more chore, go back to chapter 23 and **Analyze your writing process** ➥54 about the work you just completed, so you can keep track of the insights you gained and process improvements you made. There's always another writing assignment around the corner. If you haven't already looked at the other chapters in this book, you might want to check them out now for help with writing process problems, writing apprehension, and genres.

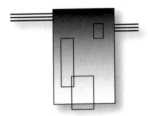

Appendix

Twenty Plays

Have you ever wished that you could tackle a writing project assisted by your own personal writing coach, who would say, "Try this first" or "If you're still having trouble with that point, try this one"? I can't provide that degree of personalization, but in the section below I offer twenty "plays," sequences of moves that take you from the first glimmerings of idea to finished product. I give each play a title that indicates what's different about the approach as well as a brief note describing the kind of person who might be drawn to that particular play. So if the title intrigues you, the note describes you, or you would appreciate someone laying out a series of steps for you, try one of these plays. As you experiment with various plays and moves, keep in mind:

- The "right" process, play, or move is simply the one that is productive—takes you a step closer to your goal—and relatively painless. What works for you on a particular project may not work for you on the next project and may never work for anyone else.

- Successful writing processes tend to be recursive rather than linear—that is, writers loop back around, rewriting, rethinking, rediscovering, rather than starting with something like freewriting and working straight through a sequence of moves to the finished product.
- There's nothing magical about these plays or doing these moves in this order. These are just suggestions. You can always substitute other moves for the ones suggested, though you may want to stay with a move from the same chapter. If it works, use it.

Remember that the arrow (➡) indicates "move number." Most plays end with simple reminders to revise and present. Revising rituals (chapter 30) and presentation approaches (chapter 31) depend on the individual writer and situation, so I have made only a few suggestions for those steps.

1. Step by step—For those who like doing what the teacher asks, and doing it well.

    a. Freewrite ➡72
    b. Change your perspective ➡44
    c. Use a double-entry journal ➡106
    d. Integrate sources ➡133
    e. Brainstorm titles ➡142
    f. Answer readers' questions ➡159
    g. Draft by outline ➡172
    h. Outline your draft ➡160
    i. Revise (chapter 30)
    j. Present (chapter 31)

2. Jump right in—For those eager to fill the screen with words.

    a. Draft by freewriting ➡171
    b. Outline your draft ➡160
    c. Brainstorm titles ➡142
    d. Brainstorm leads ➡143
    e. Ask yourself the "So what?" question ➡156
    f. Revise for meaning, coherence, language ➡203
    g. Present (chapter 31)

3. On a scratch pad—For those who like to do a lot on paper before heading for the computer and full sentences.

    a. Freewrite ➡72
    b. Expand ➡92
    c. Brainstorm titles ➡142
    d. Brainstorm leads ➡143
    e. Brainstorm ends ➡144
    f. Develop a thesis ➡97
    g. Answer readers' questions ➡159

   h. Draft by freewriting—longhand ➥171

   i. Outline your draft ➥160

   j. Revise (chapter 30)

   k. Present (chapter 31)

4. Analyze, then write—There's a lot to be said for an old-fashioned rhetorical approach that focuses on why and for whom the writer is writing.

   a. Analyze audiences ➥56

   b. Analyze purposes ➥55

   c. Questions to ask your teacher or boss ➥48

   d. Develop a thesis ➥97

   e. Use a tree diagram ➥99

   f. Draft with thesis ➥175

   g. Analyze your thesis ➥169

   h. Revise (chapter 30)

   i. Present (chapter 31)

5. Hunt and gather—For those who enjoy picking mushrooms.

   a. Keep a log ➥105

   b. Brainstorm ➥69—What's the most interesting thing so far?

   c. Talk . . . and listen ➥157

   d. Freewrite on the most interesting thing ➥72

   e. Interview ➥113

   f. Use memory joggers ➥100

   g. Three times round ➥177

   h. Revise (chapter 30)

   i. Present (chapter 31)

6. Getting organized—For people who like to see a clear path ahead.

   a. Brainstorm most important aspects of your topic ➥69

   b. Treat one of your terms as a code word ➥93

   c. Group, label, and order ➥162

   d. Outline ➥95

   e. Draft by outline ➥172

   f. Outline your draft ➥160

   g. Analyze your thesis ➥169

   h. Revise (chapter 30)

   i. Present (chapter 31)

7. Focus first—For those obsessed with the "So what?" question.

   a. Brainstorm potential paper topics ➥69

   b. Focus with freewriting ➥140

   c. Expand then choose ➥152

    d. Brainstorm titles ➡142
    e. Brainstorm leads ➡143
    f. Draft recursively ➡176
    g. Ask yourself the "So what?" question ➡156
    h. Analyze your thesis ➡169
    i. Examine the links ➡198
    j. Revise (chapter 30)
    k. Present (chapter 31)

8. Drafting, drafting—For those who don't mind writing but hate revising.
    a. Three times round ➡177
    b. Outline your draft ➡160
    c. Analyze your thesis ➡169
    d. Revise (chapter 30)
    e. Present (chapter 31)

9. It's all in the thesis—For those who want to be sure the reader gets it.
    a. Develop a thesis ➡97
    b. Brainstorm titles ➡142
    c. Brainstorm leads ➡143
    d. Ask yourself the "So what?" question ➡156
    e. Draft with thesis ➡175
    f. Make ends meet ➡197
    g. Analyze your thesis ➡169
    h. Examine the links ➡198
    i. Revise (chapter 30)
    j. Present (chapter 31)

10. Top down—For those who want to start with a thought, then branch.
    a. Brainstorm ideas for the paper topic ➡69
    b. Choose ➡76
    c. Brainstorm titles ➡142
    d. Brainstorm leads ➡143
    e. Use a tree diagram ➡99
    f. Draft by outline ➡172
    g. Revise (chapter 30)
    h. Present (chapter 31)

11. Discovering all the way—For those who don't like to be pinned down.
    a. Brainstorm ➡69
    b. Freewrite ➡72

    c. Map ➡73
    d. Inventory—authority on related subjects ➡62
    e. Dig into contexts and connections ➡51
    f. Graph to discover ➡77
    g. Three times round ➡177
    h. Make ends meet ➡197
    i. Revise (chapter 30)
    j. Present (chapter 31)

12. Making it personal—often makes it matter. Try the following, but at each step focus on the personal connections you can establish with your subject.
    a. Freewrite ➡72
    b. Tell your story ➡78
    c. Think like Zippy the Pinhead ➡74
    d. Find the problem/tension/conflict ➡145
    e. Sketch the organization of your paper ➡167
    f. Draft to explore ➡170
    g. Outline your draft ➡160
    h. Revise (chapter 30)
    i. Present (chapter 31)

13. Speed it up—When you have to compromise quality for speed.
    a. Draft by freewriting ➡171
    b. Make ends meet ➡197
    c. Revise (chapter 30)
    d. Present (chapter 31)

14. Make it social—For those who like to work with others.
    a. Brainstorm ➡69
    b. Talk . . . and listen ➡157
    c. Draft by freewrite ➡171
    d. Share ➡219
    e. Get some feedback ➡220
    f. Learn from feedback ➡221
    g. Revise (chapter 30)
    h. Present (chapter 31)

15. Five minutes at a time—For those forced to write in fragments.
    a. Brainstorm ➡69
    b. Freewrite ➡72
    c. Brainstorm titles ➡142
    d. Brainstorm leads ➡143
    e. Brainstorm ends ➡144
    f. Outline ➡95

  g. Draft by outline ➥172

  h. Make ends meet ➥197

  i. Revise (chapter 30)

  j. Present (chapter 31)

16. **Analyze—and build on—your strengths**—Choose this one!

  a. Analyze your writing process ➥54

  b. Analyze your strengths ➥57

  c. Brainstorm ways you could build on each strength for your writing project ➥69

  d. Outline a way to bring together all the results of step c ➥95

  e. Draft by outline ➥172

  f. Revise (chapter 30)

  g. Present (chapter 31)

17. **Key parts first**—For those who want to do their big thinking early.

  a. Brainstorm titles ➥142

  b. Brainstorm leads ➥143

  c. Brainstorm ends ➥144

  d. Brainstorm a list of contexts ➥89

  e. Summarize ➥125

  f. Draft with blinders ➥173

  g. Outline your draft ➥160

  h. Revise (chapter 30)

  i. Present (chapter 31)

18. **Right brain/left brain**—For those who appreciate balance.

  a. Brainstorm ➥69

  b. Outline ➥95

  c. Freewrite ➥72

  d. Develop a thesis ➥97

  e. Brainstorm leads ➥143

  f. Draft by outline ➥172

  g. Brainstorm titles ➥142

  h. Outline your draft ➥160

  i. Revise (chapter 30)

  j. Present (chapter 31)

19. **Gut and detail**—For those who feel before they think.

  a. Write down your gut feelings ➥67

  b. Brainstorm details that struck you about your subject ➥69

  c. Find a focusing detail ➥146

    d. Freewrite ➥72 about the meaning and importance of the detail and how it relates to your gut reaction

    e. Summarize ➥125

    f. Develop your thesis ➥97

    g. Draft with thesis ➥175

    h. Revise (chapter 30)

    i. Present (chapter 31)

20. Make your own play—Blaze a new path or return to the way you have written in the past. If you can recreate exactly what you did when your writing process succeeded in the past, try it and jot down the steps as you go.

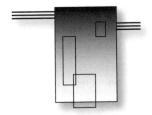

References

Bierce, Ambrose. *The Devil's Dictionary*. New York: Dover, 1958.

Boice, Robert. "Experimental and Clinical Treatments of Writing Blocks." *Journal of Consulting and Clinical Psychology* 51.2 (1983): 183–191. http://dx.doi.org/10.1037/0022-006X.51.2.183.

Brown, Greg. "If I Had Known." *Down in There*. Red House Records, 1990, CD.

Butterfield Blues Band. "I Got a Mind to Give up Living." *East-West*. Elektra, 1966, LP.

Dylan, Bob. "I Want You." *Blonde on Blonde*. Columbia, 1966.

Dylan, Bob. *Live at Budokan*. Columbia, 1979, LP.

Gilman, Charlotte Perkins. *The Yellow Wallpaper*. New York: The Feminist Press, 1996.

Johnson-Sheehan, Richard. *Technical Communication Today*, 3rd ed. Boston: Pearson, 2010.

Lee, Dickey. "Patches" (Mann, Kolber). *The Tale of Patches*. Smash, 1962, LP.

Mack, Karin, and Eric Skjei. *Overcoming Writing Blocks*. Los Angeles: J. P. Tarcher, 1979.

Meeks, Lynn Langer, and Carol Jewkes Austin. *Literacy in the Secondary English Classroom*. Boston: Pearson, 2003.

Murray, Donald. "Listening to Writing." In *The Essential Don Murray*, ed. Thomas Newkirk and Lisa C. Miller, 55–71. Portsmouth, NH: Heinemann.

Murray, Donald M. *A Writer Teaches Writing*, rev. 2nd ed. Boston: Heinle, 2003.

Oxford Dictionaries. Oxford: Oxford University Press, 2011. Web. 3 May 2011.

Palmquist, Michael, and Richard Young. "The Notion of Giftedness and Student Expectations about Writing." *Written Communication* 9.1 (1992): 137–168. http://dx.doi.org/10.1177/0741088392009001004.

Riffe, Daniel, and Don W. Stacks. "Student Characteristics and Writing Apprehension." *Journalism Educator* 47.2 (1992): 39–49. http://dx.doi.org/10.1177/107769589204700206.

Staff of the Harvard Crimson, ed. *50 Successful Harvard Application Essays*, 2nd ed. New York: St. Martin's Griffin, 2005.

Swift, Marvin. "Clear Writing Means Clear Thinking Means . . ." *Harvard Business Review* (January–February 1973).

Young, Neil. "Down by the River." *Everybody Knows This Is Nowhere*. Reprise, 1969, LP.

Young, Richard E., Alton L. Becker, and Kenneth L. Pike. *Rhetoric: Discovery and Change*. Fort Worth: Harcourt, 1970.